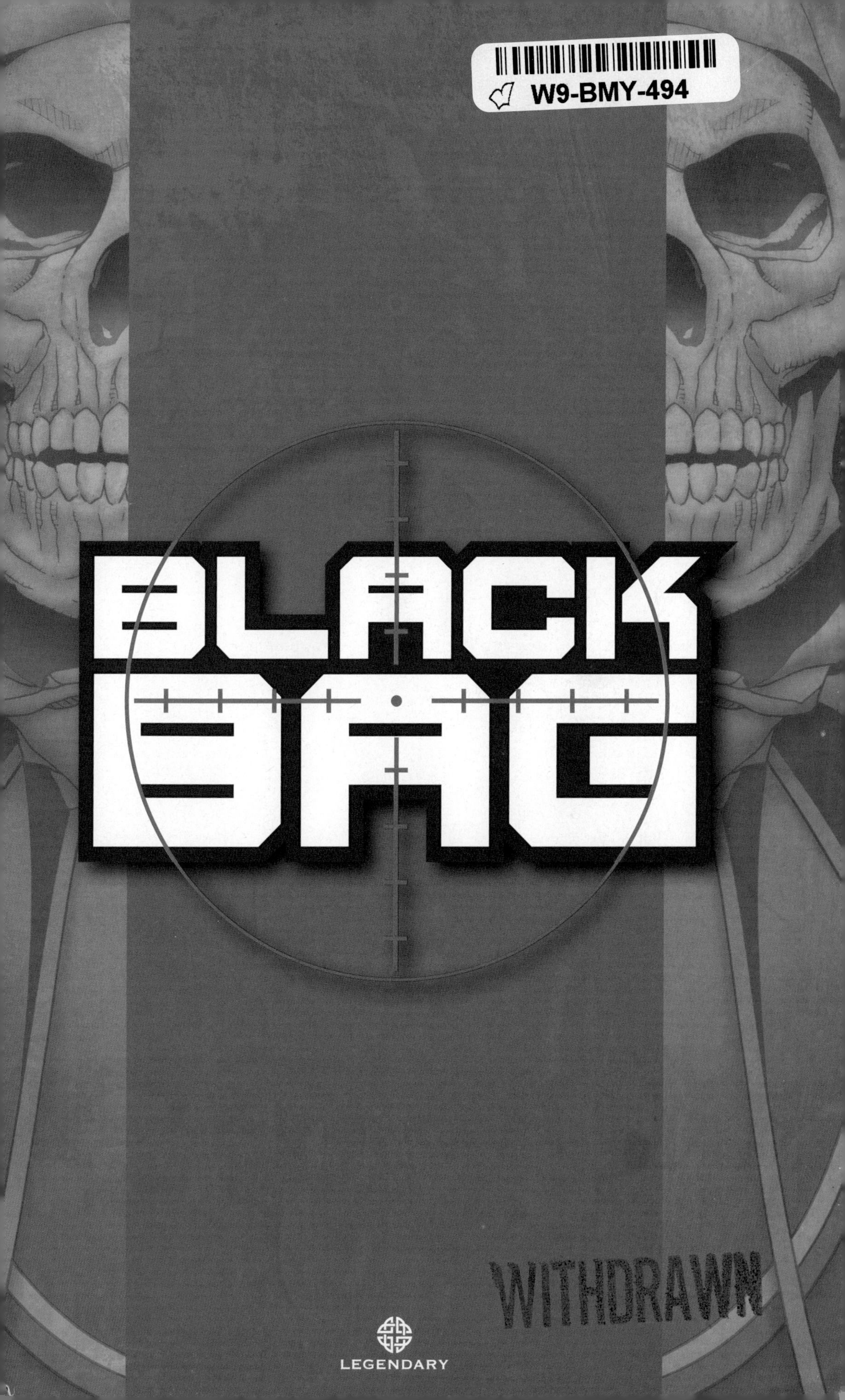
BLACK BAG
LEGENDARY
WITHDRAWN
W9-BMY-494

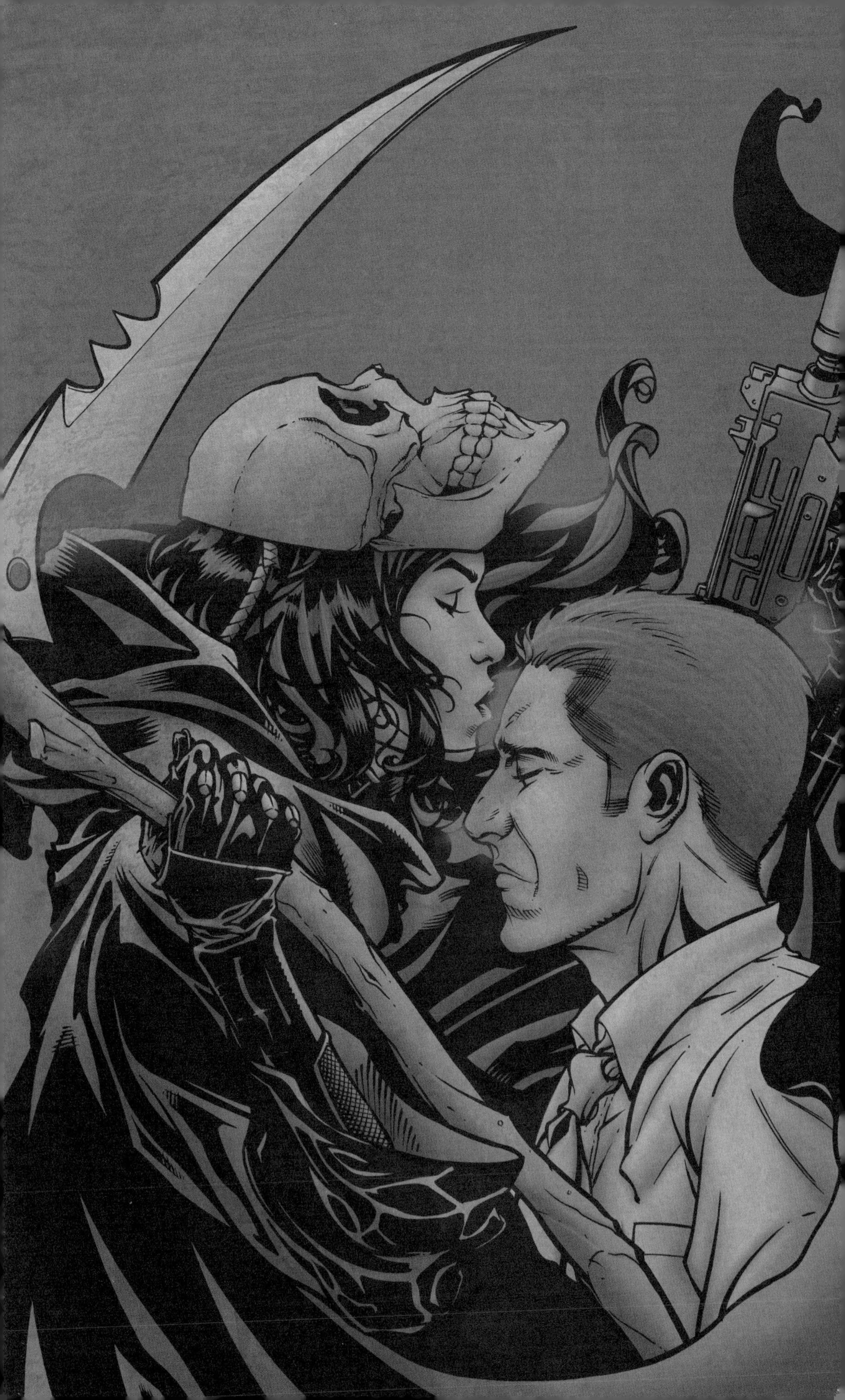

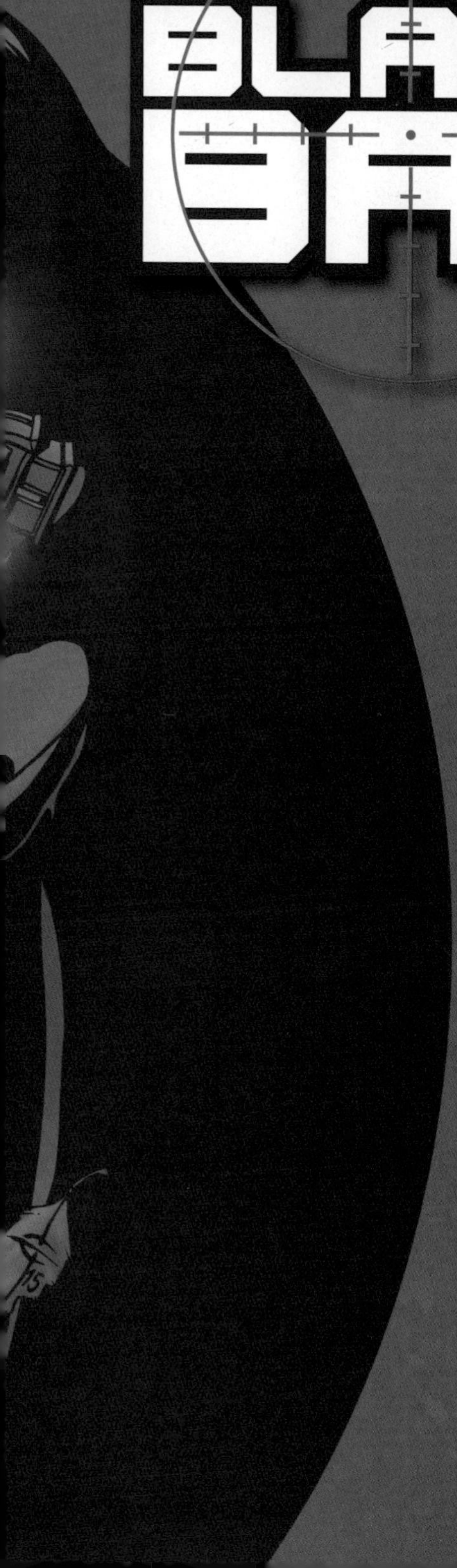

BLACK BAG

CHRIS ROBERSON
WRITER

J.B. BASTOS
PENCILER

JAMIE GRANT
COLORIST

TOM ORZECHOWSKI
LETTERER

**DREW EDWARD JOHNSON
& JAMIE GRANT**
ORIGINAL SERIES COVERS

NICOLAS SIENTY
PRE-PRESS & PRODUCTION

JOHN J. HILL
BOOK & LOGO DESIGNER

GREG TUMBARELLO
EDITOR

**CREATED BY
THOMAS TULL**

LEGENDARY

THOMAS TULL Chairman and Chief Executive Officer
JON JASHNI President and Chief Creative Officer
MARTY WILLHITE Chief Operating Officer & General Counsel
EMILY CASTEL Chief Marketing Officer
MIKE ROSS SVP, Business & Legal Affairs
BARNABY LEGG VP, Theatrical Strategy
DANIEL FEINBERG VP, Corporate Counsel
PEARL WIBLE Director, Digital Content
MANSI PATEL Creative Services Director

LEGENDARY COMICS

BOB SCHRECK Senior Vice President, Editor-in-Chief
ROBERT NAPTON VP, Editorial Director
DAVID SADOVE Publishing Operations Coordinator
GREG TUMBARELLO Editor

Published by LEGENDARY COMICS
2900 West Alameda Ave Suite 1500 Burbank, CA 91505

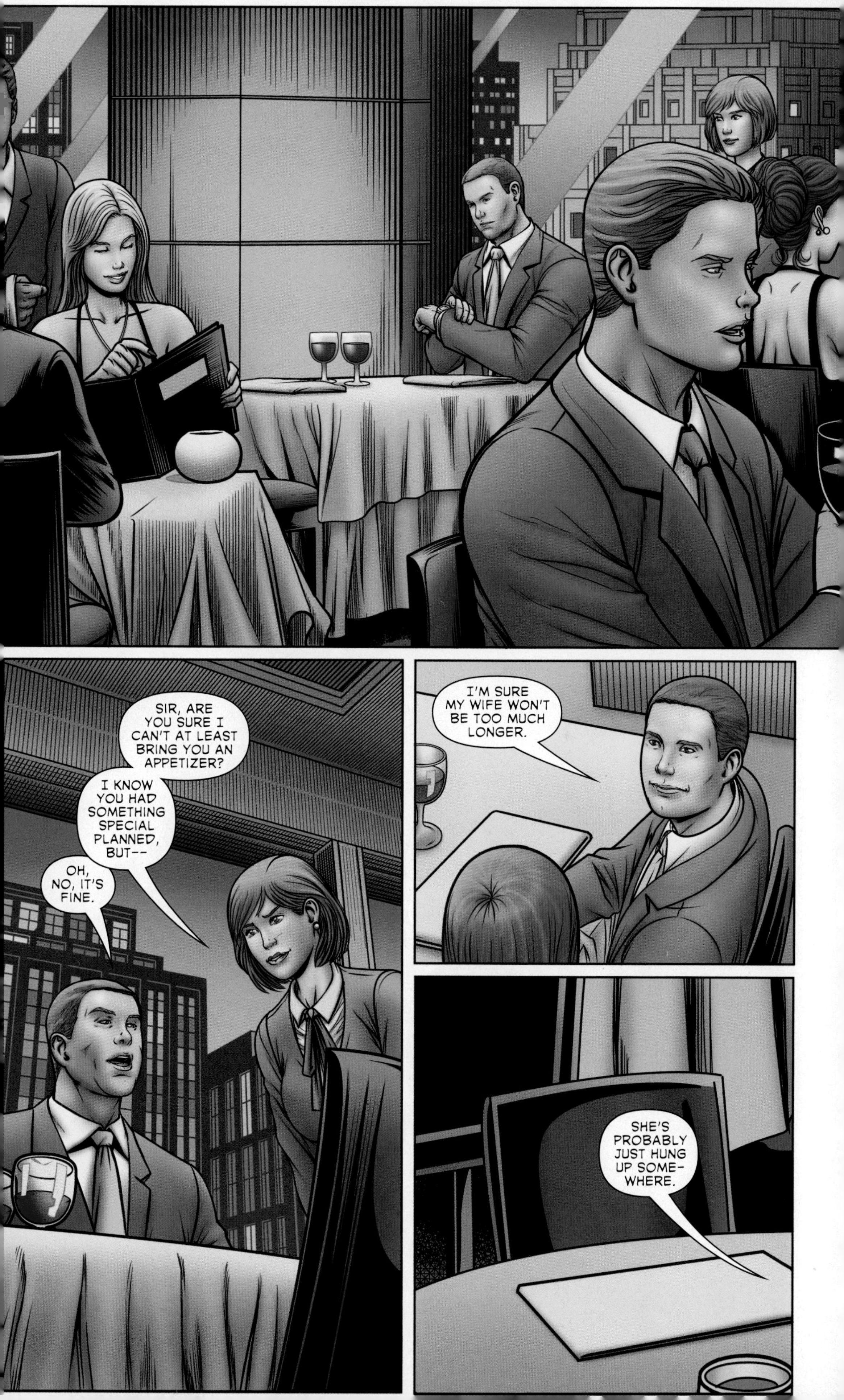

SIR, ARE YOU SURE I CAN'T AT LEAST BRING YOU AN APPETIZER?
I KNOW YOU HAD SOMETHING SPECIAL PLANNED, BUT--
OH, NO, IT'S FINE.
I'M SURE MY WIFE WON'T BE TOO MUCH LONGER.
SHE'S PROBABLY JUST HUNG UP SOME-WHERE.

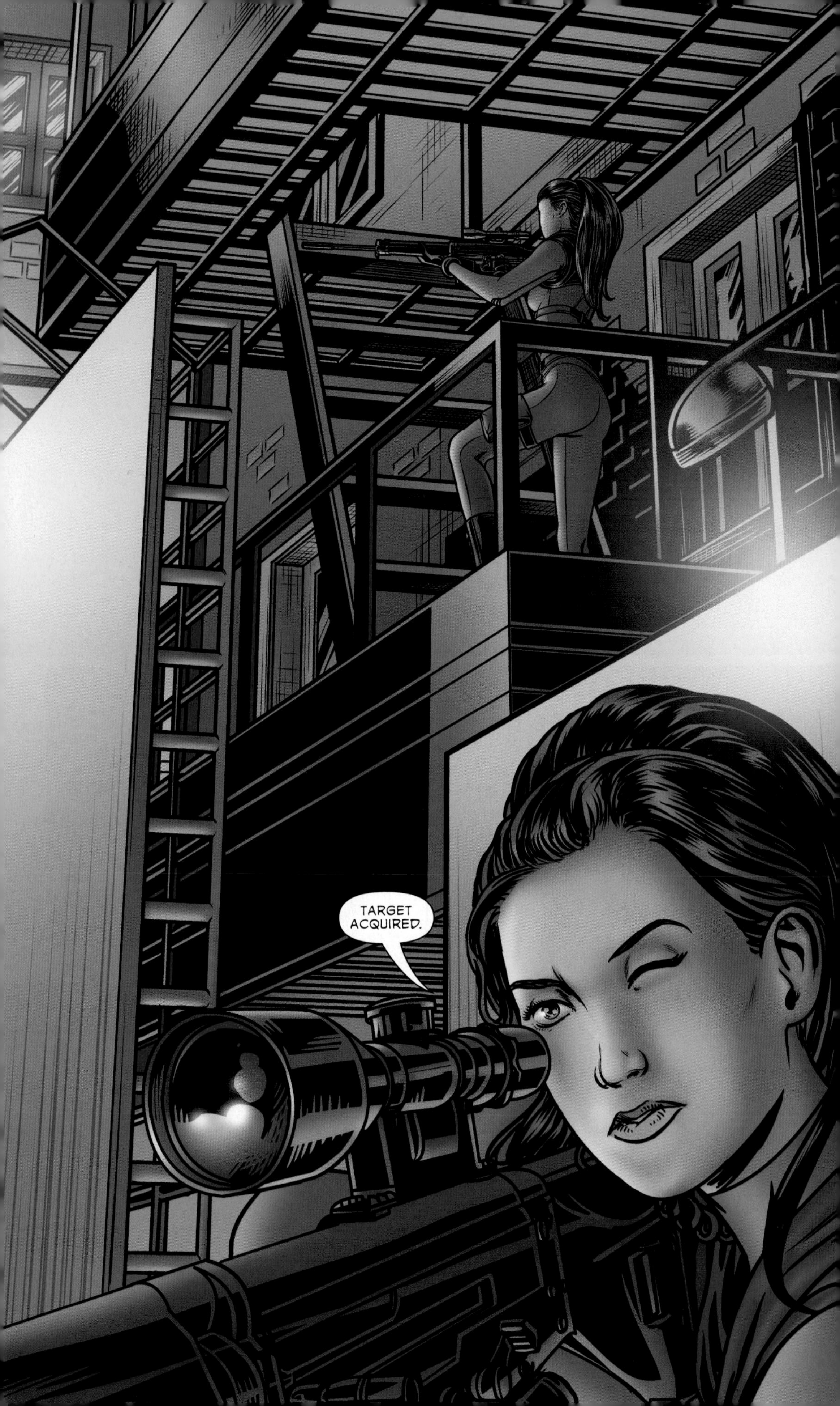
TARGET ACQUIRED.

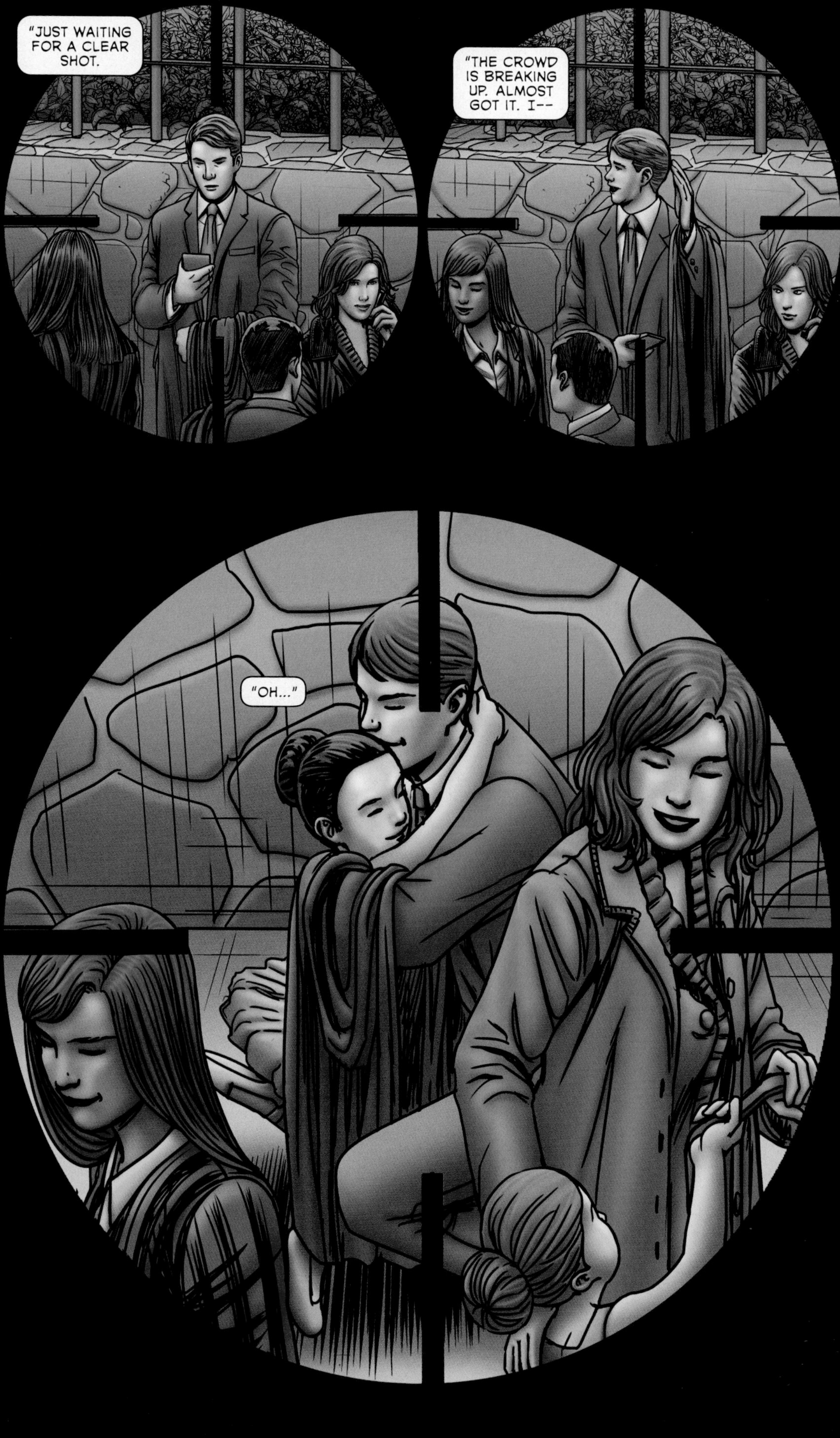
"JUST WAITING FOR A CLEAR SHOT.
"THE CROWD IS BREAKING UP. ALMOST GOT IT. I--
"OH..."

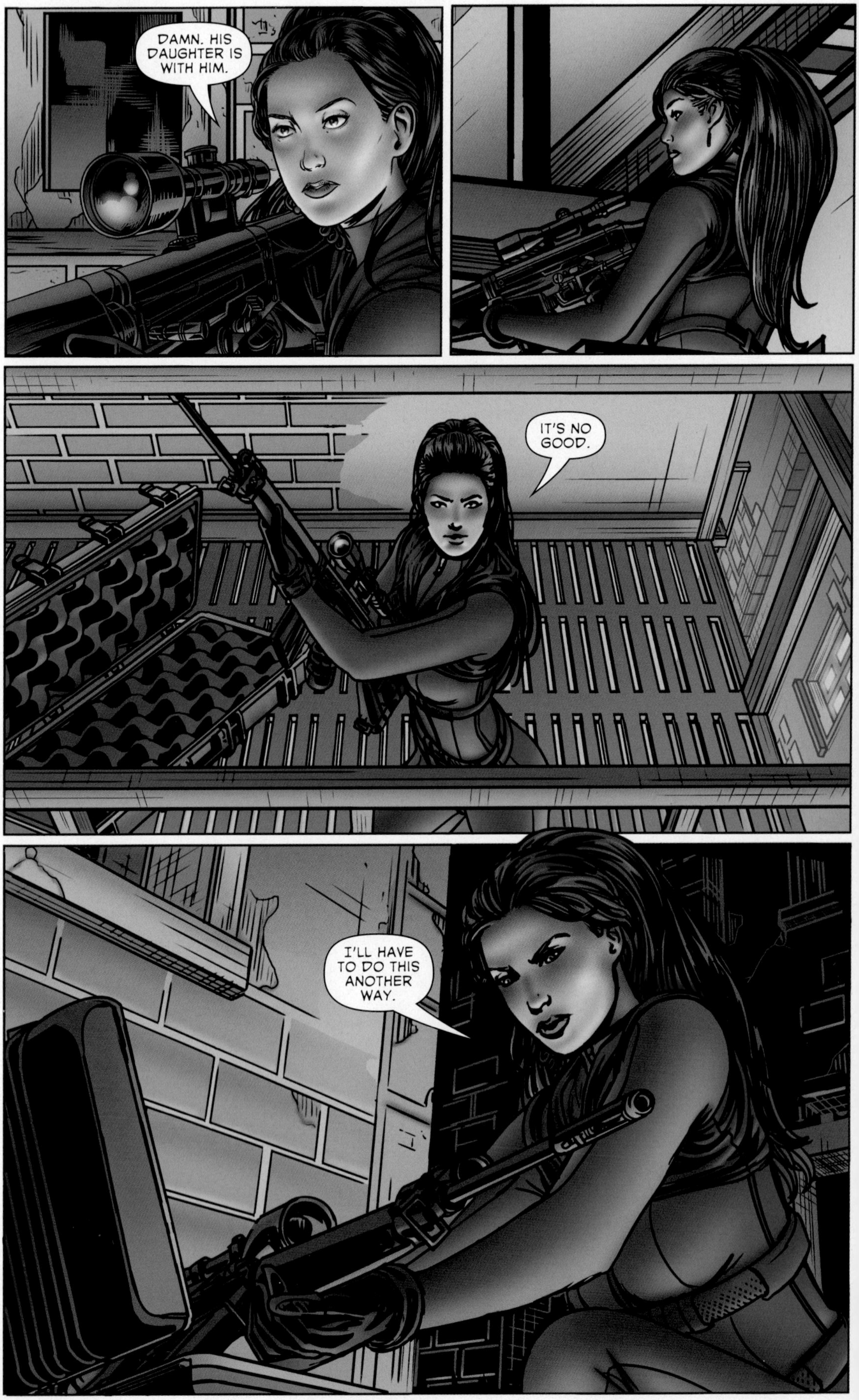
DAMN. HIS DAUGHTER IS WITH HIM.
IT'S NO GOOD.
I'LL HAVE TO DO THIS ANOTHER WAY.

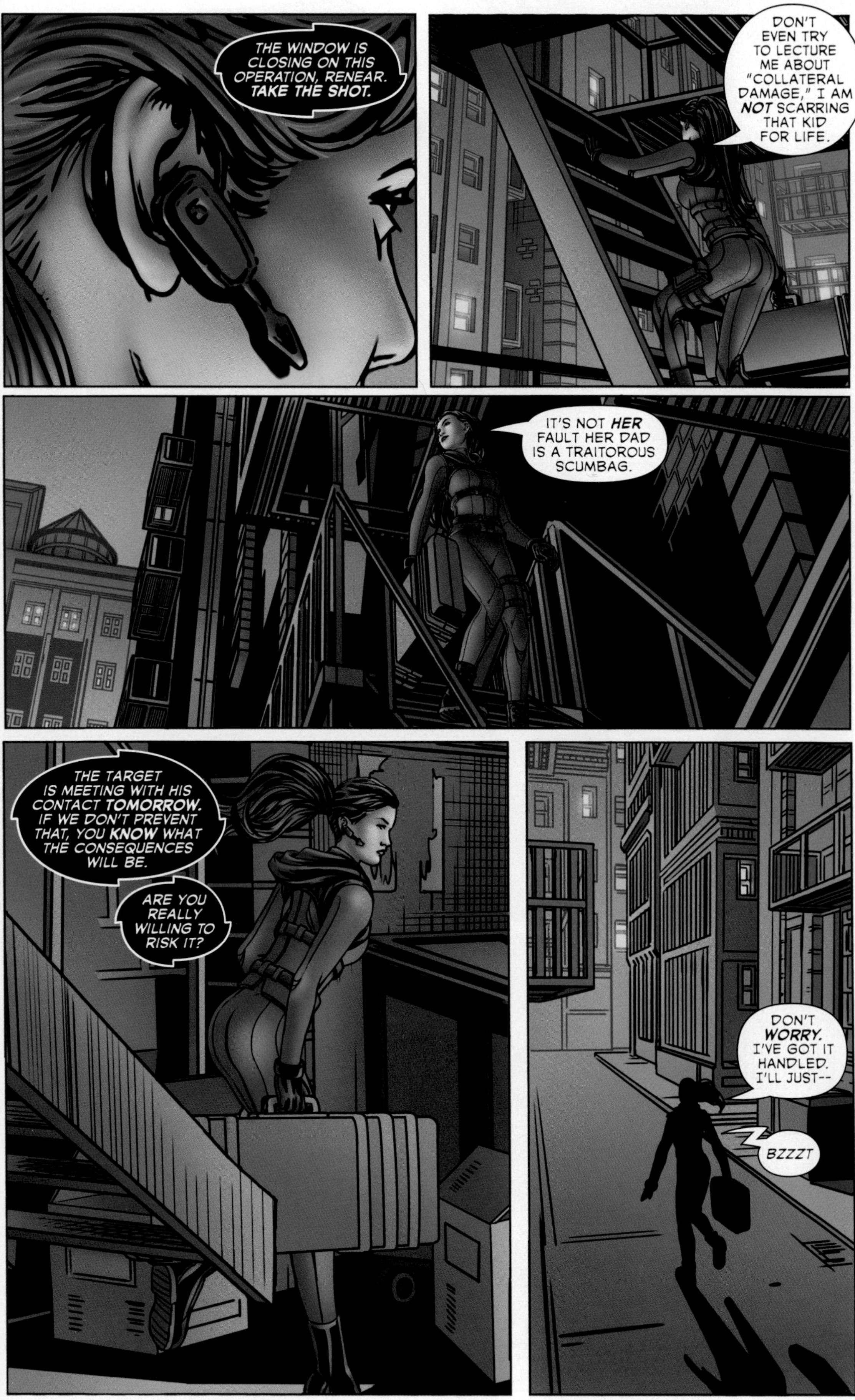
THE WINDOW IS CLOSING ON THIS OPERATION, RENEAR. TAKE THE SHOT.
DON'T EVEN TRY TO LECTURE ME ABOUT "COLLATERAL DAMAGE," I AM NOT SCARRING THAT KID FOR LIFE.
IT'S NOT HER FAULT HER DAD IS A TRAITOROUS SCUMBAG.
THE TARGET IS MEETING WITH HIS CONTACT TOMORROW. IF WE DON'T PREVENT THAT, YOU KNOW WHAT THE CONSEQUENCES WILL BE.
ARE YOU REALLY WILLING TO RISK IT?
DON'T WORRY. I'VE GOT IT HANDLED. I'LL JUST--
BZZZT

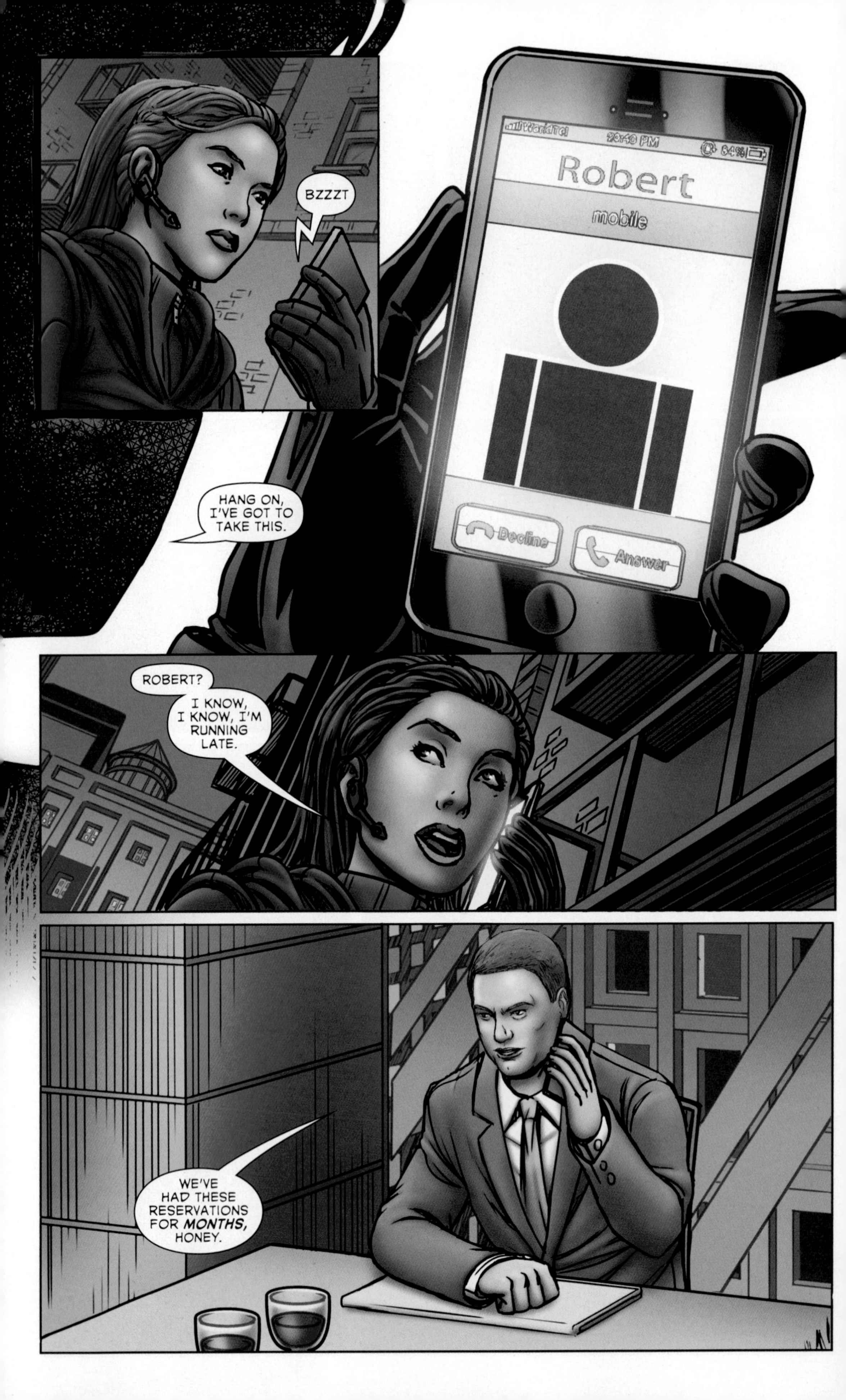
BZZZT
WorldTel
20:40 PM
84%
Robert
mobile
Decline
Answer
HANG ON, I'VE GOT TO TAKE THIS.
ROBERT?
I KNOW, I KNOW, I'M RUNNING LATE.
WE'VE HAD THESE RESERVATIONS FOR *MONTHS,* HONEY.

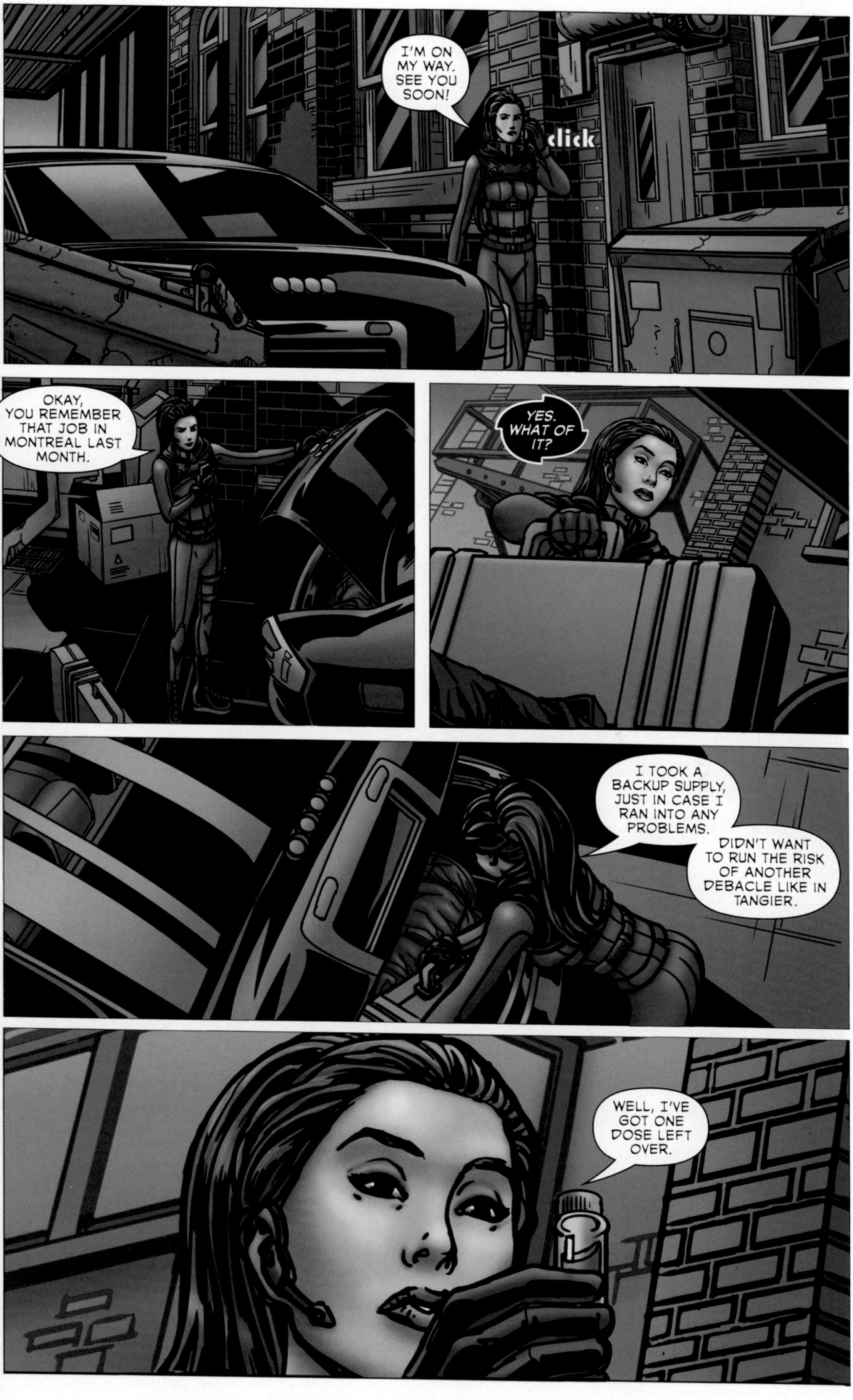
I'M ON MY WAY. SEE YOU SOON!
click
OKAY, YOU REMEMBER THAT JOB IN MONTREAL LAST MONTH.
YES. WHAT OF IT?
I TOOK A BACKUP SUPPLY, JUST IN CASE I RAN INTO ANY PROBLEMS.
DIDN'T WANT TO RUN THE RISK OF ANOTHER DEBACLE LIKE IN TANGIER.
WELL, I'VE GOT ONE DOSE LEFT OVER.

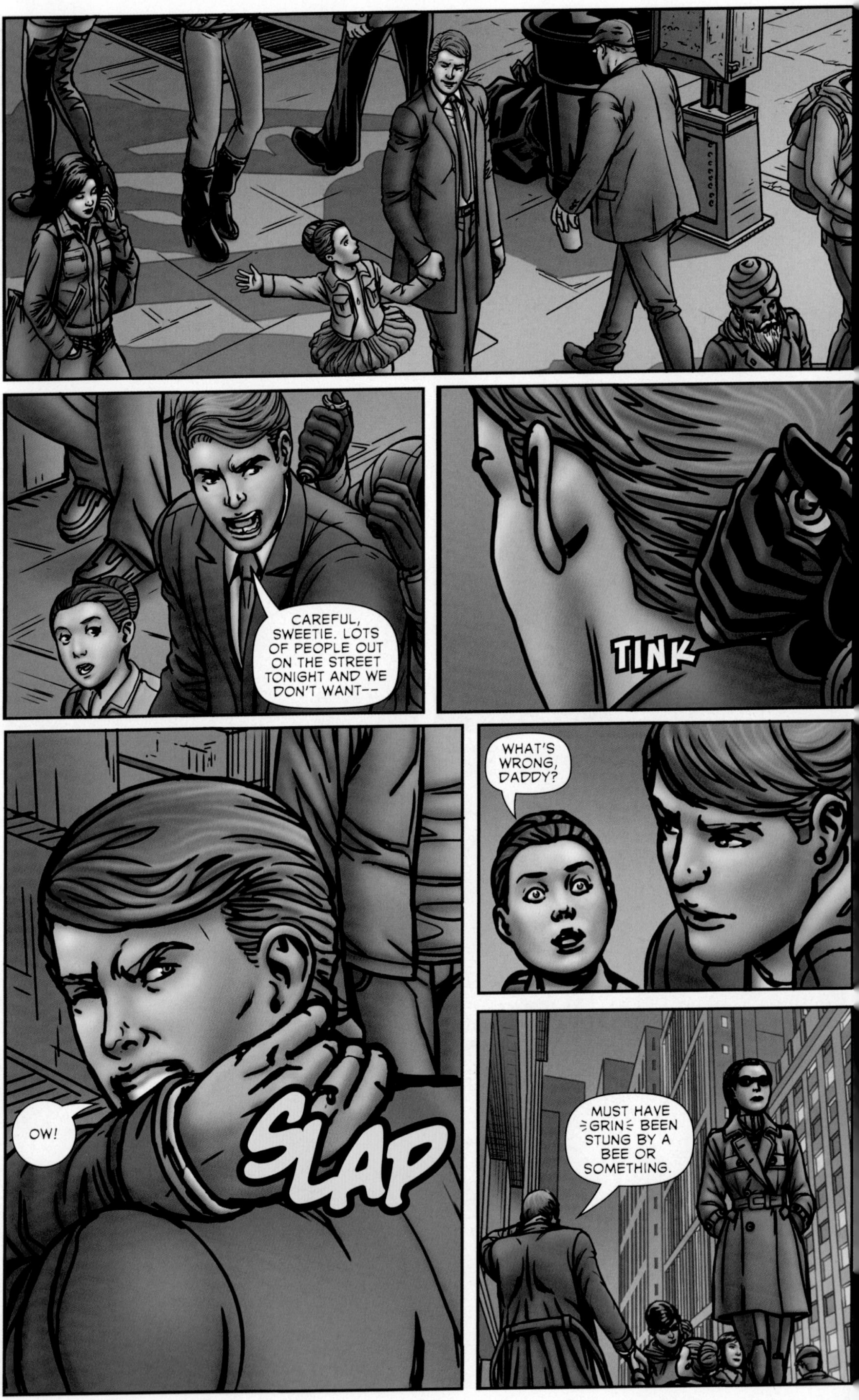

CAREFUL, SWEETIE. LOTS OF PEOPLE OUT ON THE STREET TONIGHT AND WE DON'T WANT--
TINK
OW!
SLAP
WHAT'S WRONG, DADDY?
MUST HAVE =GRIN= BEEN STUNG BY A BEE OR SOMETHING.

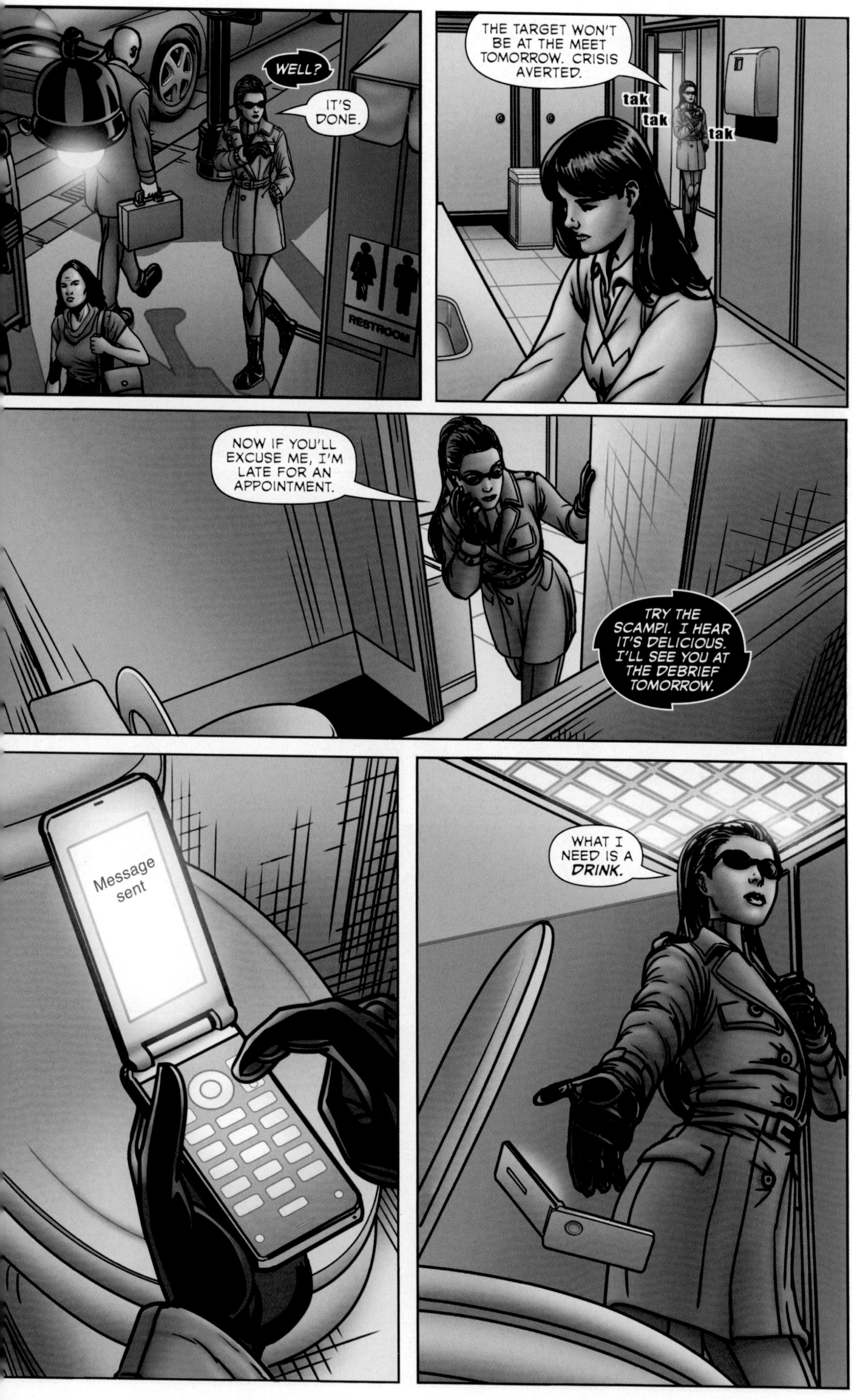
WELL?
IT'S DONE.
THE TARGET WON'T BE AT THE MEET TOMORROW. CRISIS AVERTED.
tak
tak
tak
RESTROOM
NOW IF YOU'LL EXCUSE ME, I'M LATE FOR AN APPOINTMENT.
TRY THE SCAMPI. I HEAR IT'S DELICIOUS. I'LL SEE YOU AT THE DEBRIEF TOMORROW.
Message sent
WHAT I NEED IS A DRINK.

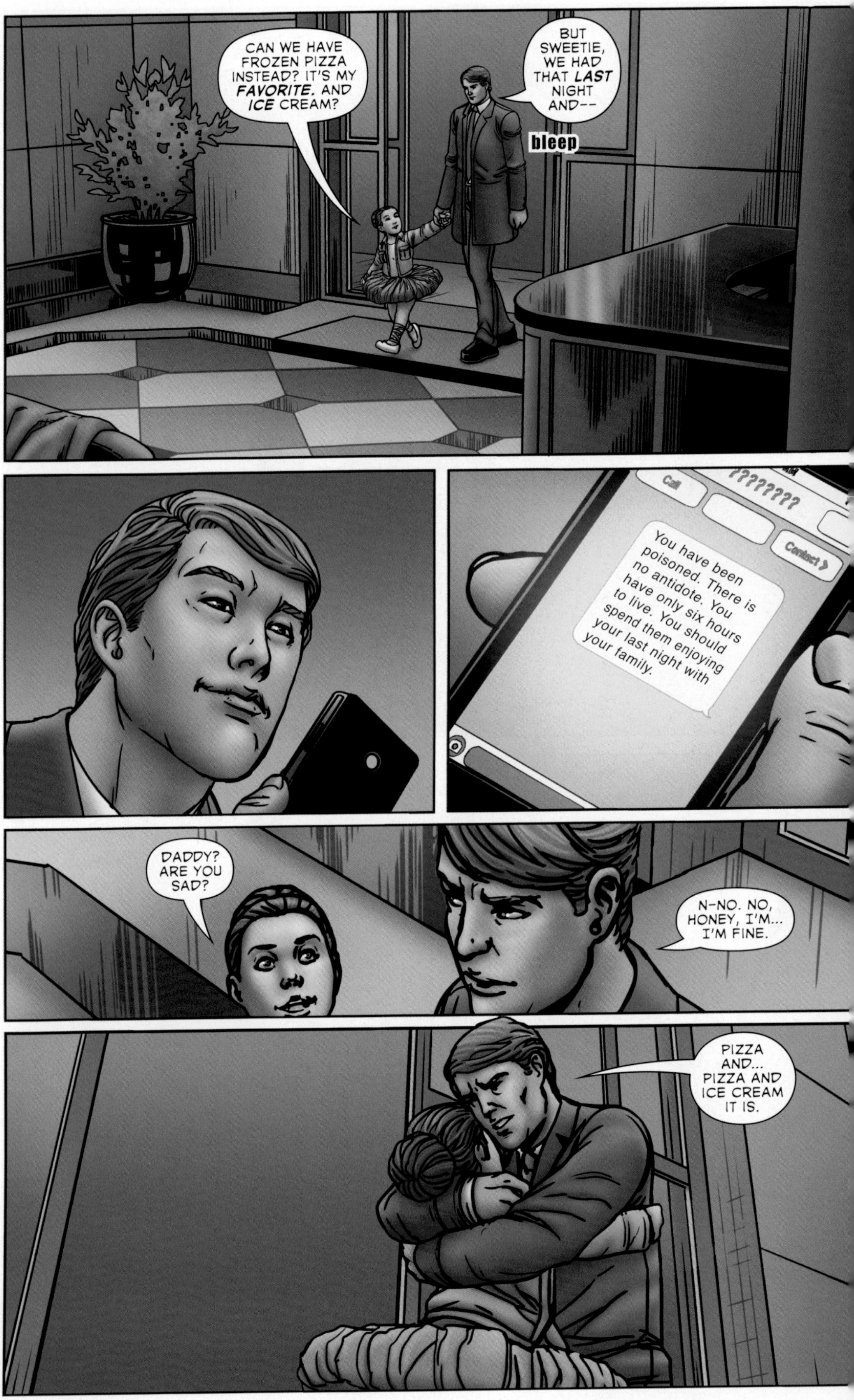
CAN WE HAVE FROZEN PIZZA INSTEAD? IT'S MY FAVORITE. AND ICE CREAM?
BUT SWEETIE, WE HAD THAT LAST NIGHT AND--
bleep
Call
????????
Contact
You have been poisoned. There is no antidote. You have only six hours to live. You should spend them enjoying your last night with your family.
DADDY? ARE YOU SAD?
N-NO. NO, HONEY, I'M... I'M FINE.
PIZZA AND... PIZZA AND ICE CREAM IT IS.

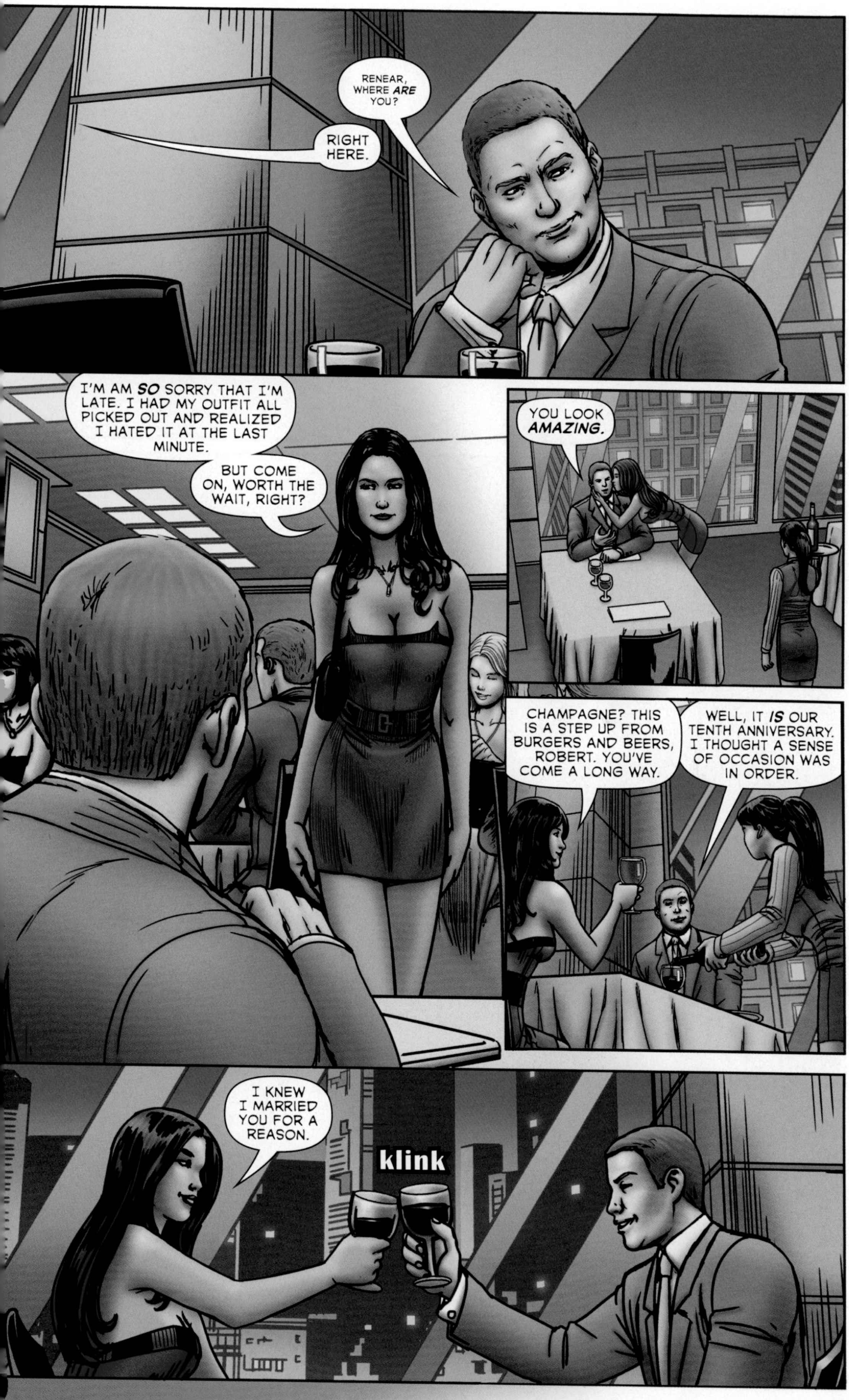
RENEAR, WHERE ARE YOU?
RIGHT HERE.
I'M AM SO SORRY THAT I'M LATE. I HAD MY OUTFIT ALL PICKED OUT AND REALIZED I HATED IT AT THE LAST MINUTE.
BUT COME ON, WORTH THE WAIT, RIGHT?
YOU LOOK AMAZING.
CHAMPAGNE? THIS IS A STEP UP FROM BURGERS AND BEERS, ROBERT. YOU'VE COME A LONG WAY.
WELL, IT IS OUR TENTH ANNIVERSARY. I THOUGHT A SENSE OF OCCASION WAS IN ORDER.
I KNEW I MARRIED YOU FOR A REASON.
klink

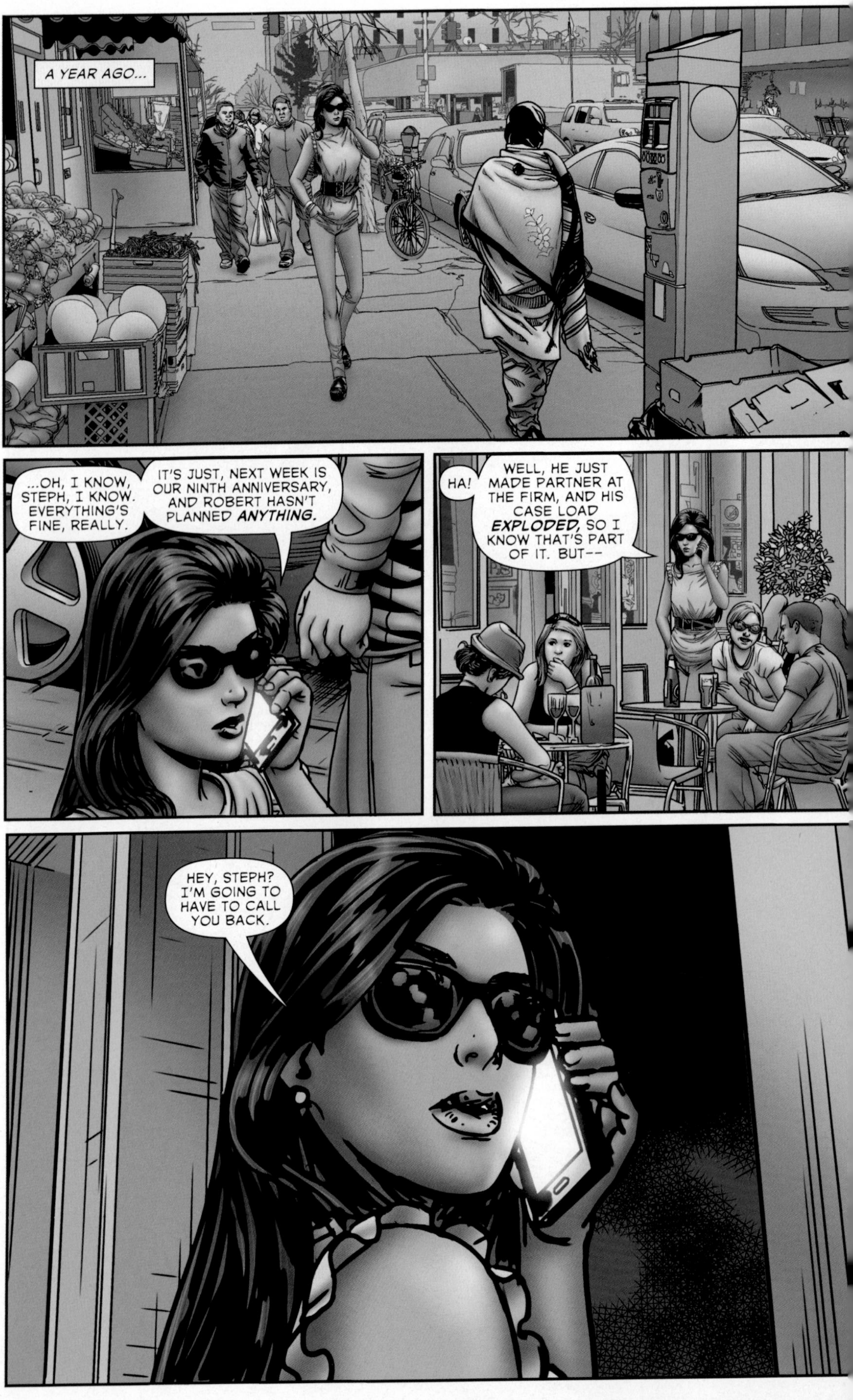
A YEAR AGO...
...OH, I KNOW, STEPH, I KNOW. EVERYTHING'S FINE, REALLY.
IT'S JUST, NEXT WEEK IS OUR NINTH ANNIVERSARY, AND ROBERT HASN'T PLANNED ANYTHING.
HA!
WELL, HE JUST MADE PARTNER AT THE FIRM, AND HIS CASE LOAD EXPLODED, SO I KNOW THAT'S PART OF IT. BUT--
HEY, STEPH? I'M GOING TO HAVE TO CALL YOU BACK.

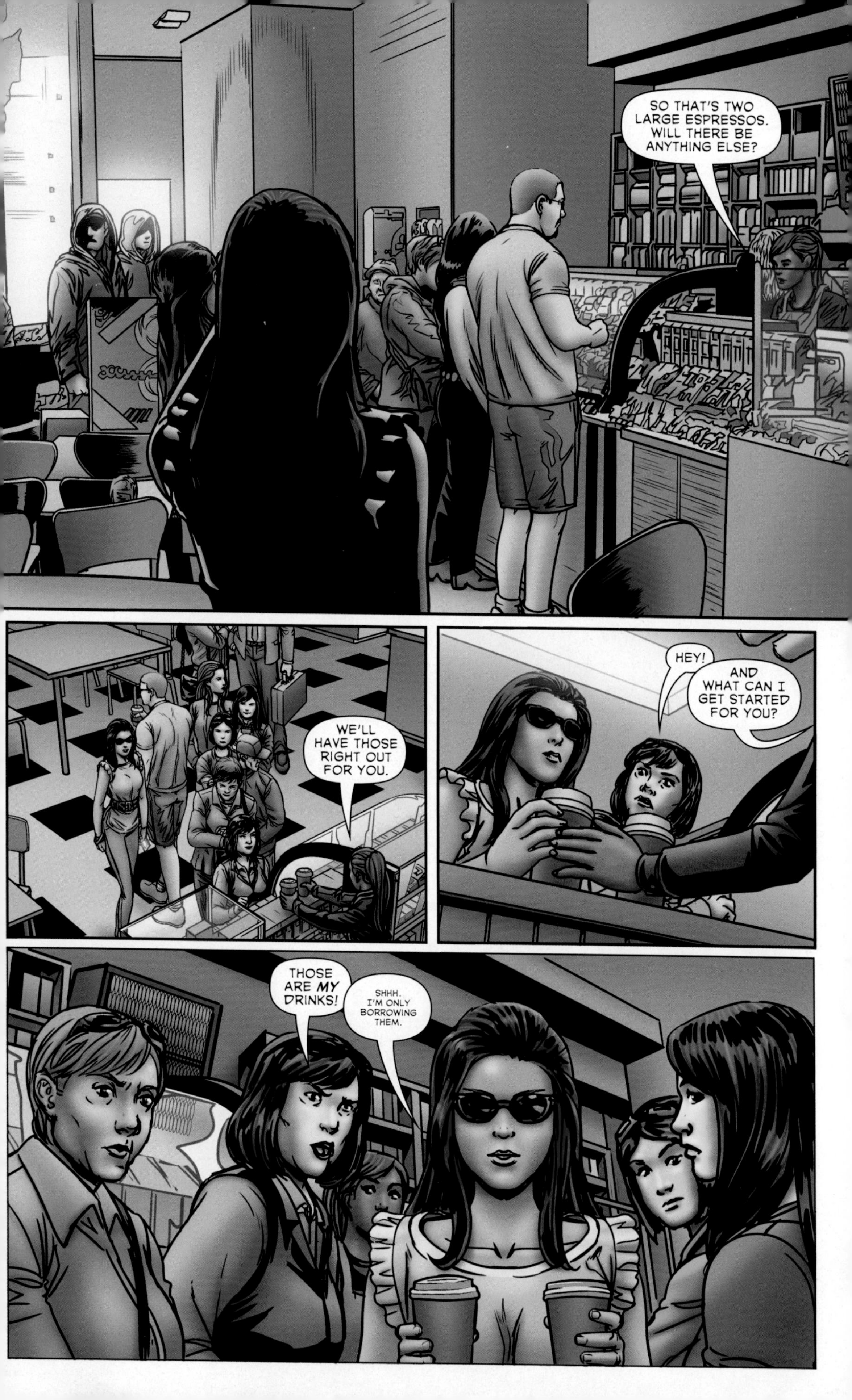
SO THAT'S TWO LARGE ESPRESSOS. WILL THERE BE ANYTHING ELSE?
WE'LL HAVE THOSE RIGHT OUT FOR YOU.
HEY!
AND WHAT CAN I GET STARTED FOR YOU?
THOSE ARE MY DRINKS!
SHHH. I'M ONLY BORROWING THEM.

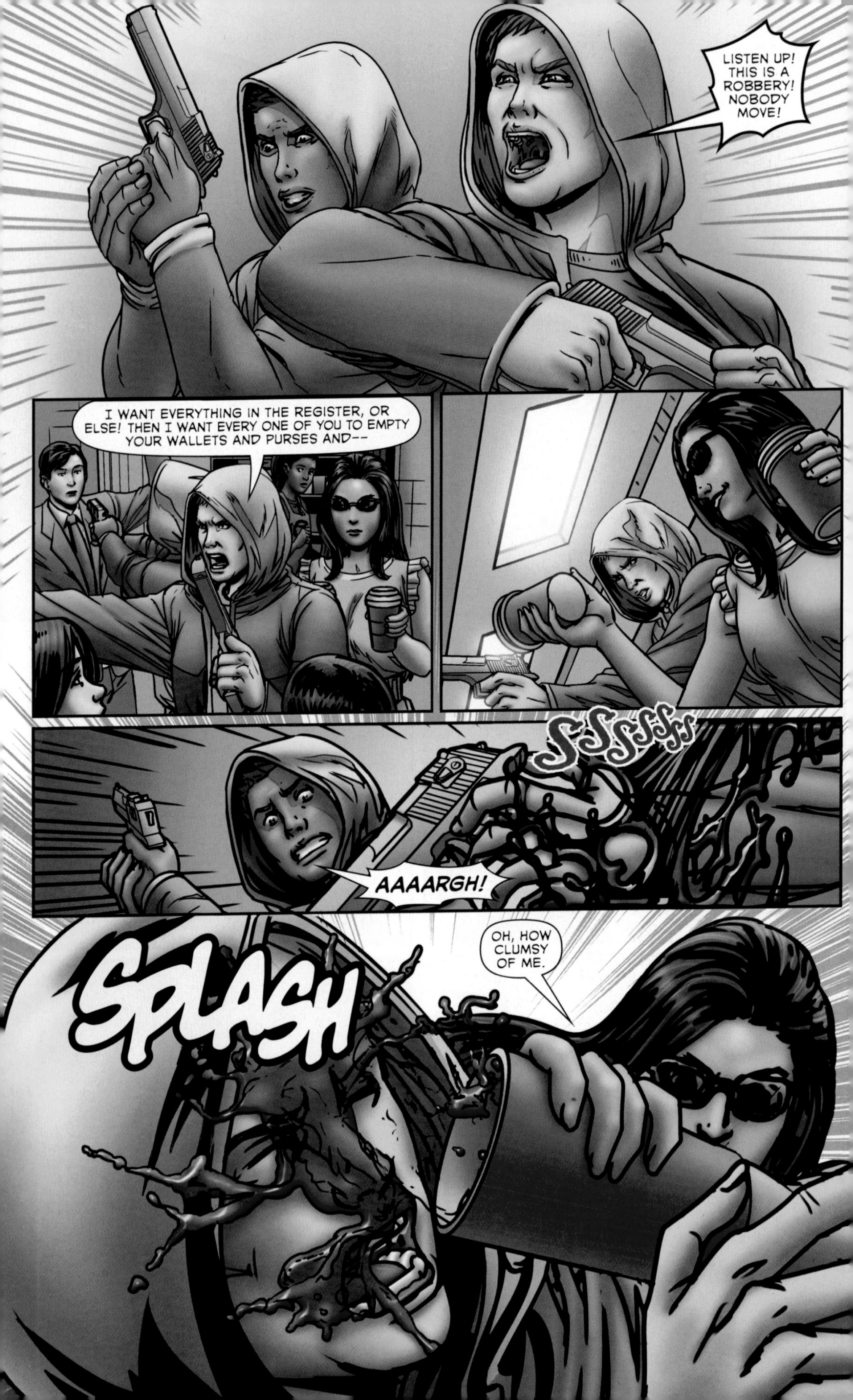
LISTEN UP! THIS IS A ROBBERY! NOBODY MOVE!
I WANT EVERYTHING IN THE REGISTER, OR ELSE! THEN I WANT EVERY ONE OF YOU TO EMPTY YOUR WALLETS AND PURSES AND--
SSSSSSS
AAAARGH!
SPLASH
OH, HOW CLUMSY OF ME.

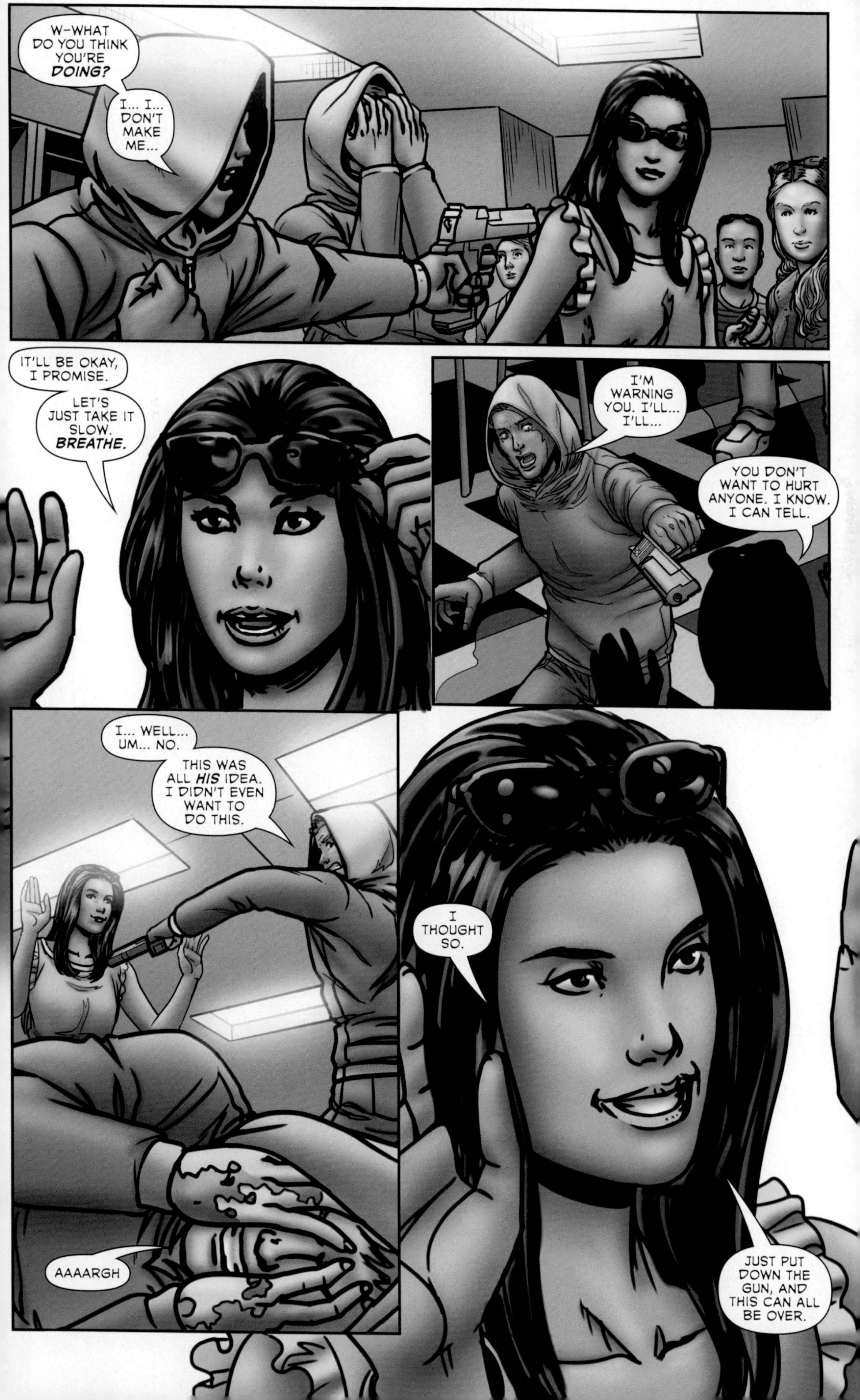
W-WHAT DO YOU THINK YOU'RE *DOING?*
I... I... DON'T MAKE ME...
IT'LL BE OKAY, I PROMISE.
LET'S JUST TAKE IT SLOW. *BREATHE.*
I'M WARNING YOU. I'LL... I'LL...
YOU DON'T WANT TO HURT ANYONE. I KNOW. I CAN TELL.
I... WELL... UM... NO.
THIS WAS ALL *HIS* IDEA. I DIDN'T EVEN WANT TO DO THIS.
AAAARGH
I THOUGHT SO.
JUST PUT DOWN THE GUN, AND THIS CAN ALL BE OVER.

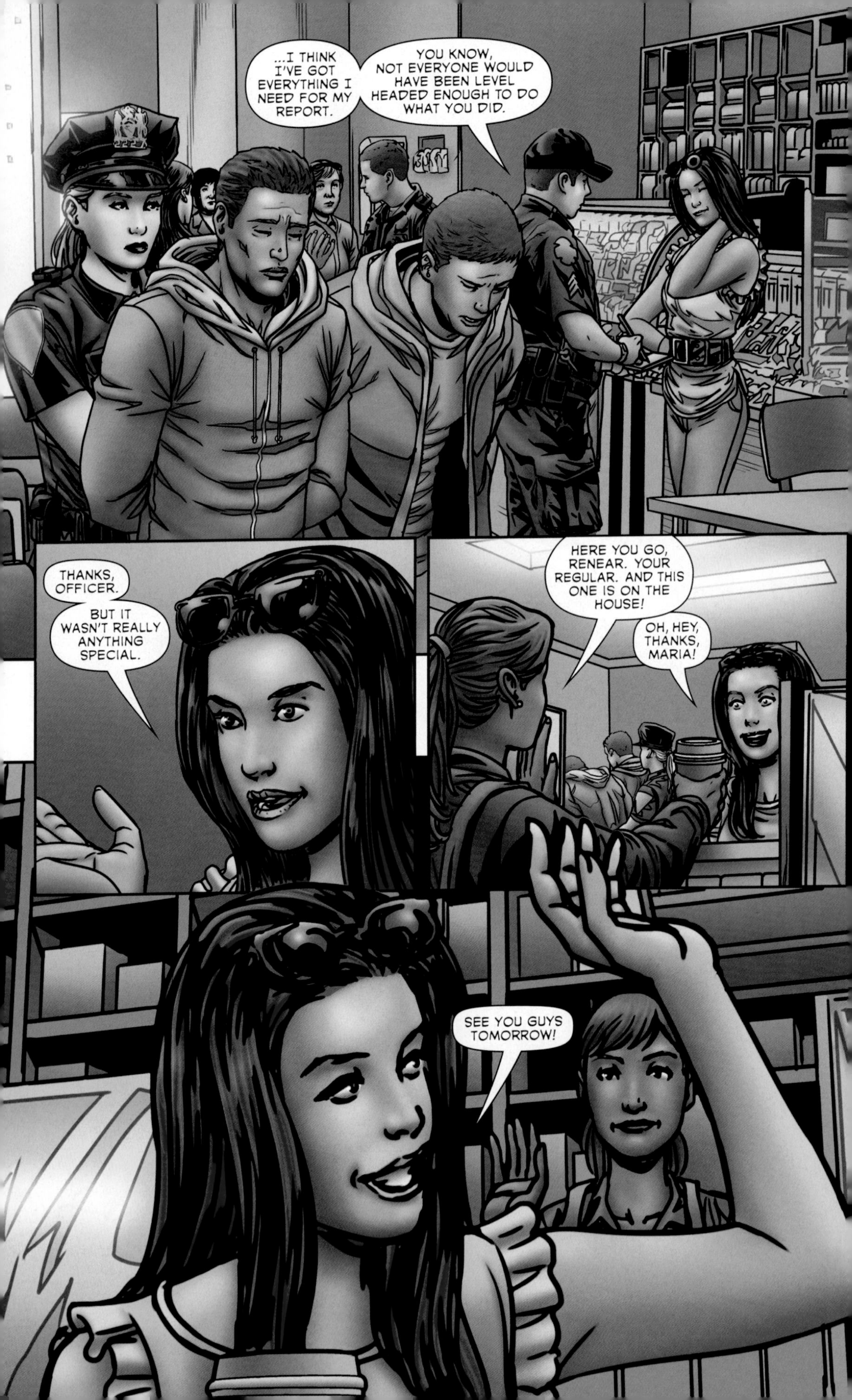

...I THINK I'VE GOT EVERYTHING I NEED FOR MY REPORT.
YOU KNOW, NOT EVERYONE WOULD HAVE BEEN LEVEL HEADED ENOUGH TO DO WHAT YOU DID.
THANKS, OFFICER.
BUT IT WASN'T REALLY ANYTHING SPECIAL.
HERE YOU GO, RENEAR. YOUR REGULAR. AND THIS ONE IS ON THE HOUSE!
OH, HEY, THANKS, MARIA!
SEE YOU GUYS TOMORROW!

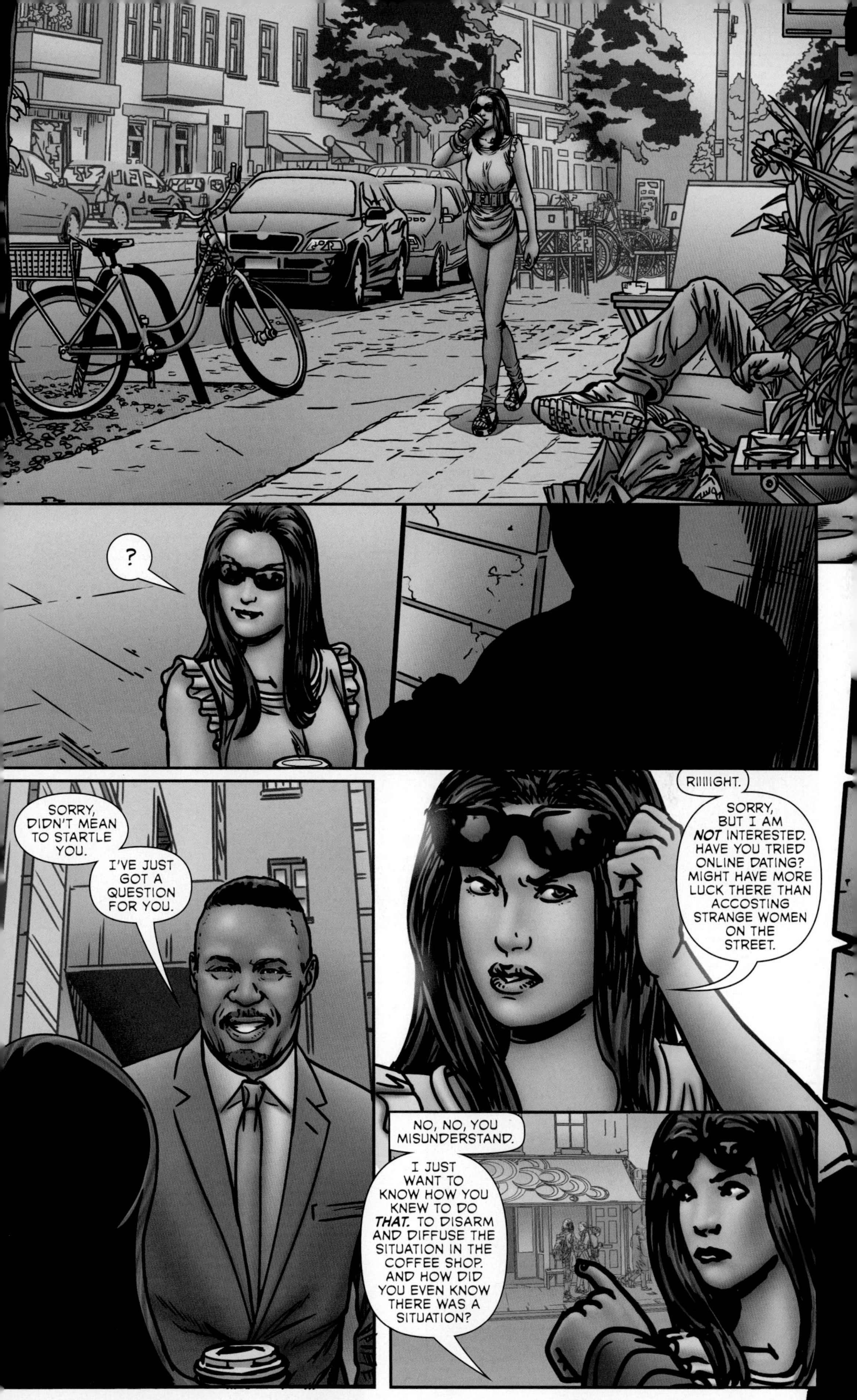
?
SORRY, DIDN'T MEAN TO STARTLE YOU.
I'VE JUST GOT A QUESTION FOR YOU.
RIIIIGHT.
SORRY, BUT I AM NOT INTERESTED. HAVE YOU TRIED ONLINE DATING? MIGHT HAVE MORE LUCK THERE THAN ACCOSTING STRANGE WOMEN ON THE STREET.
NO, NO, YOU MISUNDERSTAND.
I JUST WANT TO KNOW HOW YOU KNEW TO DO THAT. TO DISARM AND DIFFUSE THE SITUATION IN THE COFFEE SHOP. AND HOW DID YOU EVEN KNOW THERE WAS A SITUATION?

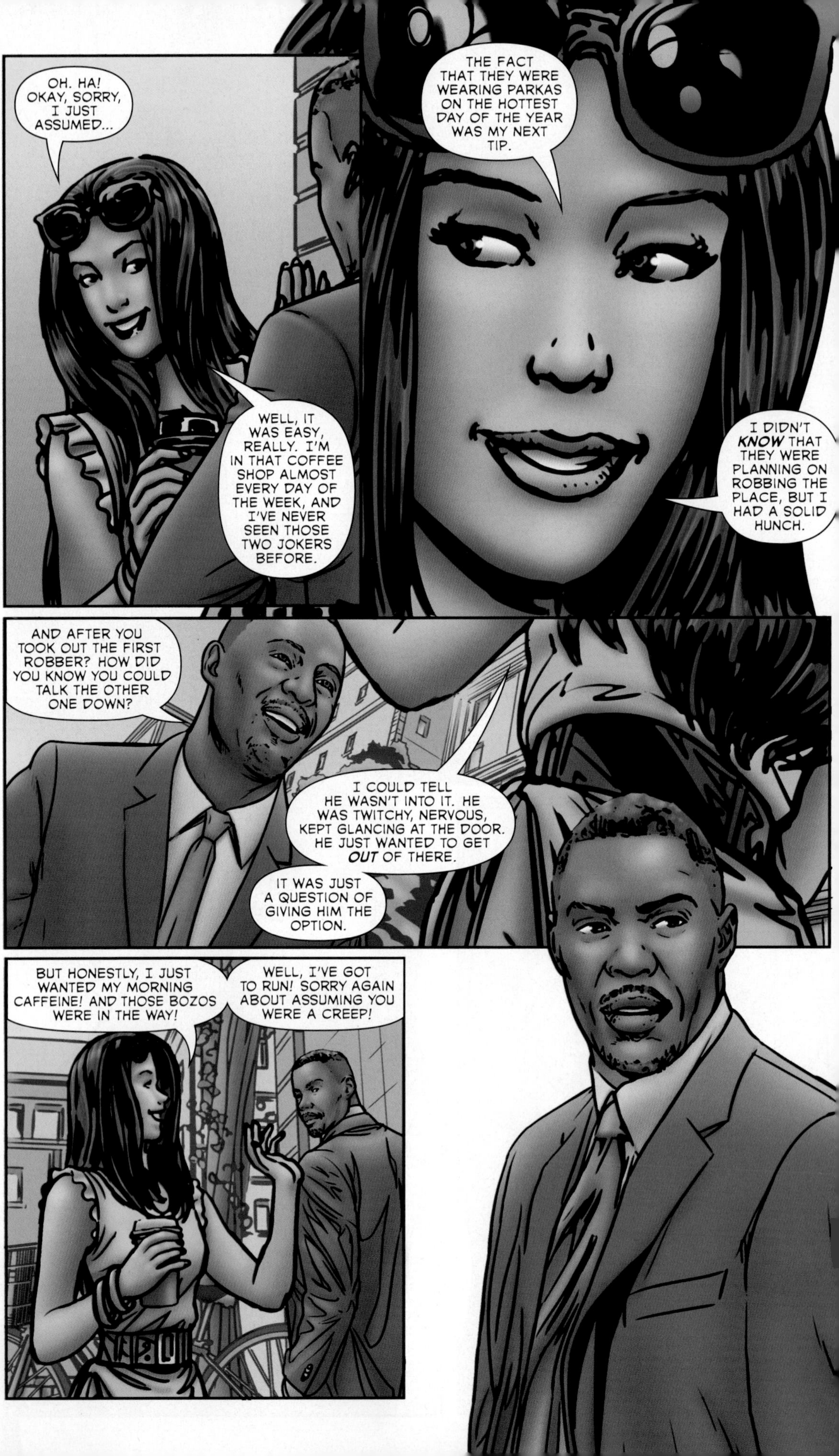

OH. HA! OKAY, SORRY, I JUST ASSUMED...
THE FACT THAT THEY WERE WEARING PARKAS ON THE HOTTEST DAY OF THE YEAR WAS MY NEXT TIP.
WELL, IT WAS EASY, REALLY. I'M IN THAT COFFEE SHOP ALMOST EVERY DAY OF THE WEEK, AND I'VE NEVER SEEN THOSE TWO JOKERS BEFORE.
I DIDN'T KNOW THAT THEY WERE PLANNING ON ROBBING THE PLACE, BUT I HAD A SOLID HUNCH.
AND AFTER YOU TOOK OUT THE FIRST ROBBER? HOW DID YOU KNOW YOU COULD TALK THE OTHER ONE DOWN?
I COULD TELL HE WASN'T INTO IT. HE WAS TWITCHY, NERVOUS, KEPT GLANCING AT THE DOOR. HE JUST WANTED TO GET OUT OF THERE.
IT WAS JUST A QUESTION OF GIVING HIM THE OPTION.
BUT HONESTLY, I JUST WANTED MY MORNING CAFFEINE! AND THOSE BOZOS WERE IN THE WAY!
WELL, I'VE GOT TO RUN! SORRY AGAIN ABOUT ASSUMING YOU WERE A CREEP!

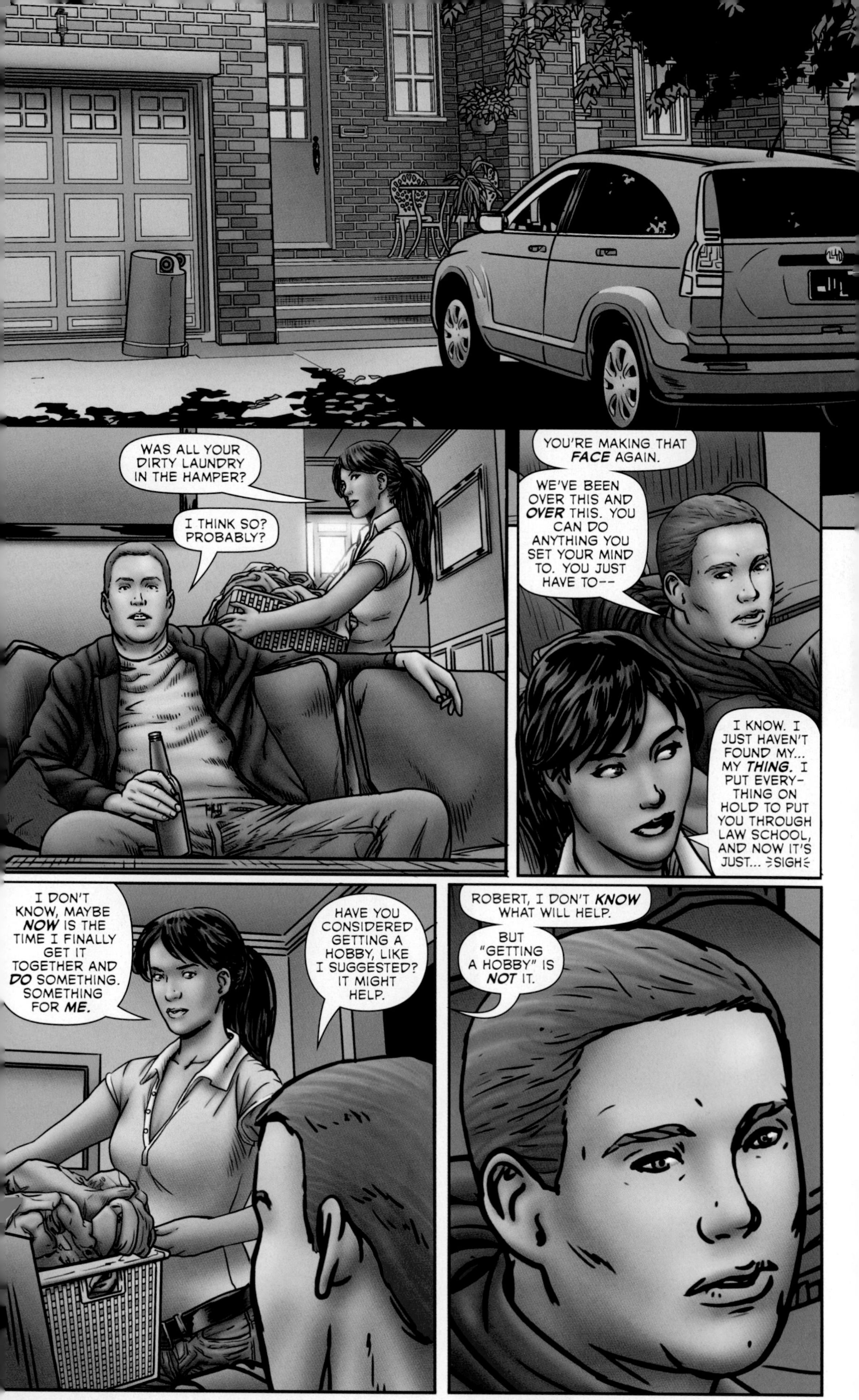
WAS ALL YOUR DIRTY LAUNDRY IN THE HAMPER?
I THINK SO? PROBABLY?
YOU'RE MAKING THAT *FACE* AGAIN.
WE'VE BEEN OVER THIS AND *OVER* THIS. YOU CAN DO ANYTHING YOU SET YOUR MIND TO. YOU JUST HAVE TO--
I KNOW. I JUST HAVEN'T FOUND MY... MY *THING.* I PUT EVERY-THING ON HOLD TO PUT YOU THROUGH LAW SCHOOL, AND NOW IT'S JUST... ⩶SIGH⩵
I DON'T KNOW, MAYBE *NOW* IS THE TIME I FINALLY GET IT TOGETHER AND *DO* SOMETHING. SOMETHING FOR *ME.*
HAVE YOU CONSIDERED GETTING A HOBBY, LIKE I SUGGESTED? IT MIGHT HELP.
ROBERT, I DON'T *KNOW* WHAT WILL HELP.
BUT "GETTING A HOBBY" IS *NOT* IT.

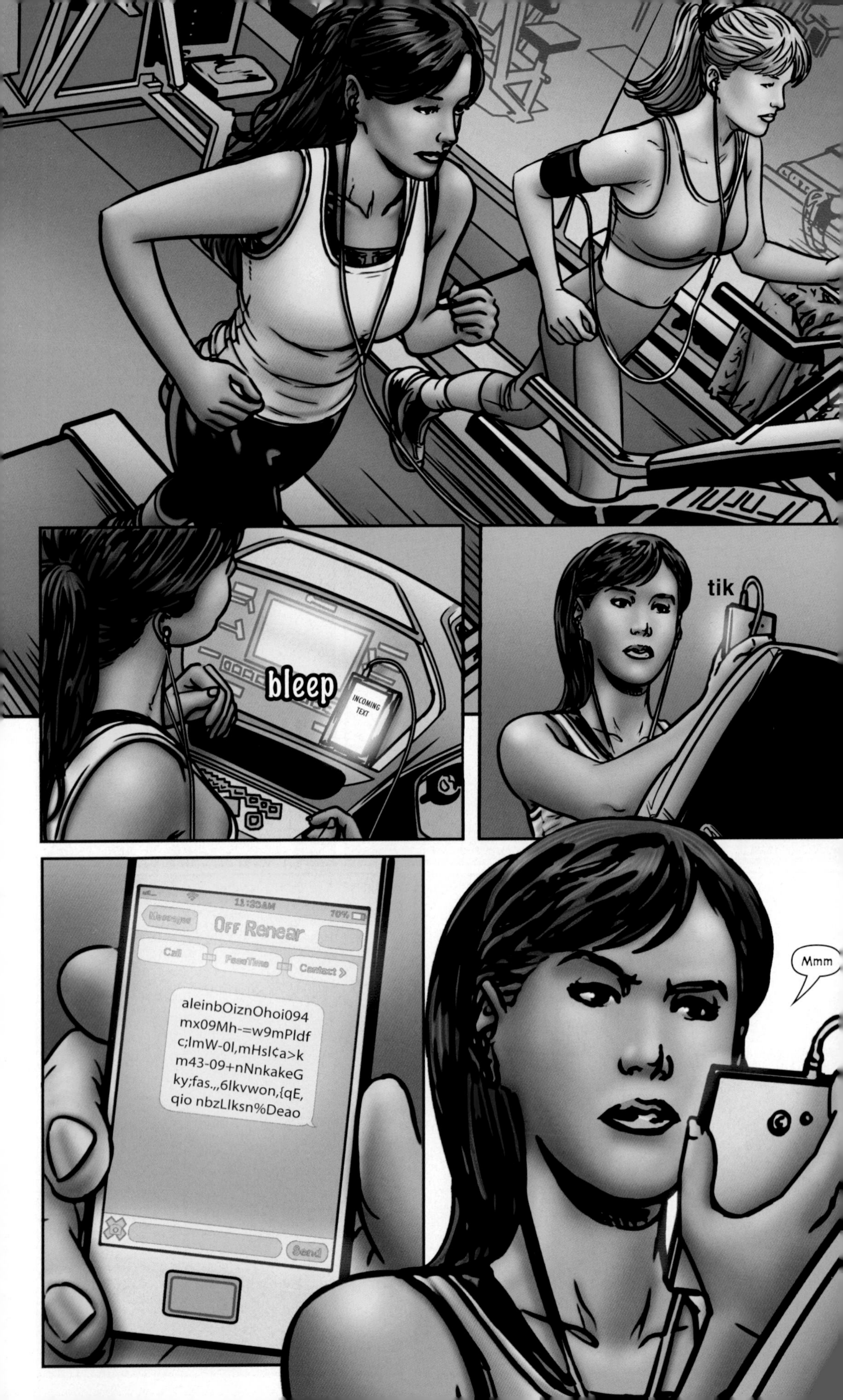
bleep
INCOMING TEXT
tik
11:30AM
70%
Off Renear
Call
FaceTime
Contact >
aleinbOiznOhoi094
mx09Mh-=w9mPldf
c;lmW-0l,mHsl¢a>k
m43-09+nNnkakeG
ky;fas.,,6lkvwon,{qE,
qio nbzLlksn%Deao
Send
Mmm

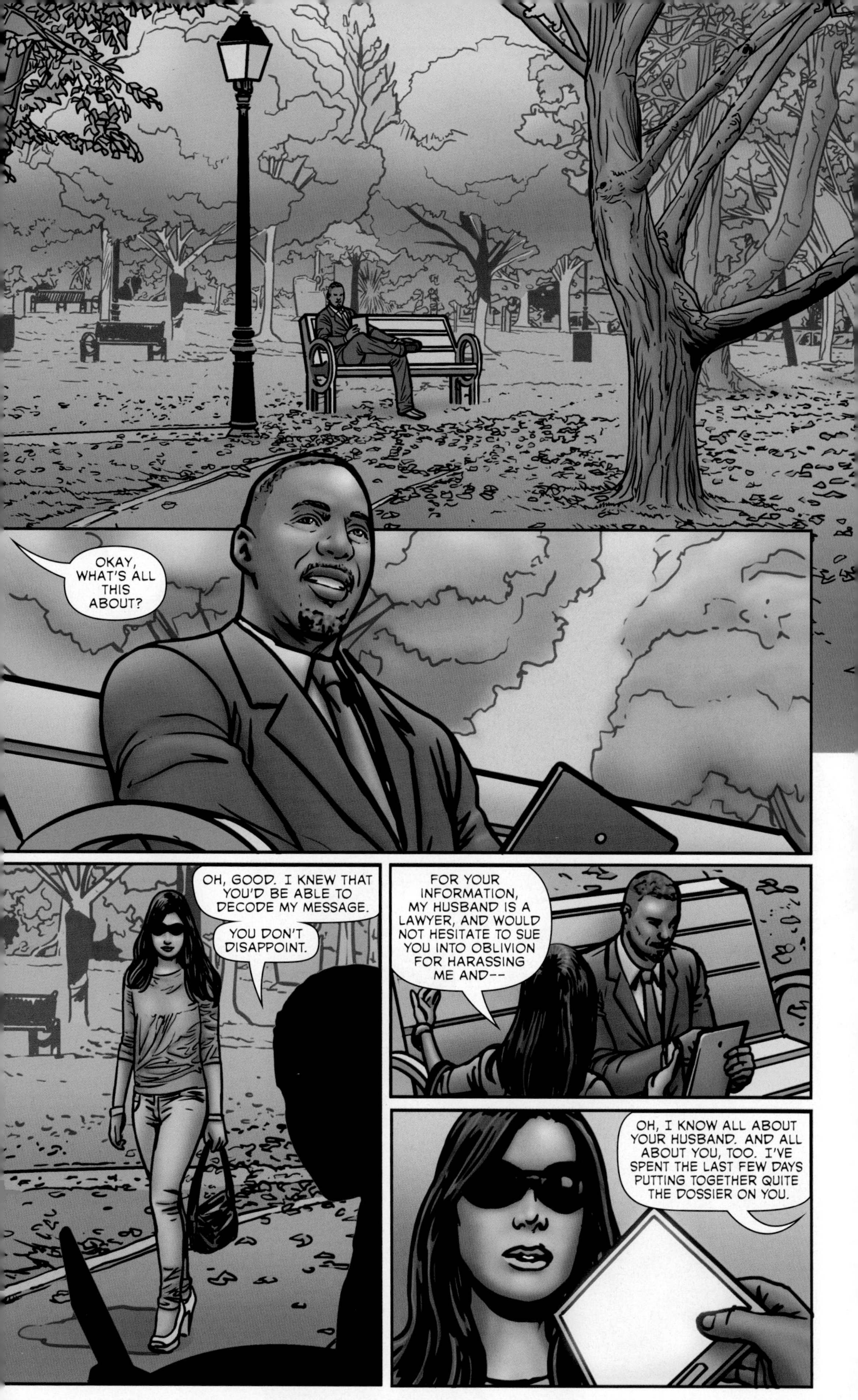
OKAY, WHAT'S ALL THIS ABOUT?
OH, GOOD. I KNEW THAT YOU'D BE ABLE TO DECODE MY MESSAGE.
YOU DON'T DISAPPOINT.
FOR YOUR INFORMATION, MY HUSBAND IS A LAWYER, AND WOULD NOT HESITATE TO SUE YOU INTO OBLIVION FOR HARASSING ME AND--
OH, I KNOW ALL ABOUT YOUR HUSBAND. AND ALL ABOUT YOU, TOO. I'VE SPENT THE LAST FEW DAYS PUTTING TOGETHER QUITE THE DOSSIER ON YOU.

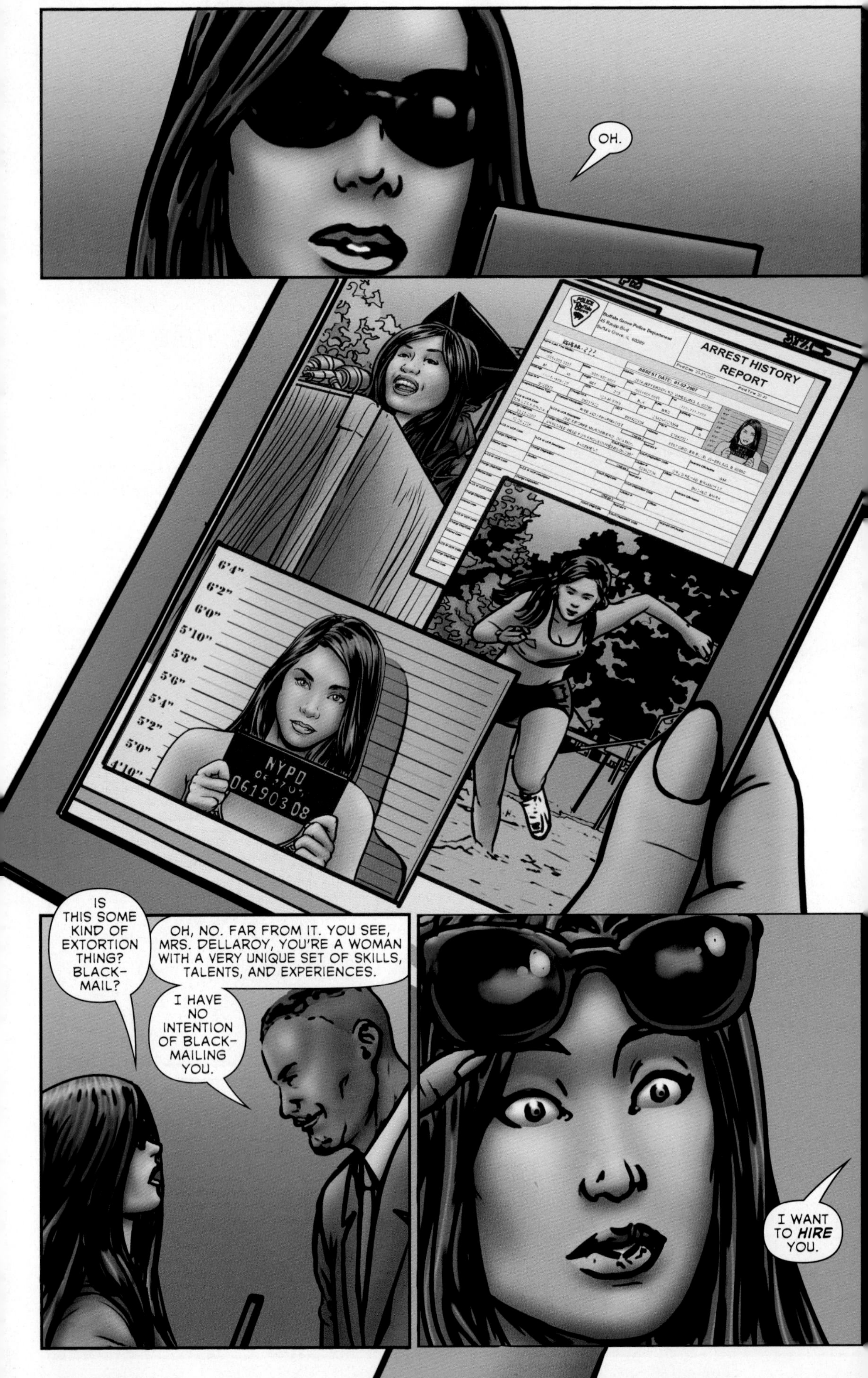
OH.
ARREST HISTORY REPORT
6'4"
6'2"
6'0"
5'10"
5'8"
5'6"
5'4"
5'2"
5'0"
4'10"
NYPD
061903 08
IS THIS SOME KIND OF EXTORTION THING? BLACK-MAIL?
OH, NO. FAR FROM IT. YOU SEE, MRS. DELLAROY, YOU'RE A WOMAN WITH A VERY UNIQUE SET OF SKILLS, TALENTS, AND EXPERIENCES.
I HAVE NO INTENTION OF BLACK-MAILING YOU.
I WANT TO ***HIRE*** YOU.

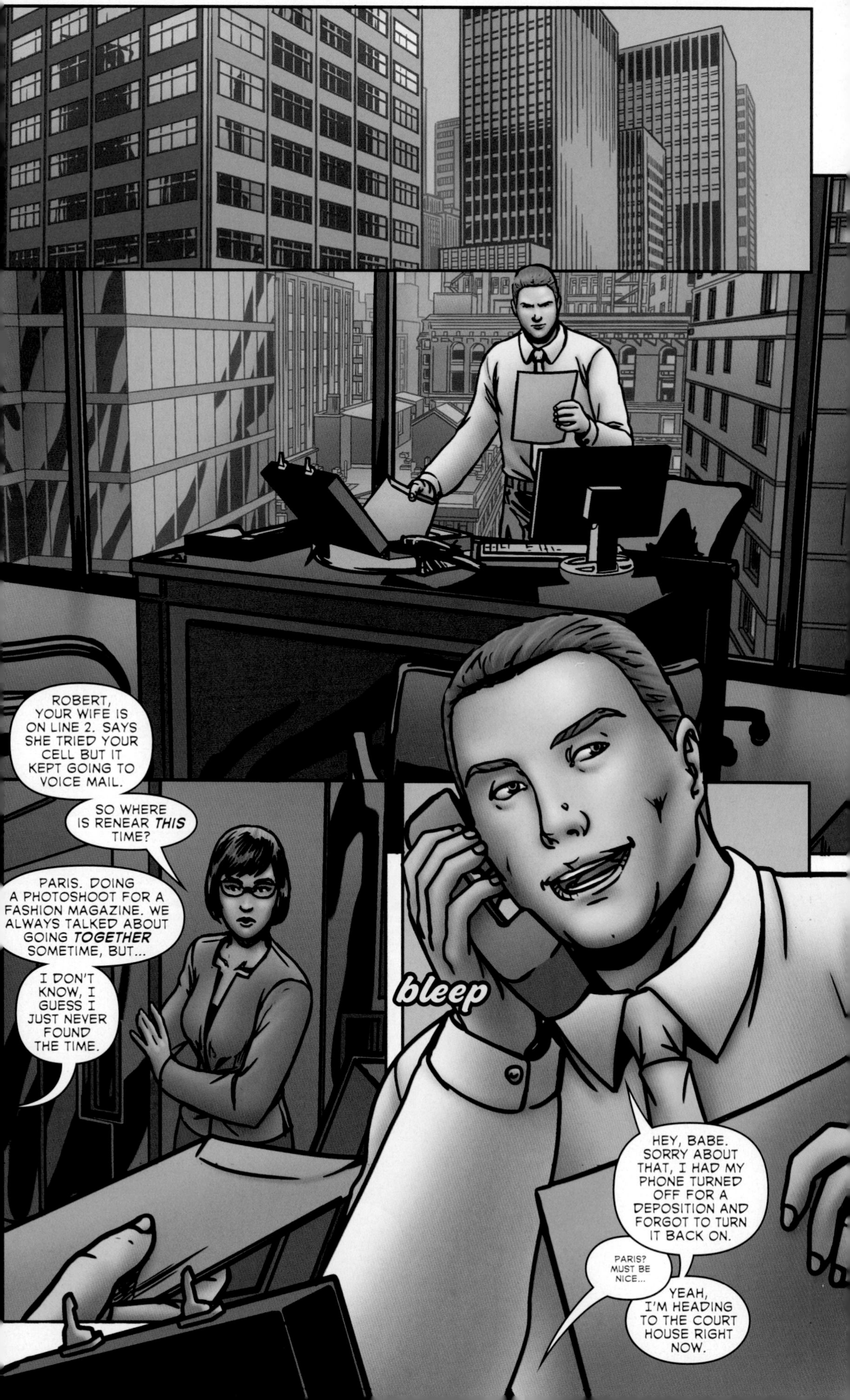
ROBERT, YOUR WIFE IS ON LINE 2. SAYS SHE TRIED YOUR CELL BUT IT KEPT GOING TO VOICE MAIL.
SO WHERE IS RENEAR *THIS* TIME?
PARIS. DOING A PHOTOSHOOT FOR A FASHION MAGAZINE. WE ALWAYS TALKED ABOUT GOING *TOGETHER* SOMETIME, BUT...
I DON'T KNOW, I GUESS I JUST NEVER FOUND THE TIME.
bleep
HEY, BABE. SORRY ABOUT THAT, I HAD MY PHONE TURNED OFF FOR A DEPOSITION AND FORGOT TO TURN IT BACK ON.
PARIS? MUST BE NICE...
YEAH, I'M HEADING TO THE COURT HOUSE RIGHT NOW.

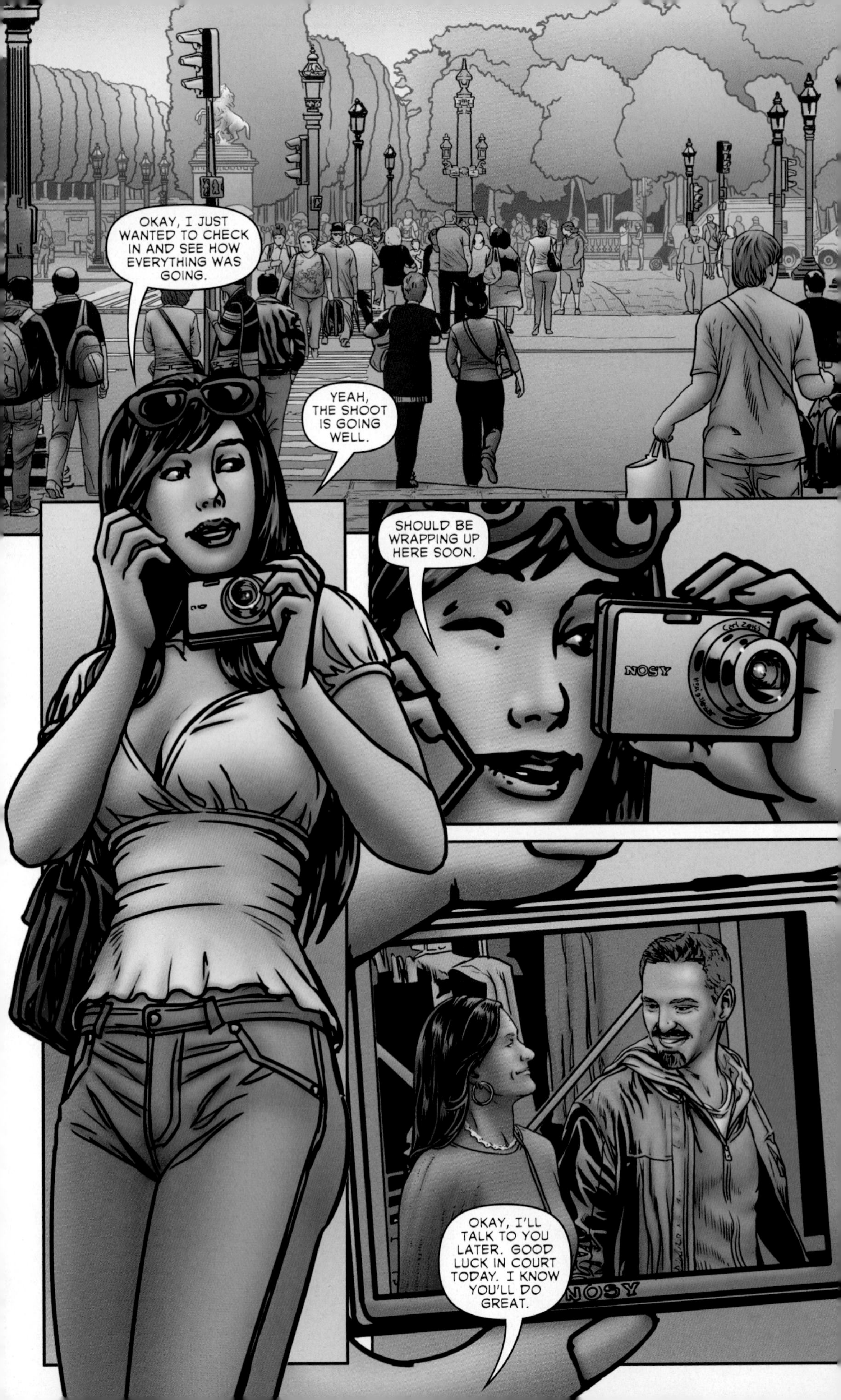

OKAY, I JUST WANTED TO CHECK IN AND SEE HOW EVERYTHING WAS GOING.
YEAH, THE SHOOT IS GOING WELL.
SHOULD BE WRAPPING UP HERE SOON.
NOSY
NOSY
OKAY, I'LL TALK TO YOU LATER. GOOD LUCK IN COURT TODAY. I KNOW YOU'LL DO GREAT.

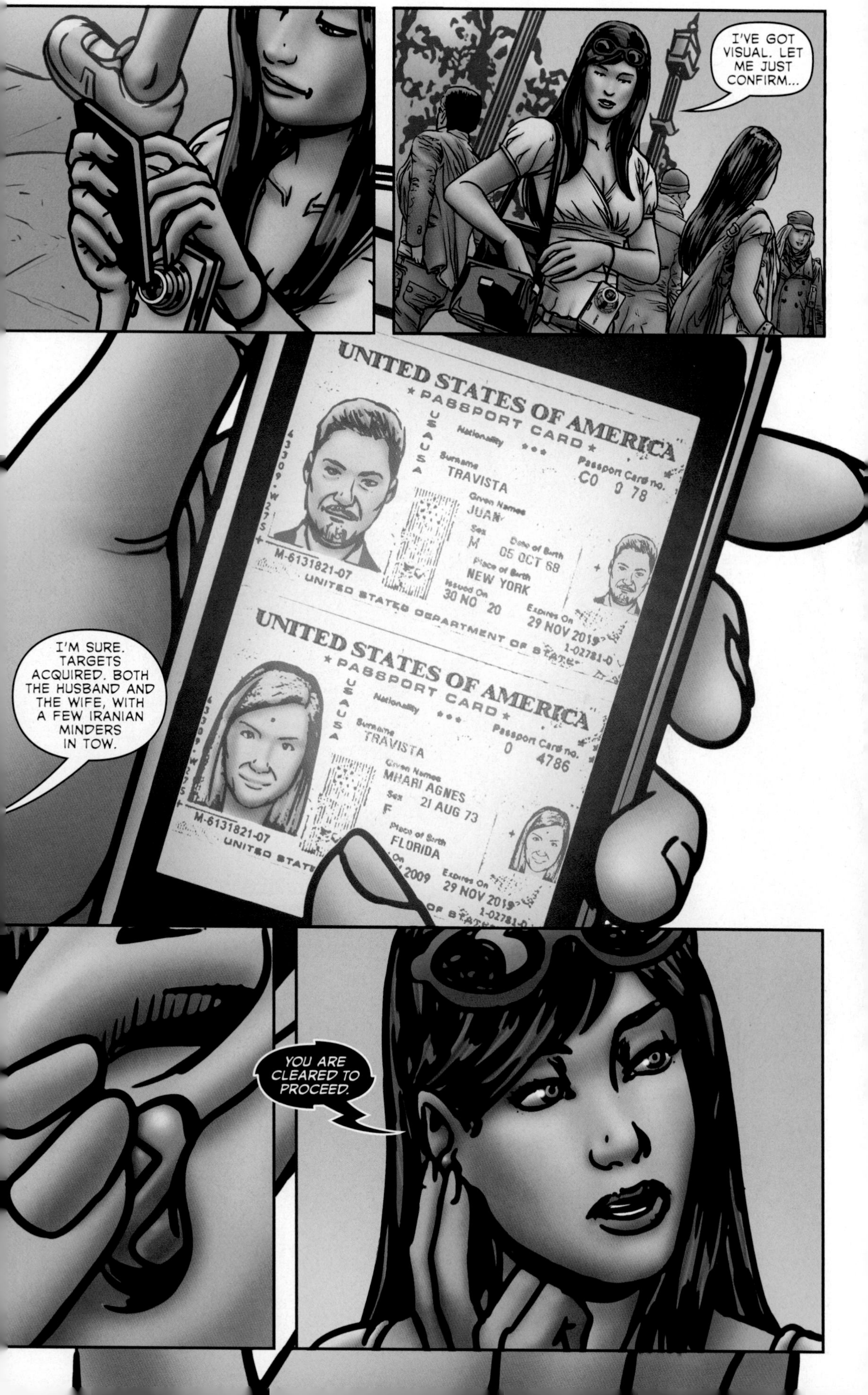
I'VE GOT VISUAL. LET ME JUST CONFIRM...
UNITED STATES OF AMERICA
PASSPORT CARD
Nationality
Surname
TRAVISTA
Passport Card no.
Given Names
JUAN
Sex
M
Date of Birth
05 OCT 68
Place of Birth
NEW YORK
Issued On
Expires On
29 NOV 2019
M-6131821-07
UNITED STATES DEPARTMENT OF STATE
I'M SURE. TARGETS ACQUIRED. BOTH THE HUSBAND AND THE WIFE, WITH A FEW IRANIAN MINDERS IN TOW.
UNITED STATES OF AMERICA
PASSPORT CARD
Nationality
Surname
TRAVISTA
Passport Card no.
4786
Given Names
MHARI AGNES
Sex
F
21 AUG 73
Place of Birth
FLORIDA
Expires On
29 NOV 2019
M-6131821-07
YOU ARE CLEARED TO PROCEED.

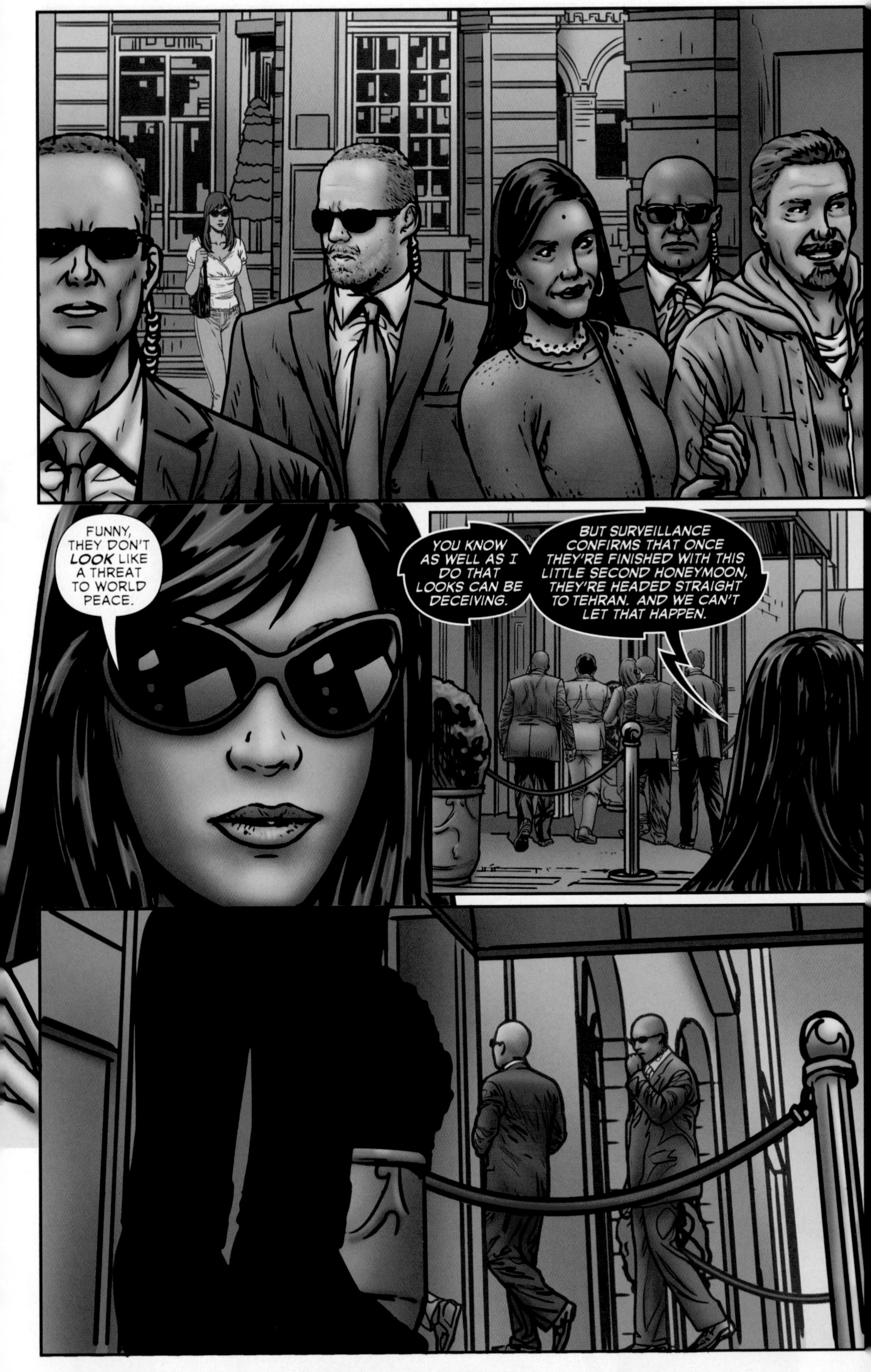
FUNNY, THEY DON'T LOOK LIKE A THREAT TO WORLD PEACE.
YOU KNOW AS WELL AS I DO THAT LOOKS CAN BE DECEIVING.
BUT SURVEILLANCE CONFIRMS THAT ONCE THEY'RE FINISHED WITH THIS LITTLE SECOND HONEYMOON, THEY'RE HEADED STRAIGHT TO TEHRAN. AND WE CAN'T LET THAT HAPPEN.

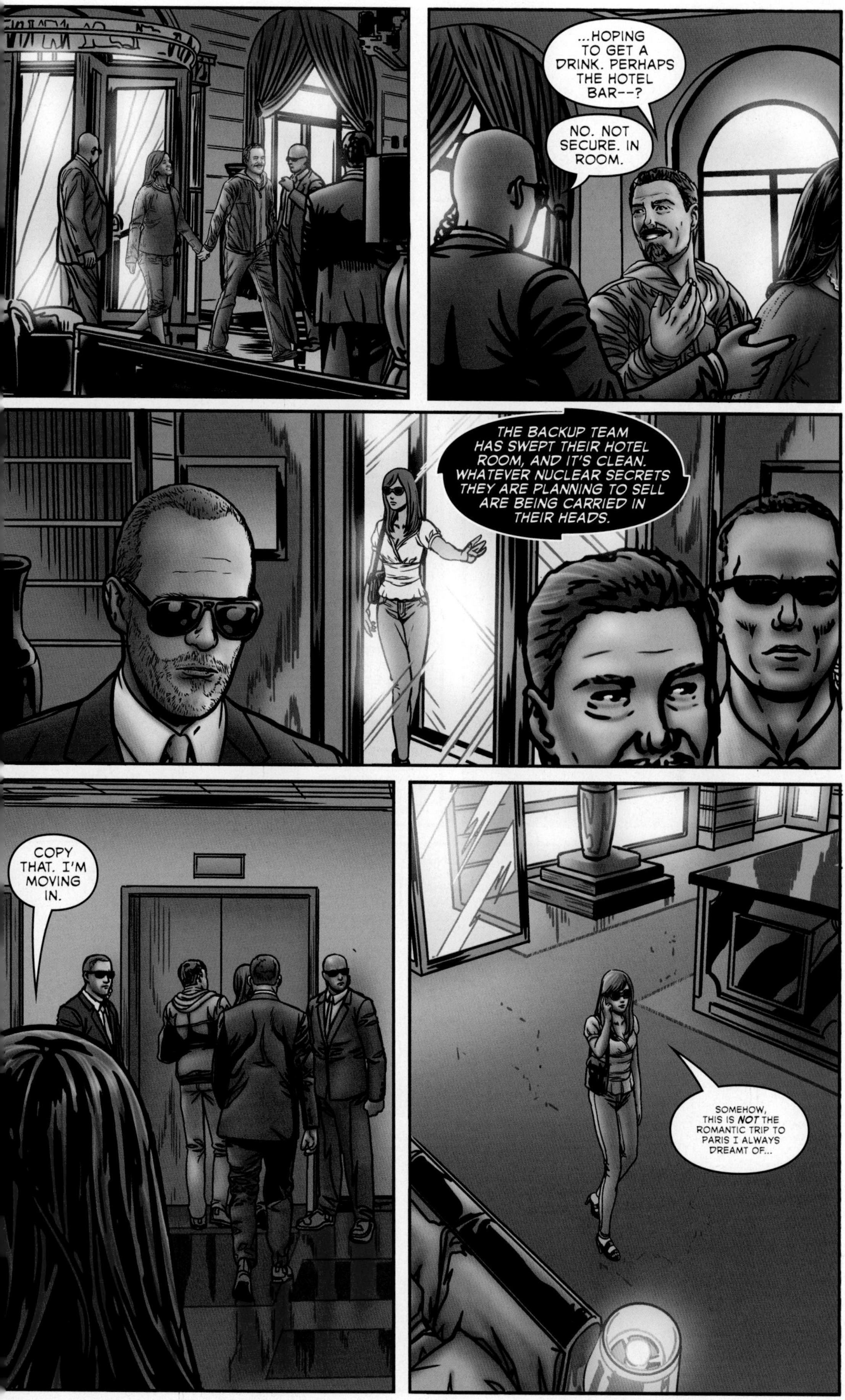
...HOPING TO GET A DRINK. PERHAPS THE HOTEL BAR--?
NO. NOT SECURE. IN ROOM.
THE BACKUP TEAM HAS SWEPT THEIR HOTEL ROOM, AND IT'S CLEAN. WHATEVER NUCLEAR SECRETS THEY ARE PLANNING TO SELL ARE BEING CARRIED IN THEIR HEADS.
COPY THAT. I'M MOVING IN.
SOMEHOW, THIS IS NOT THE ROMANTIC TRIP TO PARIS I ALWAYS DREAMT OF...

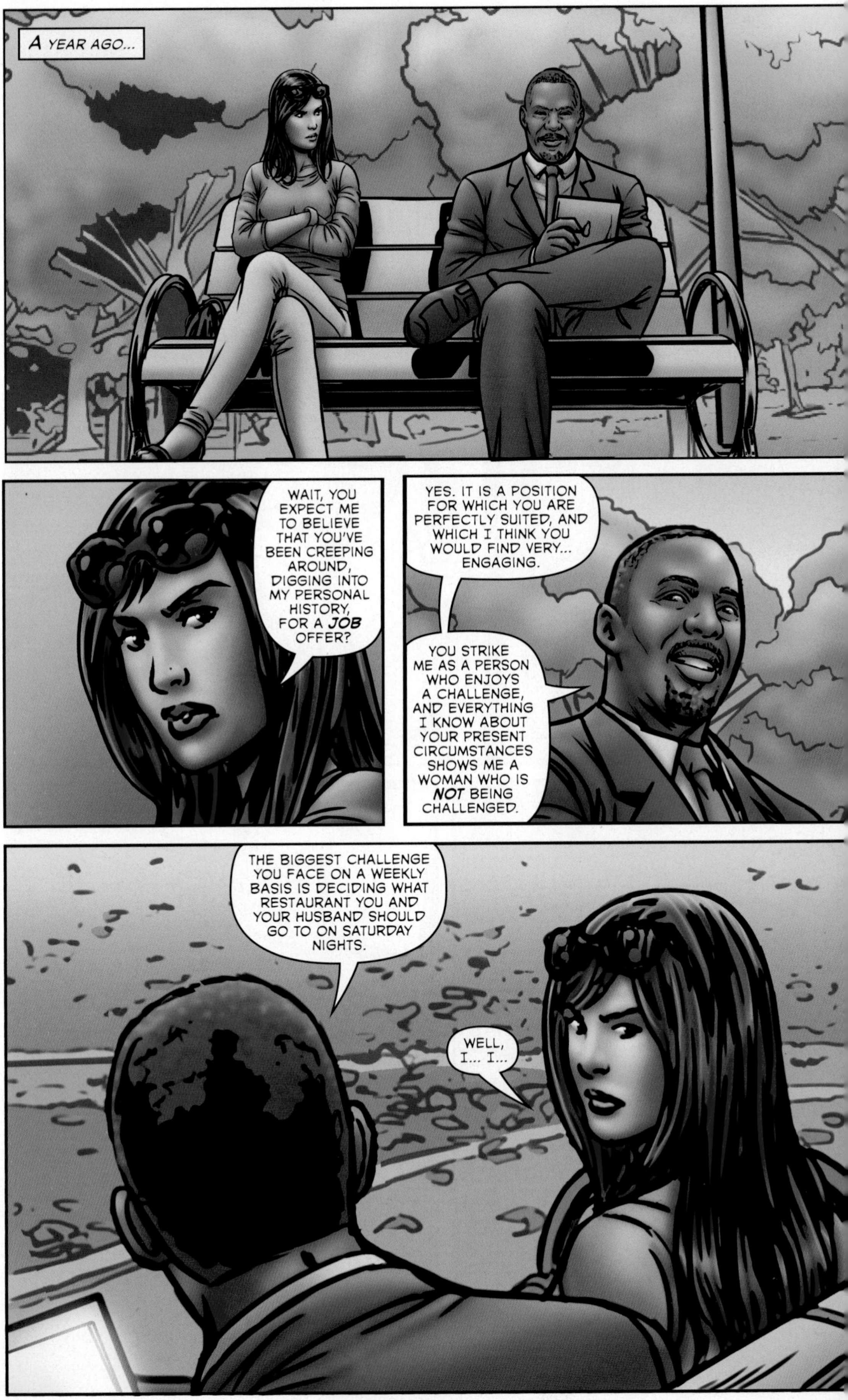

A YEAR AGO...
WAIT, YOU EXPECT ME TO BELIEVE THAT YOU'VE BEEN CREEPING AROUND, DIGGING INTO MY PERSONAL HISTORY, FOR A JOB OFFER?
YES. IT IS A POSITION FOR WHICH YOU ARE PERFECTLY SUITED, AND WHICH I THINK YOU WOULD FIND VERY... ENGAGING.
YOU STRIKE ME AS A PERSON WHO ENJOYS A CHALLENGE, AND EVERYTHING I KNOW ABOUT YOUR PRESENT CIRCUMSTANCES SHOWS ME A WOMAN WHO IS NOT BEING CHALLENGED.
THE BIGGEST CHALLENGE YOU FACE ON A WEEKLY BASIS IS DECIDING WHAT RESTAURANT YOU AND YOUR HUSBAND SHOULD GO TO ON SATURDAY NIGHTS.
WELL, I... I...

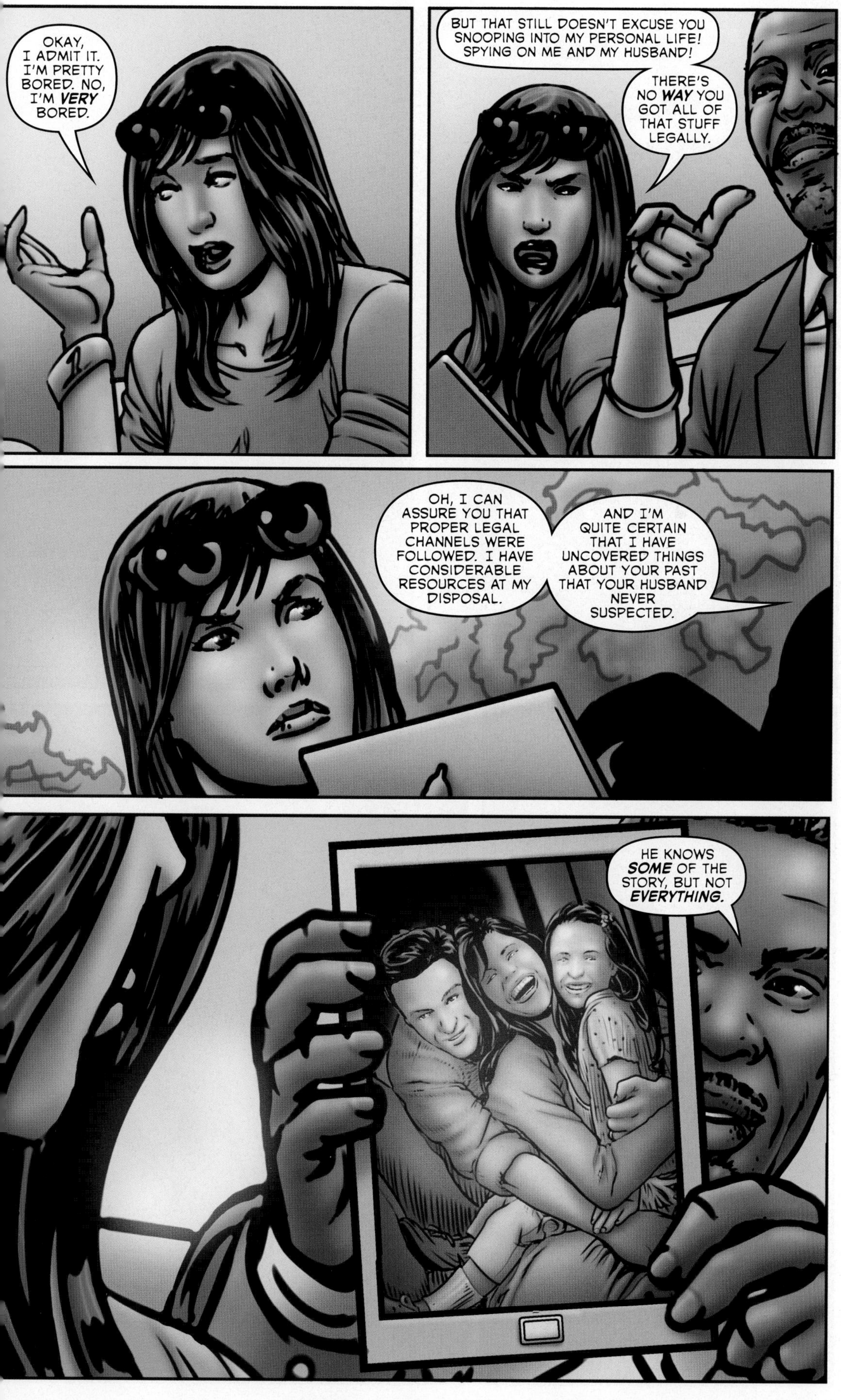

OKAY, I ADMIT IT. I'M PRETTY BORED. NO, I'M VERY BORED.
BUT THAT STILL DOESN'T EXCUSE YOU SNOOPING INTO MY PERSONAL LIFE! SPYING ON ME AND MY HUSBAND!
THERE'S NO WAY YOU GOT ALL OF THAT STUFF LEGALLY.
OH, I CAN ASSURE YOU THAT PROPER LEGAL CHANNELS WERE FOLLOWED. I HAVE CONSIDERABLE RESOURCES AT MY DISPOSAL.
AND I'M QUITE CERTAIN THAT I HAVE UNCOVERED THINGS ABOUT YOUR PAST THAT YOUR HUSBAND NEVER SUSPECTED.
HE KNOWS SOME OF THE STORY, BUT NOT EVERYTHING.

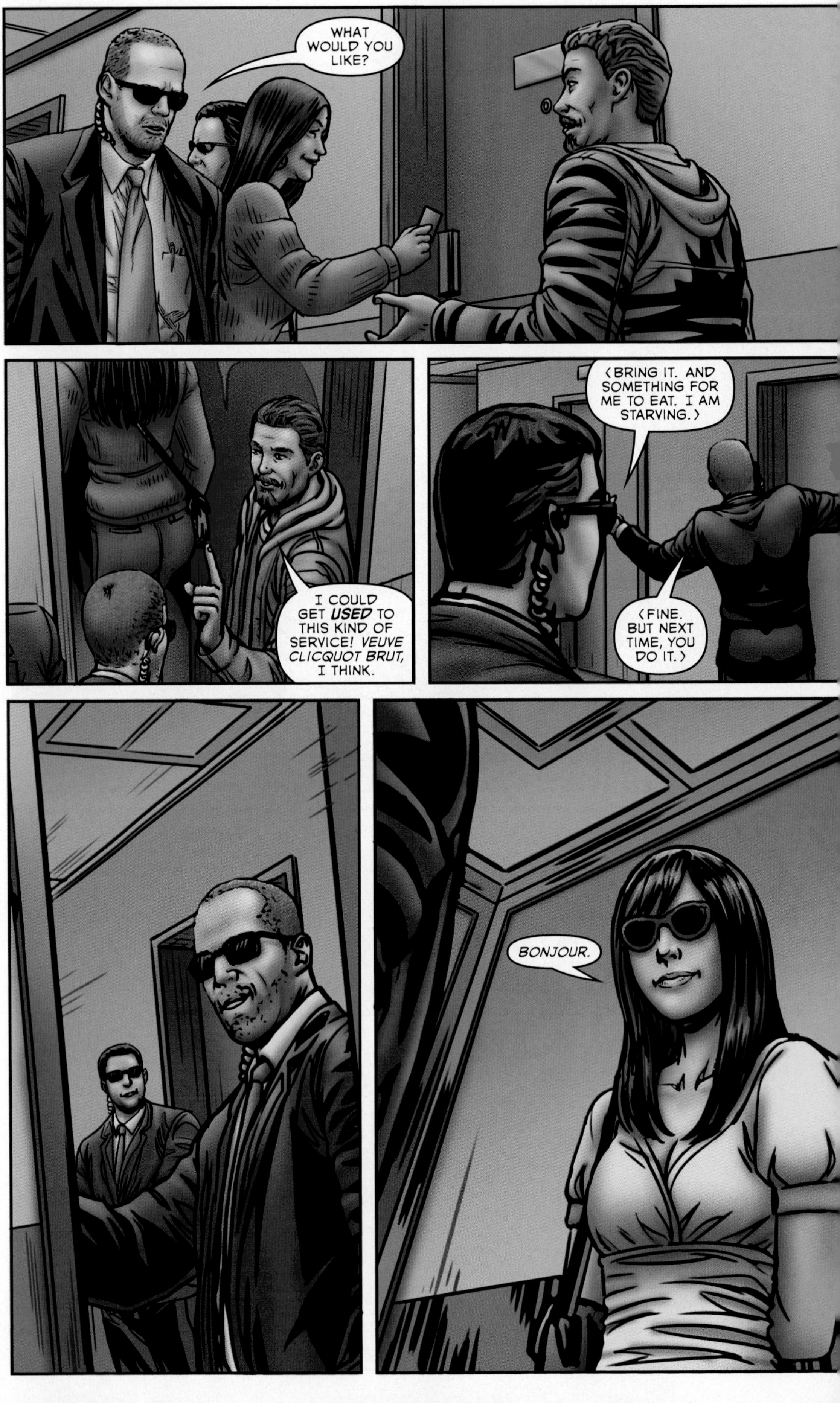
WHAT WOULD YOU LIKE?
I COULD GET *USED* TO THIS KIND OF SERVICE! *VEUVE CLICQUOT BRUT*, I THINK.
<BRING IT. AND SOMETHING FOR ME TO EAT. I AM STARVING.>
<FINE. BUT NEXT TIME, YOU DO IT.>
BONJOUR.

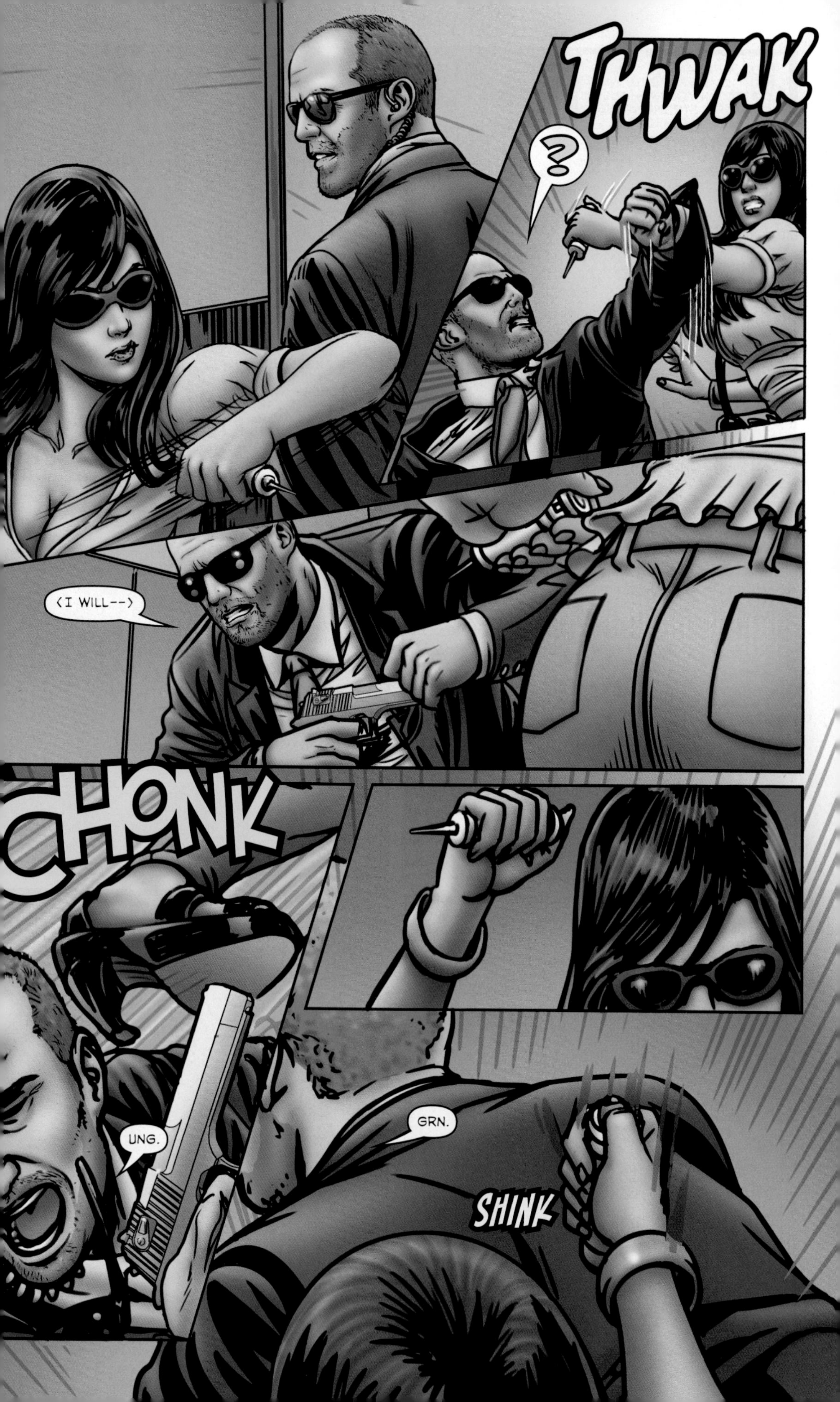
THWAK
?
<I WILL-->
CHONK
UNG.
GRN.
SHINK

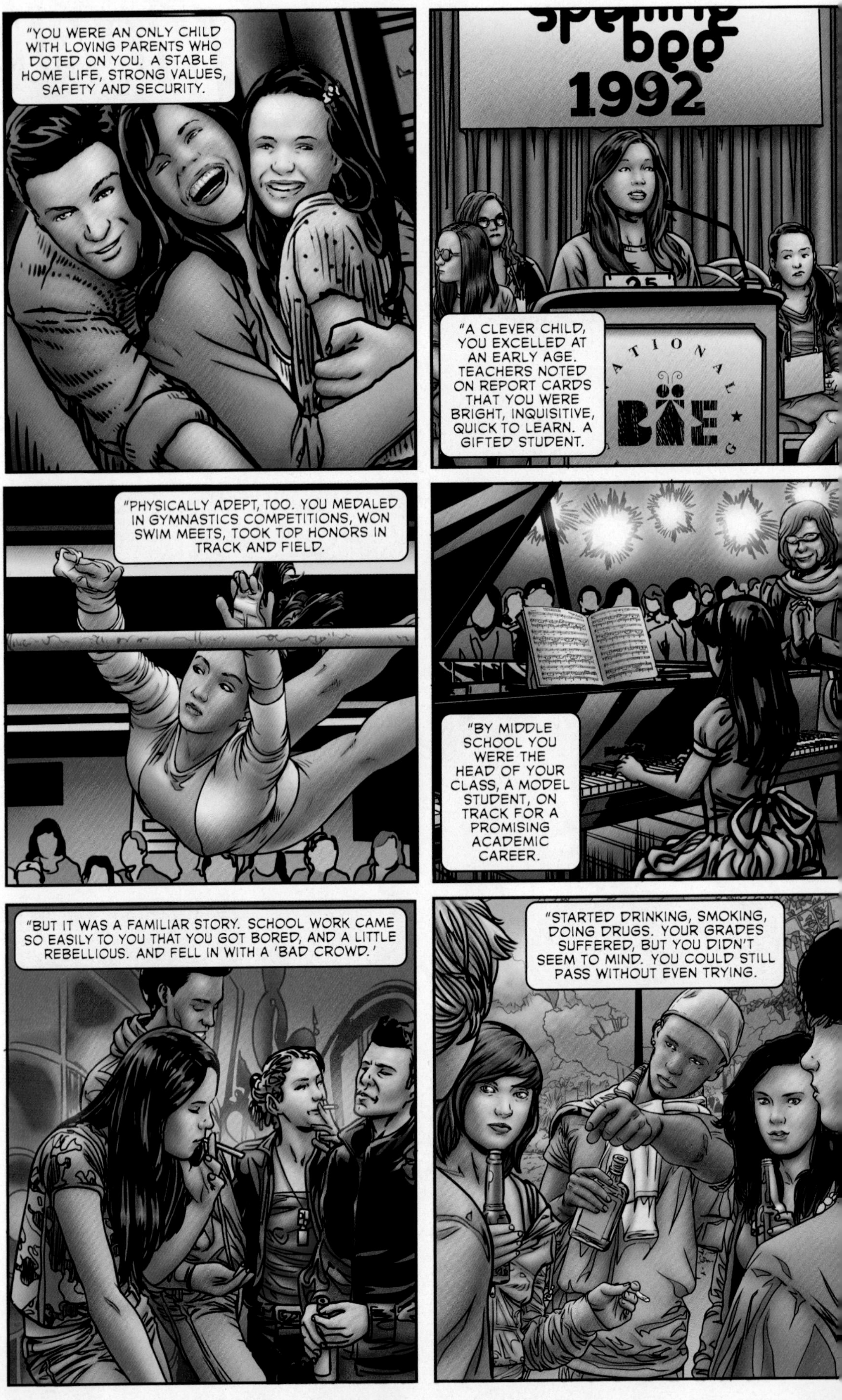

"YOU WERE AN ONLY CHILD WITH LOVING PARENTS WHO DOTED ON YOU. A STABLE HOME LIFE, STRONG VALUES, SAFETY AND SECURITY.
bee
1992
"A CLEVER CHILD, YOU EXCELLED AT AN EARLY AGE. TEACHERS NOTED ON REPORT CARDS THAT YOU WERE BRIGHT, INQUISITIVE, QUICK TO LEARN. A GIFTED STUDENT.
"PHYSICALLY ADEPT, TOO. YOU MEDALED IN GYMNASTICS COMPETITIONS, WON SWIM MEETS, TOOK TOP HONORS IN TRACK AND FIELD.
"BY MIDDLE SCHOOL YOU WERE THE HEAD OF YOUR CLASS, A MODEL STUDENT, ON TRACK FOR A PROMISING ACADEMIC CAREER.
"BUT IT WAS A FAMILIAR STORY. SCHOOL WORK CAME SO EASILY TO YOU THAT YOU GOT BORED, AND A LITTLE REBELLIOUS. AND FELL IN WITH A 'BAD CROWD.'
"STARTED DRINKING, SMOKING, DOING DRUGS. YOUR GRADES SUFFERED, BUT YOU DIDN'T SEEM TO MIND. YOU COULD STILL PASS WITHOUT EVEN TRYING.

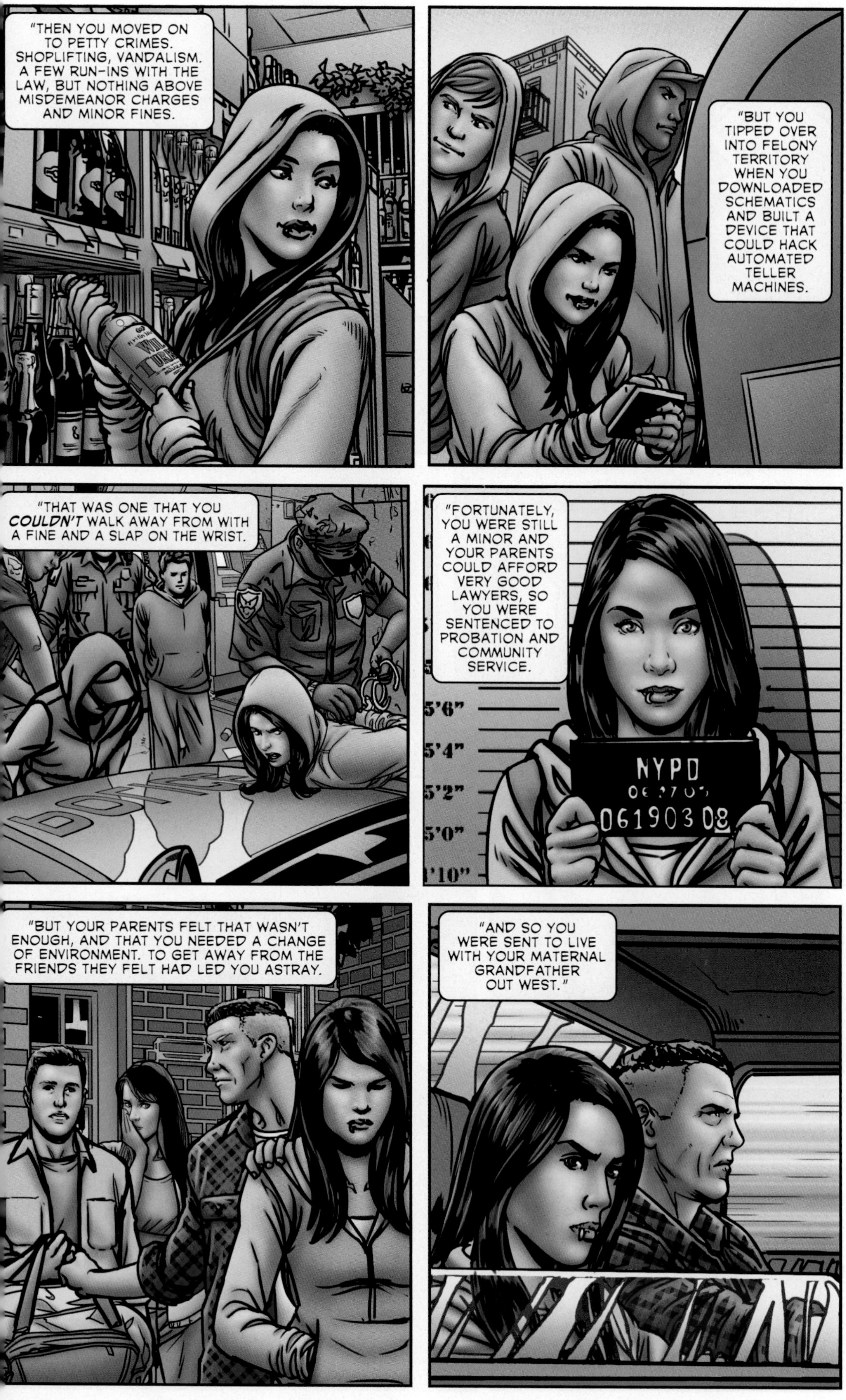
"THEN YOU MOVED ON TO PETTY CRIMES. SHOPLIFTING, VANDALISM. A FEW RUN-INS WITH THE LAW, BUT NOTHING ABOVE MISDEMEANOR CHARGES AND MINOR FINES.
"BUT YOU TIPPED OVER INTO FELONY TERRITORY WHEN YOU DOWNLOADED SCHEMATICS AND BUILT A DEVICE THAT COULD HACK AUTOMATED TELLER MACHINES.
"THAT WAS ONE THAT YOU *COULDN'T* WALK AWAY FROM WITH A FINE AND A SLAP ON THE WRIST.
"FORTUNATELY, YOU WERE STILL A MINOR AND YOUR PARENTS COULD AFFORD VERY GOOD LAWYERS, SO YOU WERE SENTENCED TO PROBATION AND COMMUNITY SERVICE.
5'6"
5'4"
5'2"
5'0"
NYPD
06190308
"BUT YOUR PARENTS FELT THAT WASN'T ENOUGH, AND THAT YOU NEEDED A CHANGE OF ENVIRONMENT. TO GET AWAY FROM THE FRIENDS THEY FELT HAD LED YOU ASTRAY.
"AND SO YOU WERE SENT TO LIVE WITH YOUR MATERNAL GRANDFATHER OUT WEST."

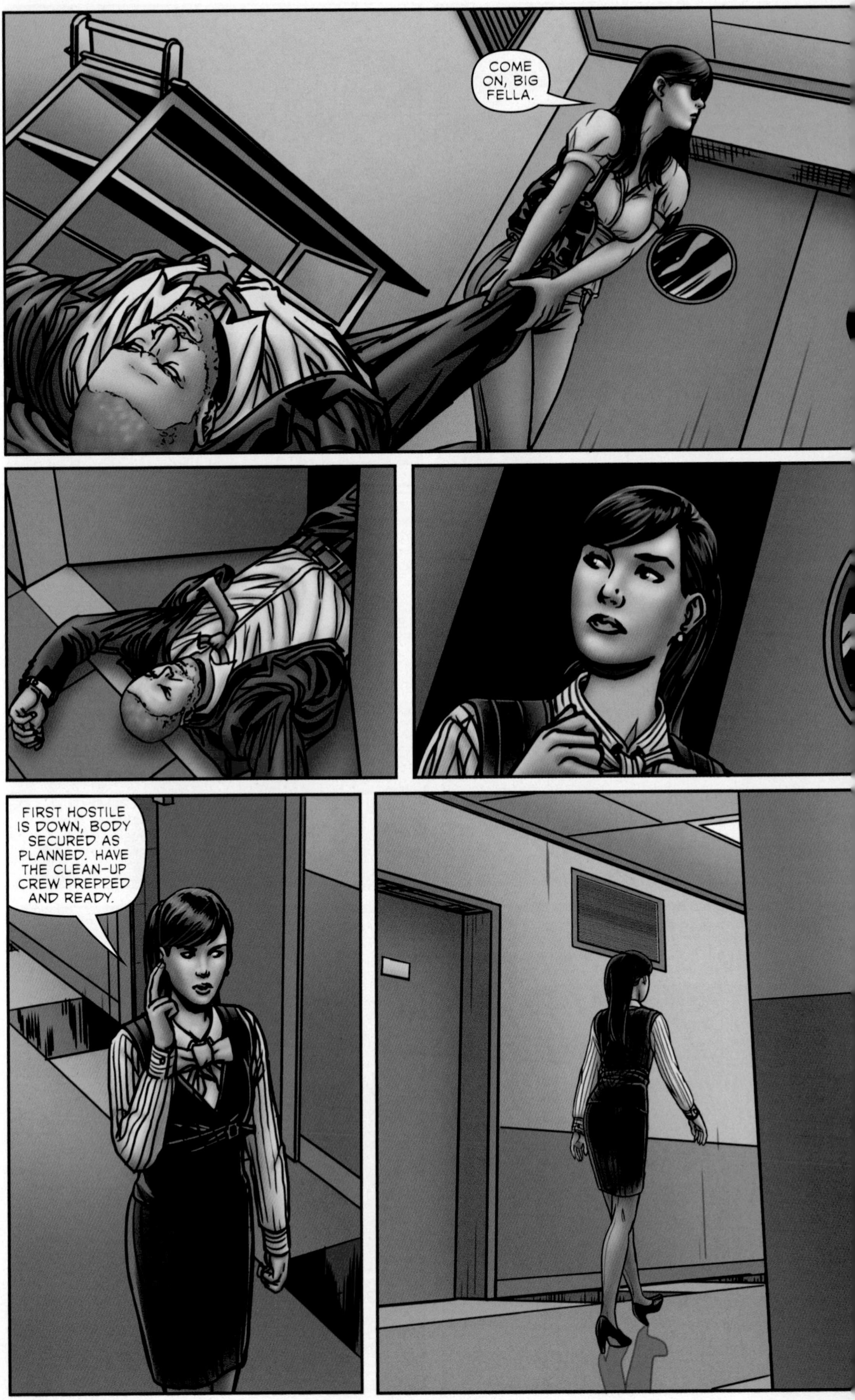
COME ON, BIG FELLA.
FIRST HOSTILE IS DOWN, BODY SECURED AS PLANNED. HAVE THE CLEAN-UP CREW PREPPED AND READY.

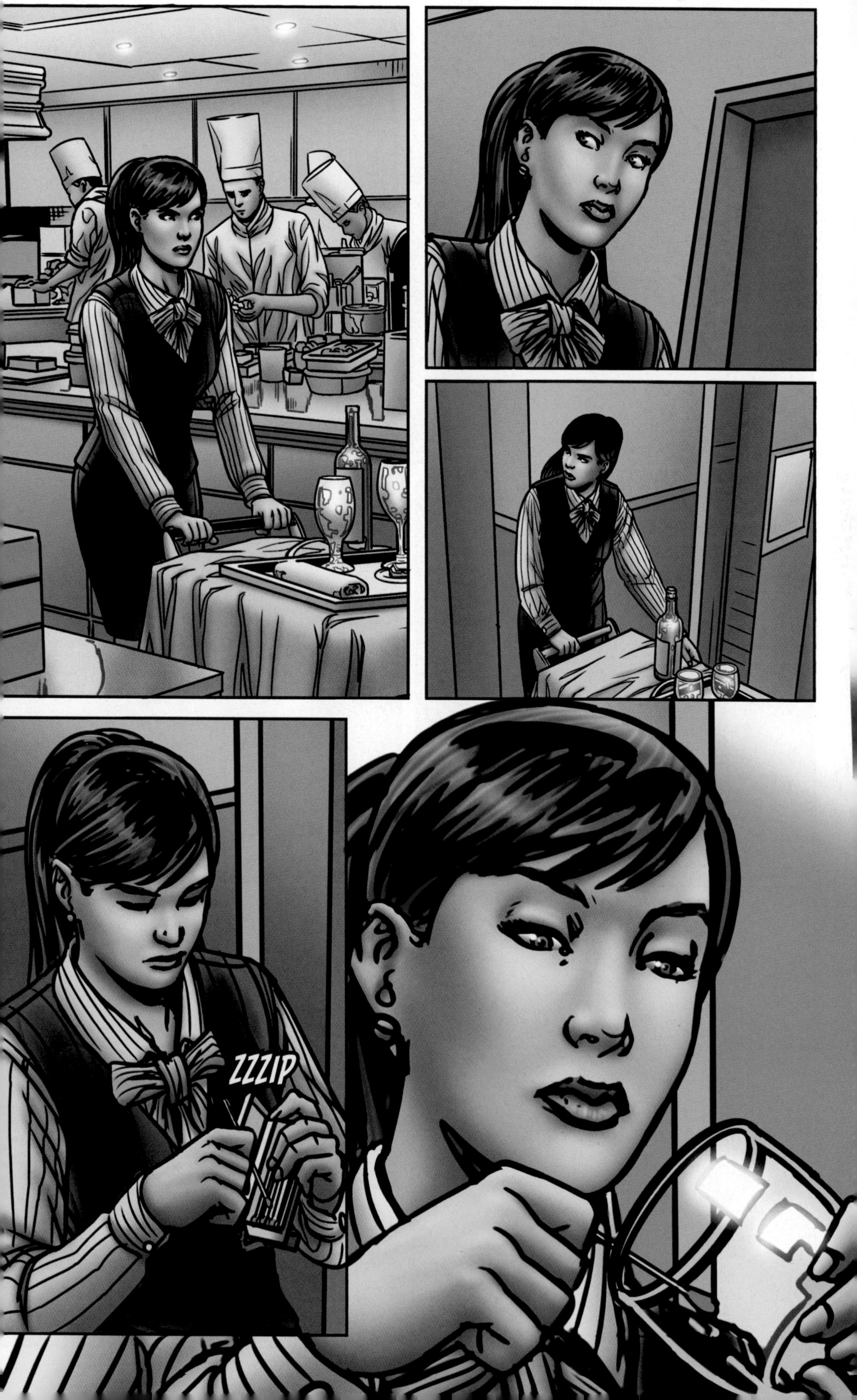
ZZZIP

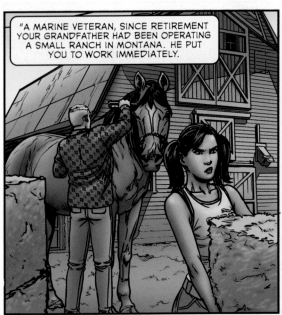

"A MARINE VETERAN, SINCE RETIREMENT YOUR GRANDFATHER HAD BEEN OPERATING A SMALL RANCH IN MONTANA. HE PUT YOU TO WORK IMMEDIATELY.

"YOUR LETTERS HOME SUGGEST THAT YOU TOOK TO YOUR NEW LIFE IN SHORT ORDER. LEARNED TO RIDE, AND CAME TO ENJOY YOUR DAILY CHORES.

"HE TAUGHT YOU TO SHOOT, HOW TO FIELD STRIP AND ASSEMBLE A RIFLE, AND UNDER HIS TUTELAGE YOU BECAME QUITE THE MARKSMAN.

"BUT PERHAPS MOST IMPORTANTLY, HE INSTILLED A SENSE OF DISCIPLINE IN YOU. A BELIEF IN THE IMPORTANCE OF DUTY, AND PATRIOTISM.

"YOU EXCELLED AT YOUR NEW SCHOOL, TOO, PARTICULARLY IN THE SCIENCES.

"YOU GRADUATED WITH HIGHEST HONORS, THE VALEDICTORIAN OF YOUR CLASS. I'M TOLD YOUR ADDRESS TO YOUR CLASSMATES WAS PARTICULARLY INSPIRING."

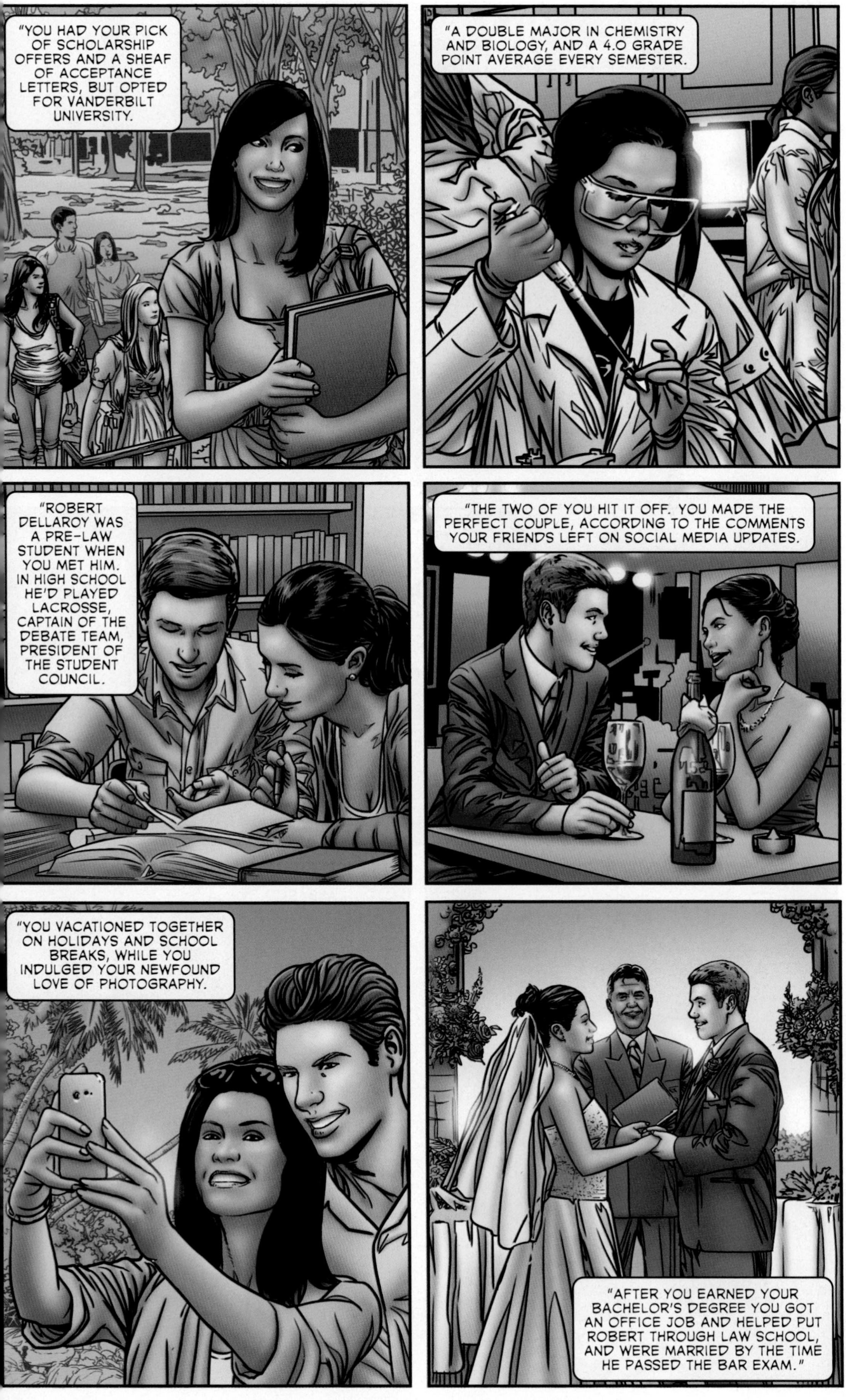
"YOU HAD YOUR PICK OF SCHOLARSHIP OFFERS AND A SHEAF OF ACCEPTANCE LETTERS, BUT OPTED FOR VANDERBILT UNIVERSITY.
"A DOUBLE MAJOR IN CHEMISTRY AND BIOLOGY, AND A 4.0 GRADE POINT AVERAGE EVERY SEMESTER.
"ROBERT DELLAROY WAS A PRE-LAW STUDENT WHEN YOU MET HIM. IN HIGH SCHOOL HE'D PLAYED LACROSSE, CAPTAIN OF THE DEBATE TEAM, PRESIDENT OF THE STUDENT COUNCIL.
"THE TWO OF YOU HIT IT OFF. YOU MADE THE PERFECT COUPLE, ACCORDING TO THE COMMENTS YOUR FRIENDS LEFT ON SOCIAL MEDIA UPDATES.
"YOU VACATIONED TOGETHER ON HOLIDAYS AND SCHOOL BREAKS, WHILE YOU INDULGED YOUR NEWFOUND LOVE OF PHOTOGRAPHY.
"AFTER YOU EARNED YOUR BACHELOR'S DEGREE YOU GOT AN OFFICE JOB AND HELPED PUT ROBERT THROUGH LAW SCHOOL, AND WERE MARRIED BY THE TIME HE PASSED THE BAR EXAM."

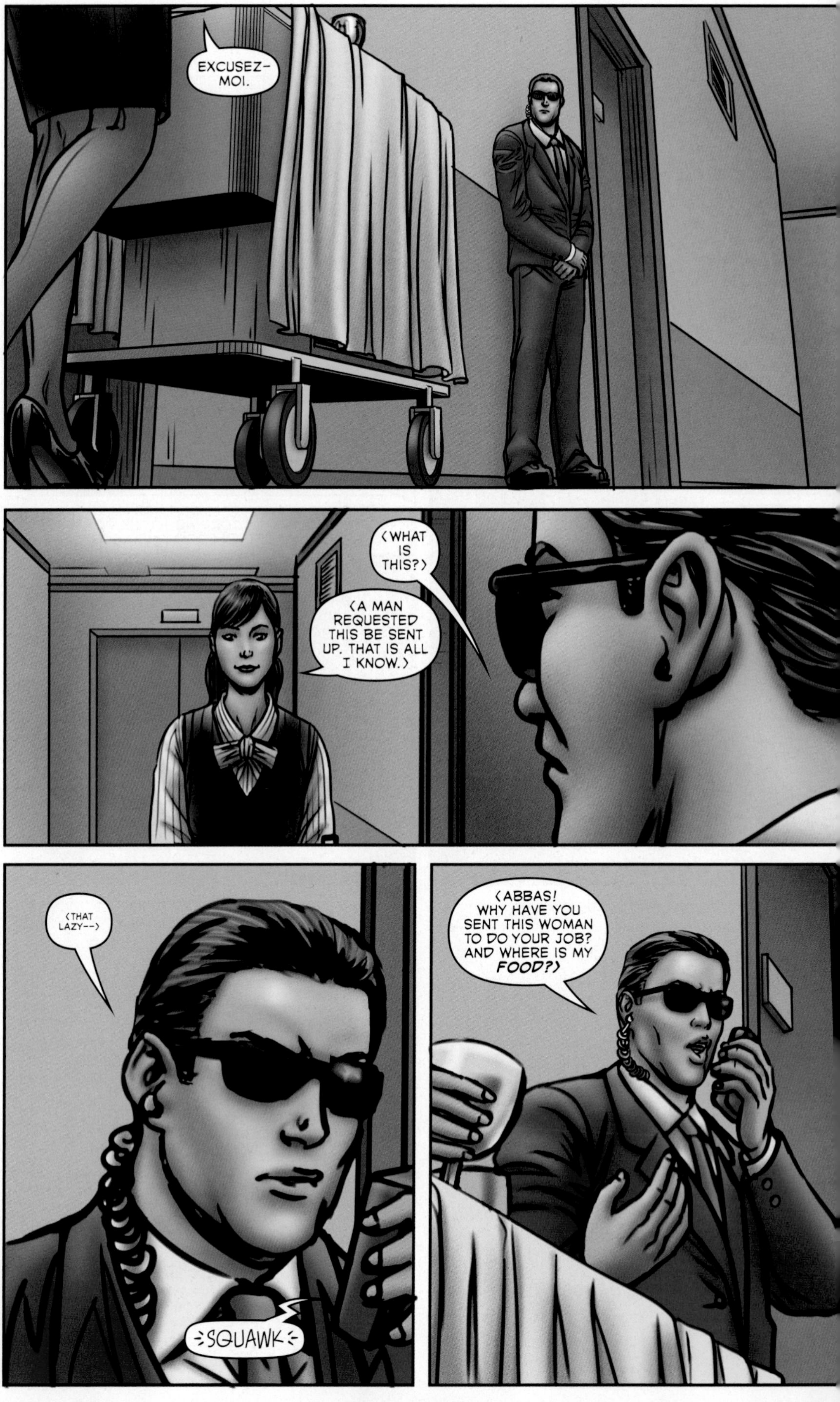
EXCUSEZ-MOI.
‹WHAT IS THIS?›
‹A MAN REQUESTED THIS BE SENT UP. THAT IS ALL I KNOW.›
‹THAT LAZY--›
SQUAWK
‹ABBAS! WHY HAVE YOU SENT THIS WOMAN TO DO YOUR JOB? AND WHERE IS MY *FOOD?*›

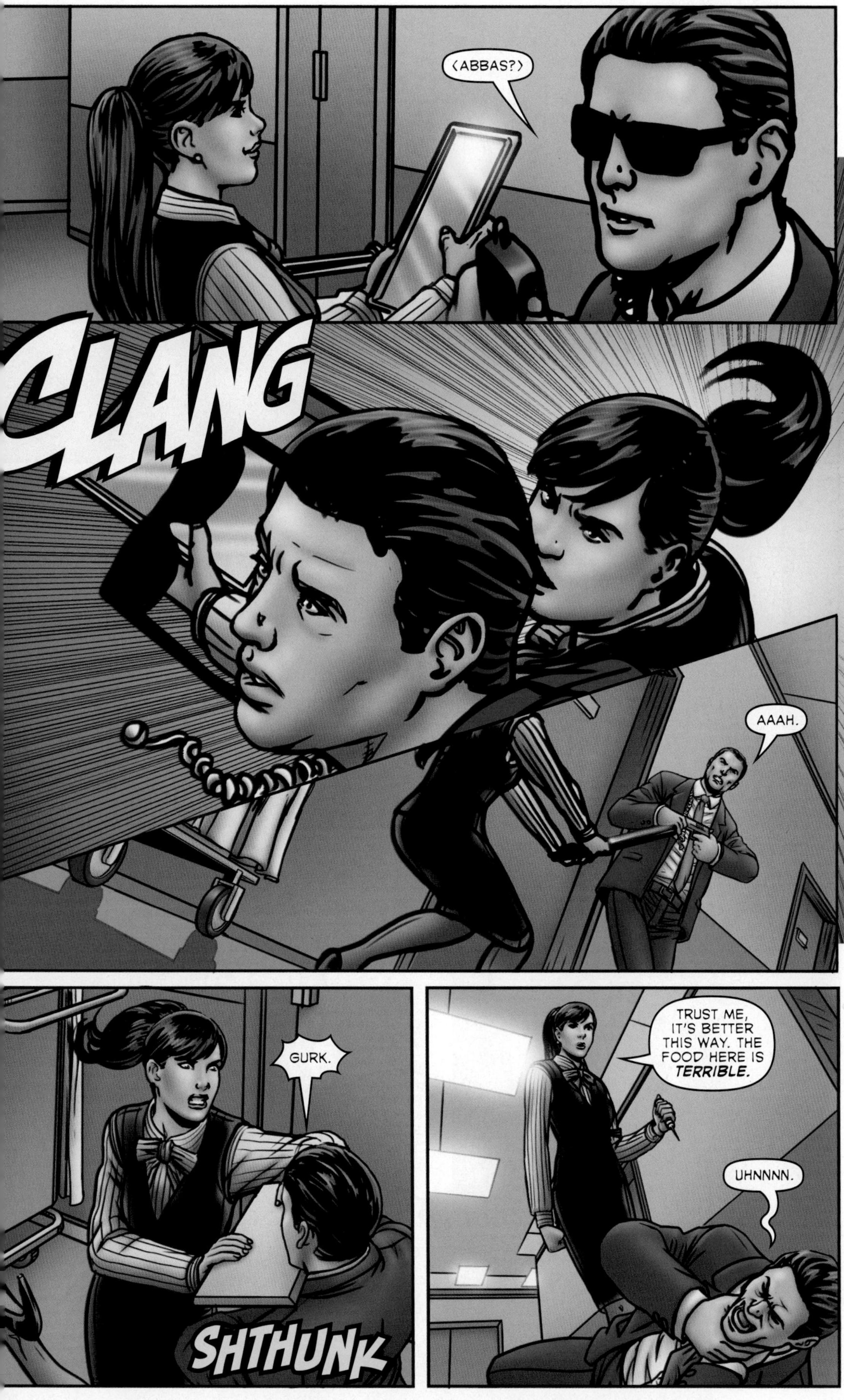

‹ABBAS?›
CLANG
AAAH.
GURK.
SHTHUNK
TRUST ME, IT'S BETTER THIS WAY. THE FOOD HERE IS *TERRIBLE.*
UHNNNN.

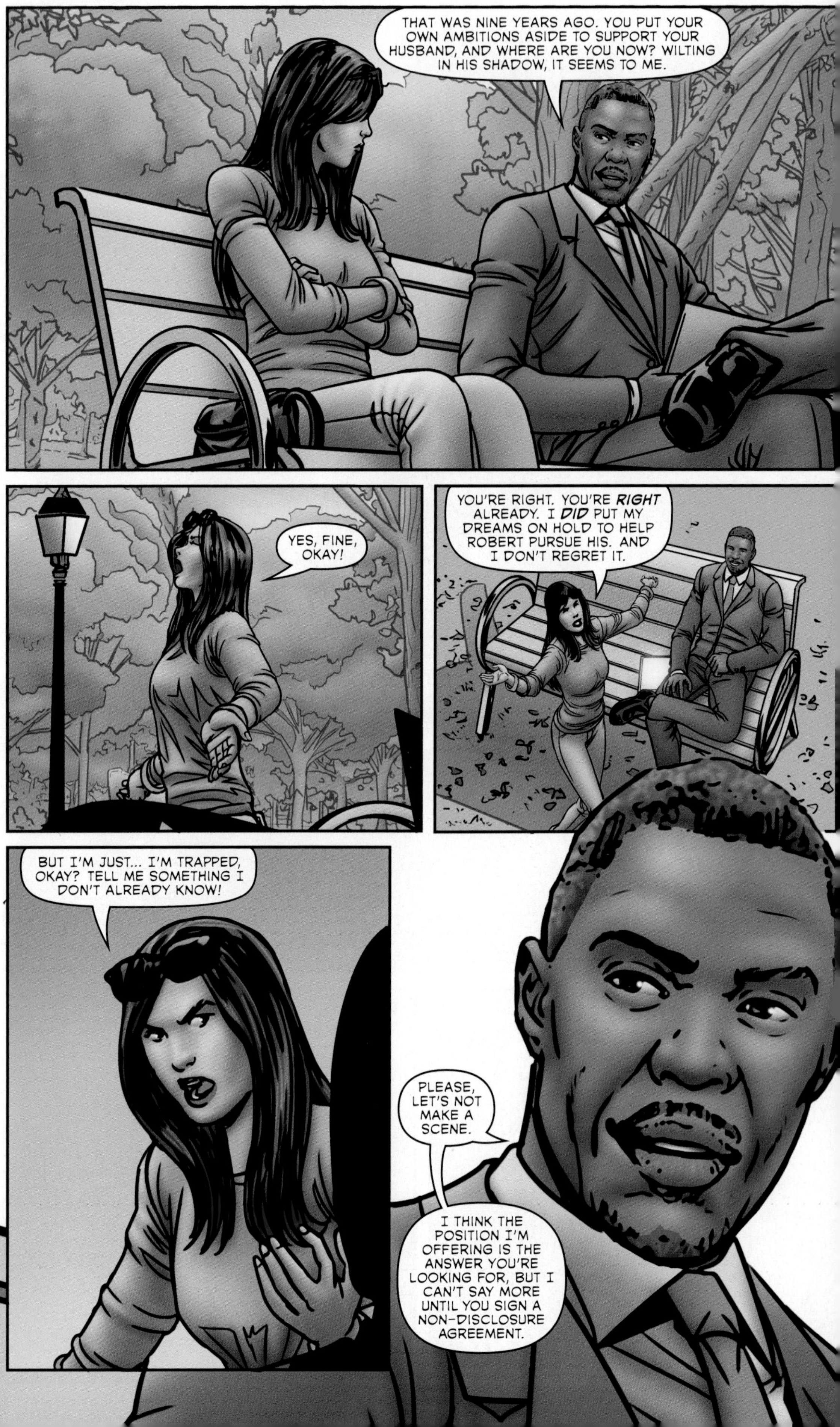
THAT WAS NINE YEARS AGO. YOU PUT YOUR OWN AMBITIONS ASIDE TO SUPPORT YOUR HUSBAND, AND WHERE ARE YOU NOW? WILTING IN HIS SHADOW, IT SEEMS TO ME.
YES, FINE, OKAY!
YOU'RE RIGHT. YOU'RE *RIGHT* ALREADY. I *DID* PUT MY DREAMS ON HOLD TO HELP ROBERT PURSUE HIS. AND I DON'T REGRET IT.
BUT I'M JUST... I'M TRAPPED, OKAY? TELL ME SOMETHING I DON'T ALREADY KNOW!
PLEASE, LET'S NOT MAKE A SCENE.
I THINK THE POSITION I'M OFFERING IS THE ANSWER YOU'RE LOOKING FOR, BUT I CAN'T SAY MORE UNTIL YOU SIGN A NON-DISCLOSURE AGREEMENT.

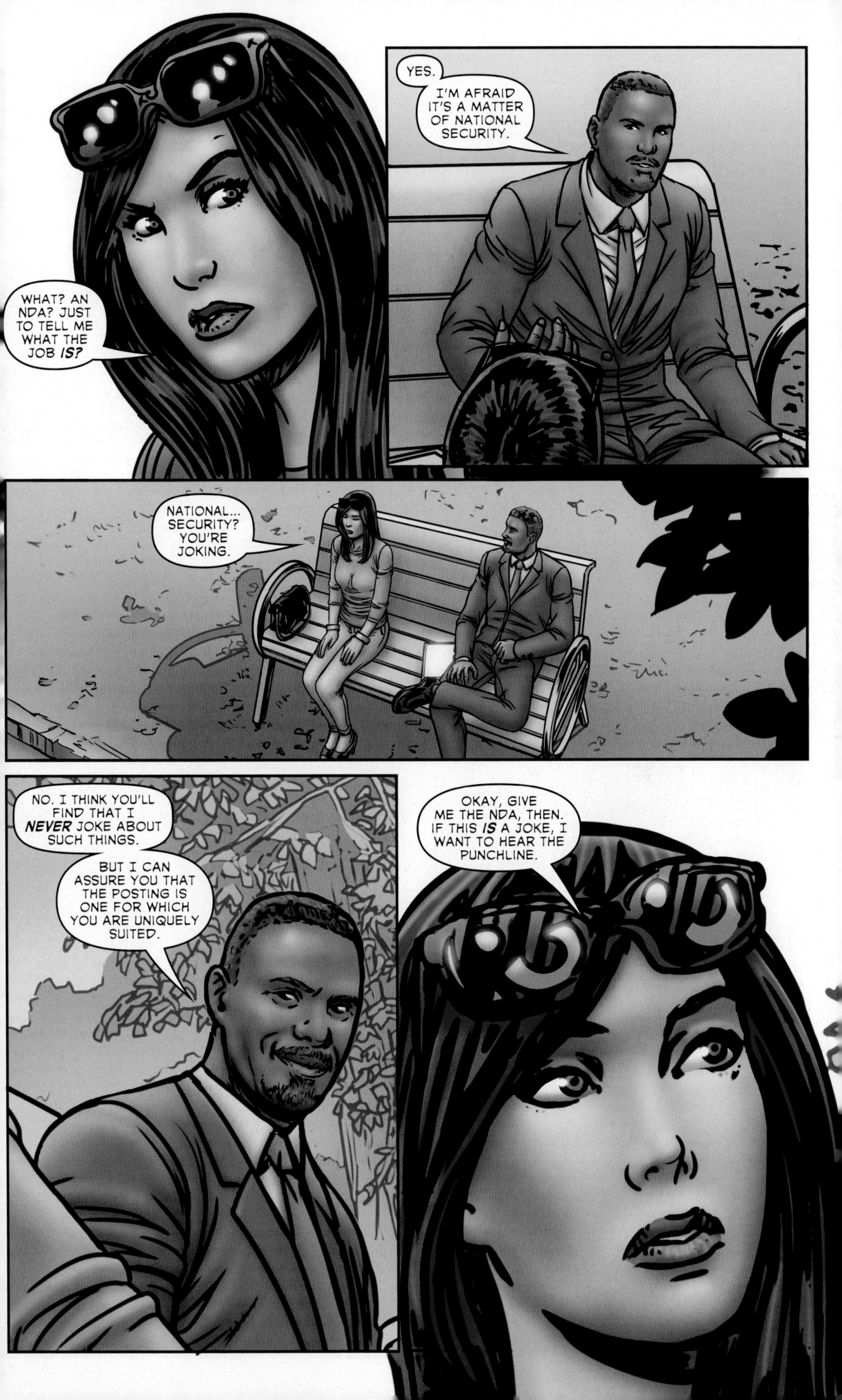
WHAT? AN NDA? JUST TO TELL ME WHAT THE JOB *IS?*
YES.
I'M AFRAID IT'S A MATTER OF NATIONAL SECURITY.
NATIONAL... SECURITY? YOU'RE JOKING.
NO. I THINK YOU'LL FIND THAT I ***NEVER*** JOKE ABOUT SUCH THINGS.
BUT I CAN ASSURE YOU THAT THE POSTING IS ONE FOR WHICH YOU ARE UNIQUELY SUITED.
OKAY, GIVE ME THE NDA, THEN. IF THIS *IS* A JOKE, I WANT TO HEAR THE PUNCHLINE.

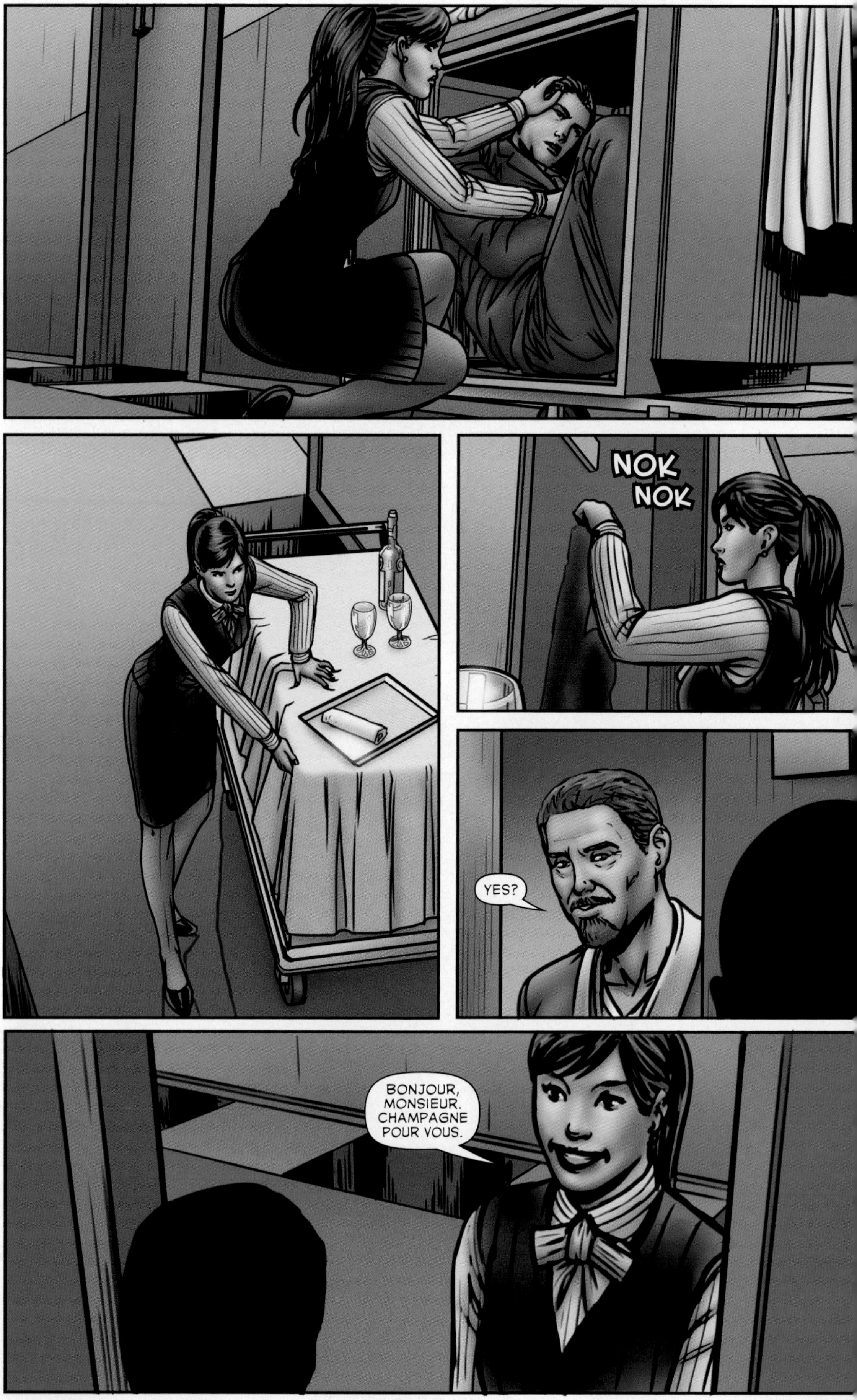
NOK
NOK
YES?
BONJOUR, MONSIEUR. CHAMPAGNE POUR VOUS.

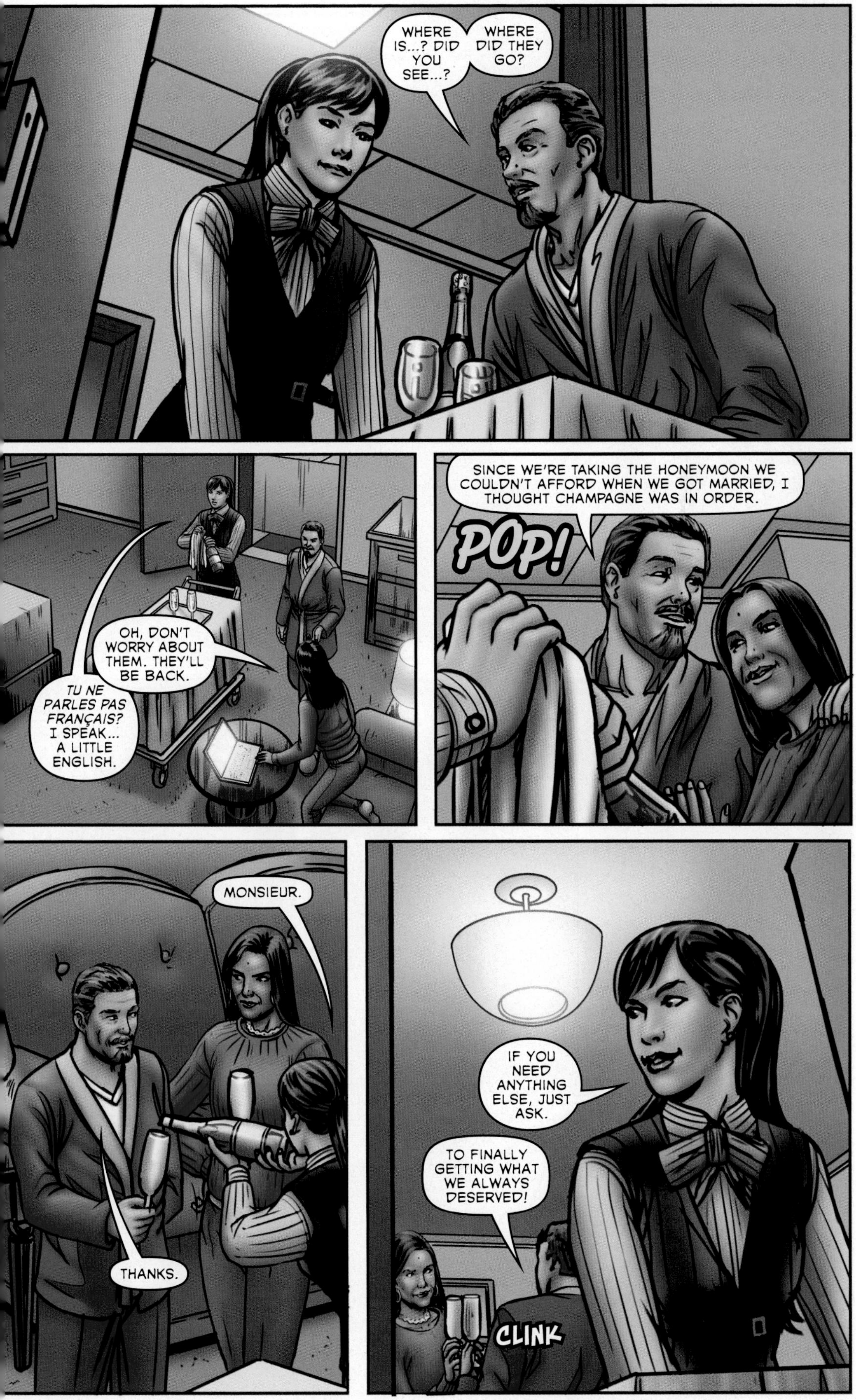
WHERE IS...? DID YOU SEE...?
WHERE DID THEY GO?
TU NE PARLES PAS FRANÇAIS? I SPEAK... A LITTLE ENGLISH.
OH, DON'T WORRY ABOUT THEM. THEY'LL BE BACK.
POP!
SINCE WE'RE TAKING THE HONEYMOON WE COULDN'T AFFORD WHEN WE GOT MARRIED, I THOUGHT CHAMPAGNE WAS IN ORDER.
MONSIEUR.
THANKS.
IF YOU NEED ANYTHING ELSE, JUST ASK.
TO FINALLY GETTING WHAT WE ALWAYS DESERVED!
CLINK

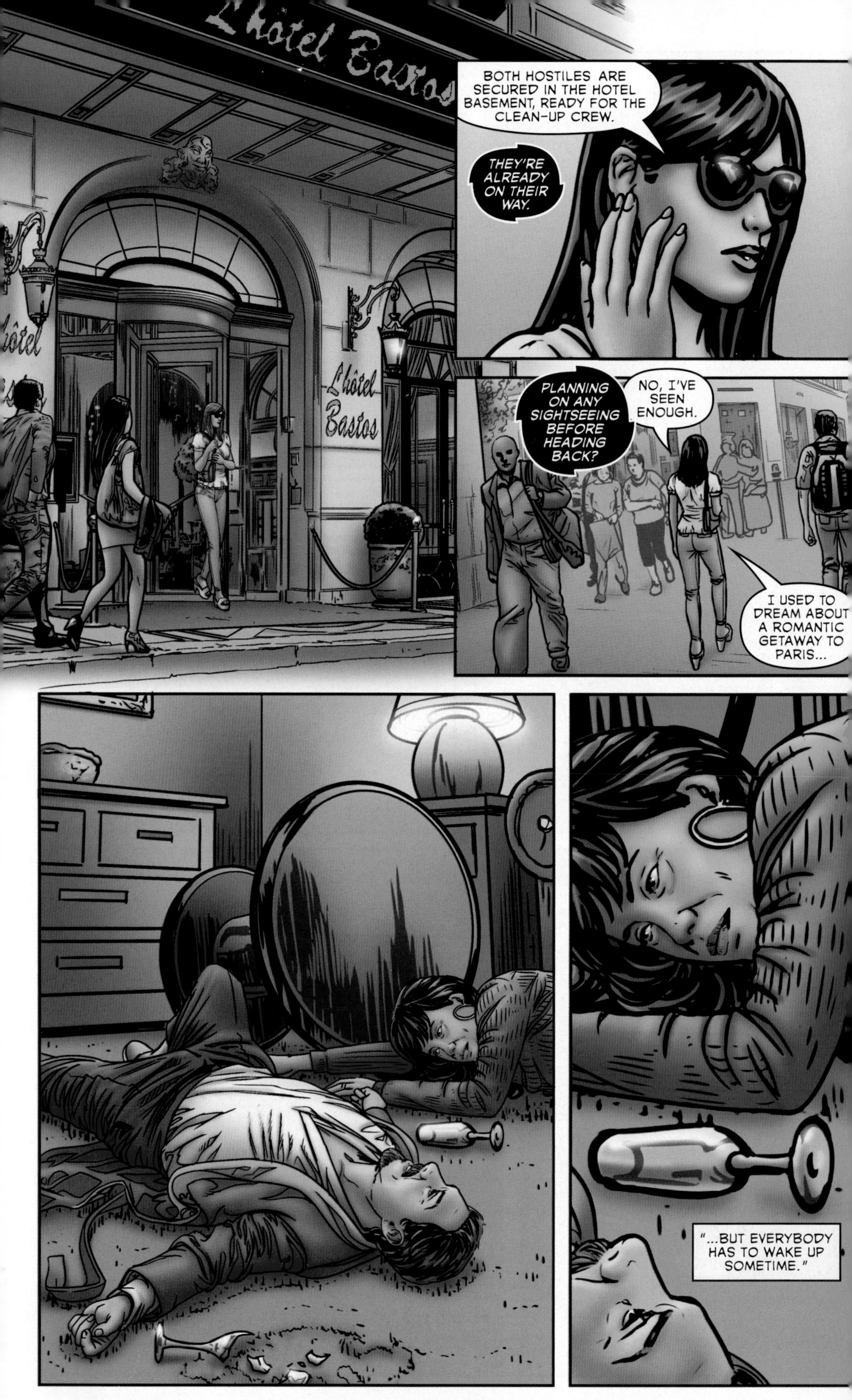

L'hôtel Bastos
BOTH HOSTILES ARE SECURED IN THE HOTEL BASEMENT, READY FOR THE CLEAN-UP CREW.
THEY'RE ALREADY ON THEIR WAY.
L'hôtel Bastos
PLANNING ON ANY SIGHTSEEING BEFORE HEADING BACK?
NO, I'VE SEEN ENOUGH.
I USED TO DREAM ABOUT A ROMANTIC GETAWAY TO PARIS...
"...BUT EVERYBODY HAS TO WAKE UP SOMETIME."

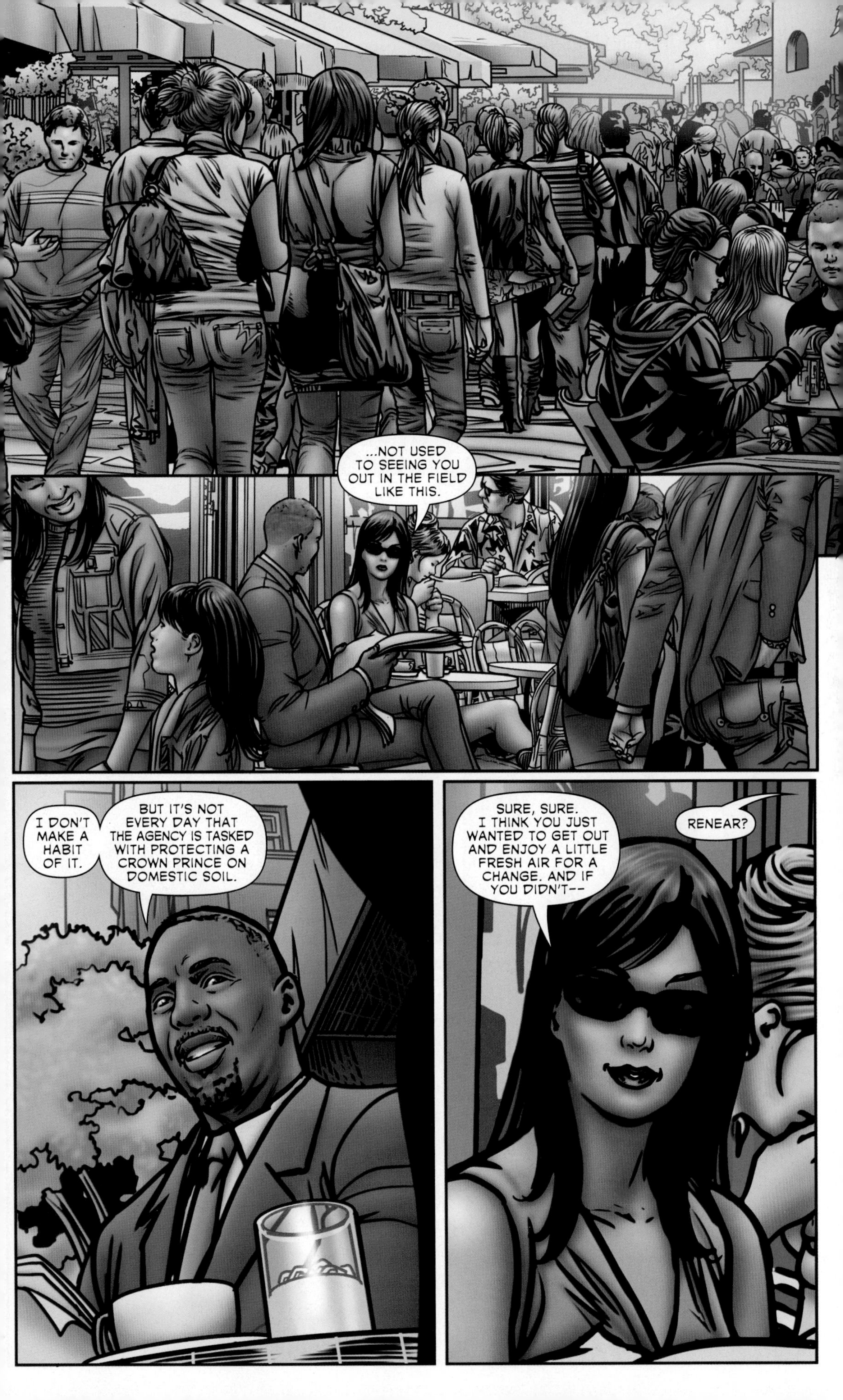
...NOT USED TO SEEING YOU OUT IN THE FIELD LIKE THIS.
I DON'T MAKE A HABIT OF IT.
BUT IT'S NOT EVERY DAY THAT THE AGENCY IS TASKED WITH PROTECTING A CROWN PRINCE ON DOMESTIC SOIL.
SURE, SURE. I THINK YOU JUST WANTED TO GET OUT AND ENJOY A LITTLE FRESH AIR FOR A CHANGE. AND IF YOU DIDN'T--
RENEAR?

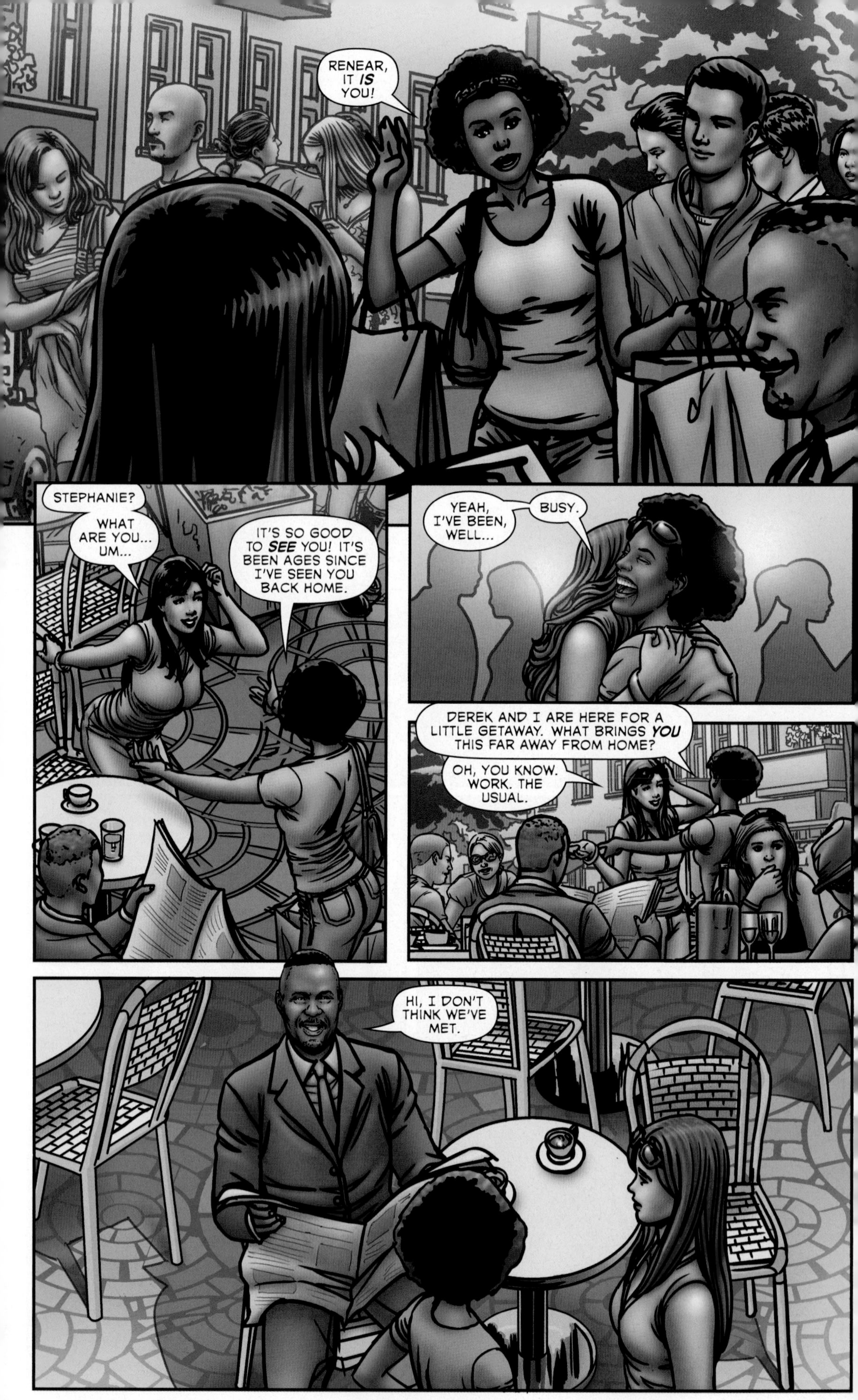
RENEAR, IT IS YOU!
STEPHANIE?
WHAT ARE YOU... UM...
IT'S SO GOOD TO SEE YOU! IT'S BEEN AGES SINCE I'VE SEEN YOU BACK HOME.
YEAH, I'VE BEEN, WELL...
BUSY.
DEREK AND I ARE HERE FOR A LITTLE GETAWAY. WHAT BRINGS YOU THIS FAR AWAY FROM HOME?
OH, YOU KNOW. WORK. THE USUAL.
HI, I DON'T THINK WE'VE MET.

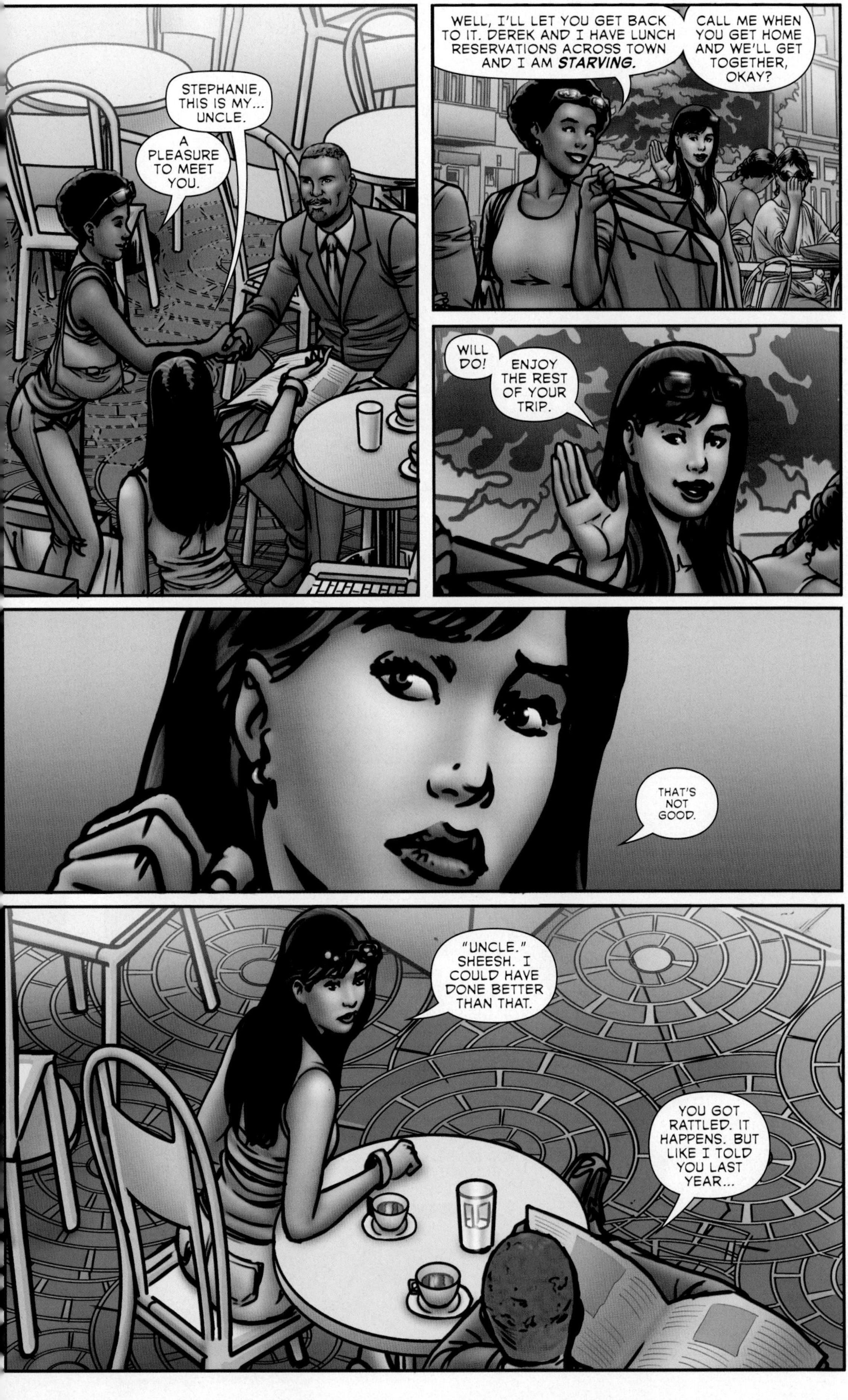
STEPHANIE, THIS IS MY... UNCLE.
A PLEASURE TO MEET YOU.
WELL, I'LL LET YOU GET BACK TO IT. DEREK AND I HAVE LUNCH RESERVATIONS ACROSS TOWN AND I AM STARVING.
CALL ME WHEN YOU GET HOME AND WE'LL GET TOGETHER, OKAY?
WILL DO!
ENJOY THE REST OF YOUR TRIP.
THAT'S NOT GOOD.
"UNCLE." SHEESH. I COULD HAVE DONE BETTER THAN THAT.
YOU GOT RATTLED. IT HAPPENS. BUT LIKE I TOLD YOU LAST YEAR...

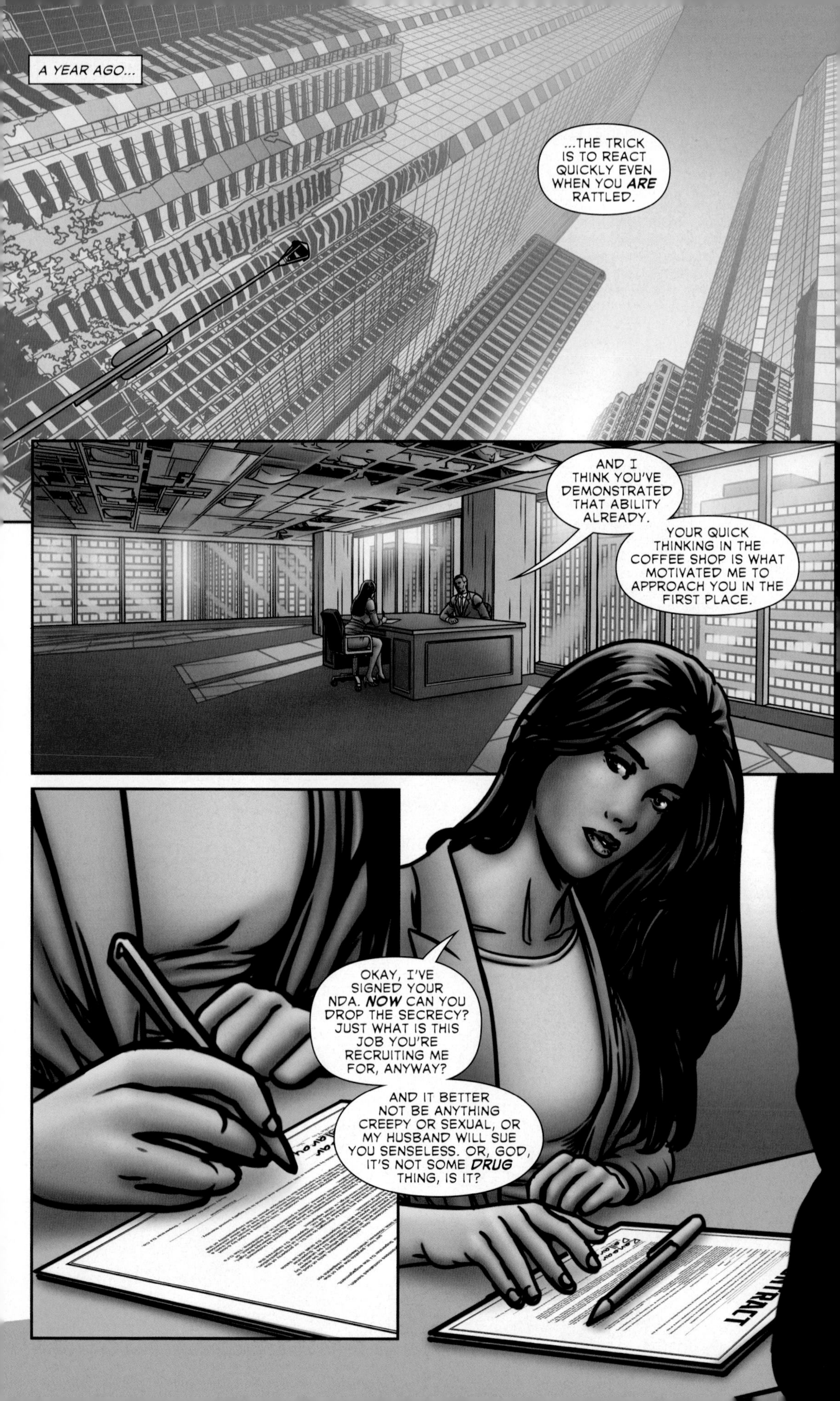
A YEAR AGO...
...THE TRICK IS TO REACT QUICKLY EVEN WHEN YOU *ARE* RATTLED.
AND I THINK YOU'VE DEMONSTRATED THAT ABILITY ALREADY.
YOUR QUICK THINKING IN THE COFFEE SHOP IS WHAT MOTIVATED ME TO APPROACH YOU IN THE FIRST PLACE.
OKAY, I'VE SIGNED YOUR NDA. *NOW* CAN YOU DROP THE SECRECY? JUST WHAT IS THIS JOB YOU'RE RECRUITING ME FOR, ANYWAY?
AND IT BETTER NOT BE ANYTHING CREEPY OR SEXUAL, OR MY HUSBAND WILL SUE YOU SENSELESS. OR, GOD, IT'S NOT SOME *DRUG* THING, IS IT?

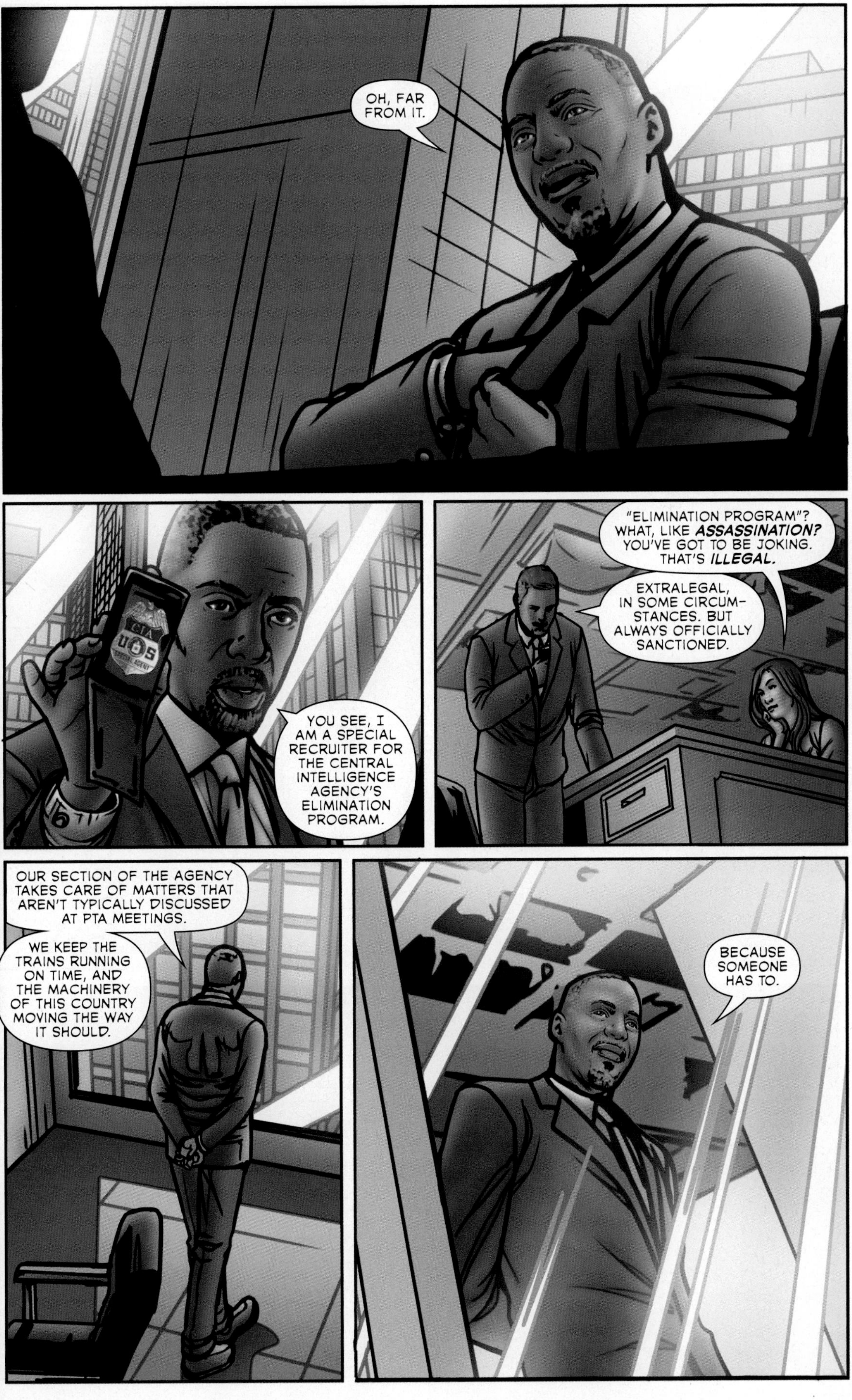

OH, FAR FROM IT.
YOU SEE, I AM A SPECIAL RECRUITER FOR THE CENTRAL INTELLIGENCE AGENCY'S ELIMINATION PROGRAM.
"ELIMINATION PROGRAM"? WHAT, LIKE ASSASSINATION? YOU'VE GOT TO BE JOKING. THAT'S ILLEGAL.
EXTRALEGAL, IN SOME CIRCUM-STANCES. BUT ALWAYS OFFICIALLY SANCTIONED.
OUR SECTION OF THE AGENCY TAKES CARE OF MATTERS THAT AREN'T TYPICALLY DISCUSSED AT PTA MEETINGS.
WE KEEP THE TRAINS RUNNING ON TIME, AND THE MACHINERY OF THIS COUNTRY MOVING THE WAY IT SHOULD.
BECAUSE SOMEONE HAS TO.

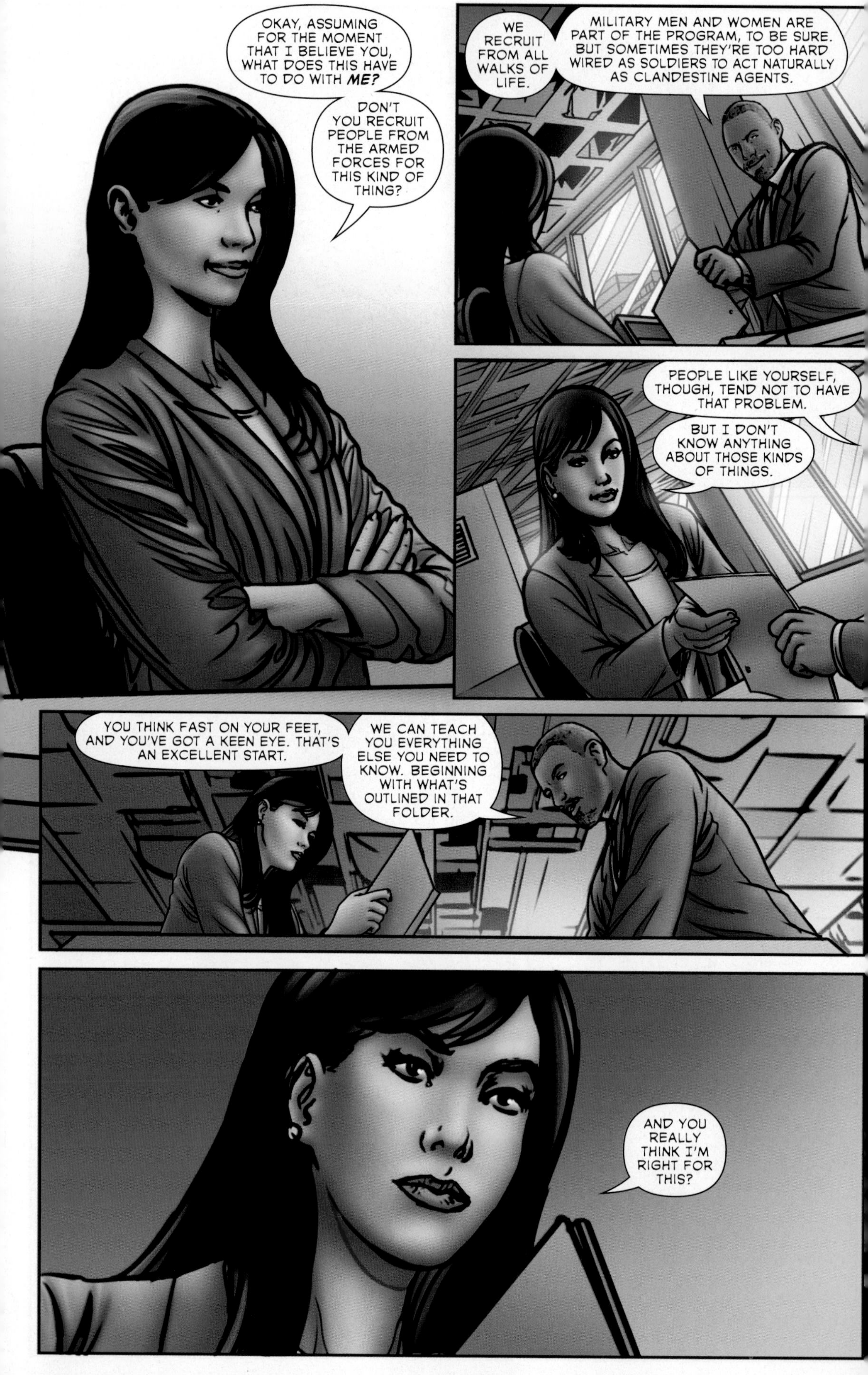

OKAY, ASSUMING FOR THE MOMENT THAT I BELIEVE YOU, WHAT DOES THIS HAVE TO DO WITH *ME?*
DON'T YOU RECRUIT PEOPLE FROM THE ARMED FORCES FOR THIS KIND OF THING?
WE RECRUIT FROM ALL WALKS OF LIFE.
MILITARY MEN AND WOMEN ARE PART OF THE PROGRAM, TO BE SURE. BUT SOMETIMES THEY'RE TOO HARD WIRED AS SOLDIERS TO ACT NATURALLY AS CLANDESTINE AGENTS.
PEOPLE LIKE YOURSELF, THOUGH, TEND NOT TO HAVE THAT PROBLEM.
BUT I DON'T KNOW ANYTHING ABOUT THOSE KINDS OF THINGS.
YOU THINK FAST ON YOUR FEET, AND YOU'VE GOT A KEEN EYE. THAT'S AN EXCELLENT START.
WE CAN TEACH YOU EVERYTHING ELSE YOU NEED TO KNOW. BEGINNING WITH WHAT'S OUTLINED IN THAT FOLDER.
AND YOU REALLY THINK I'M RIGHT FOR THIS?

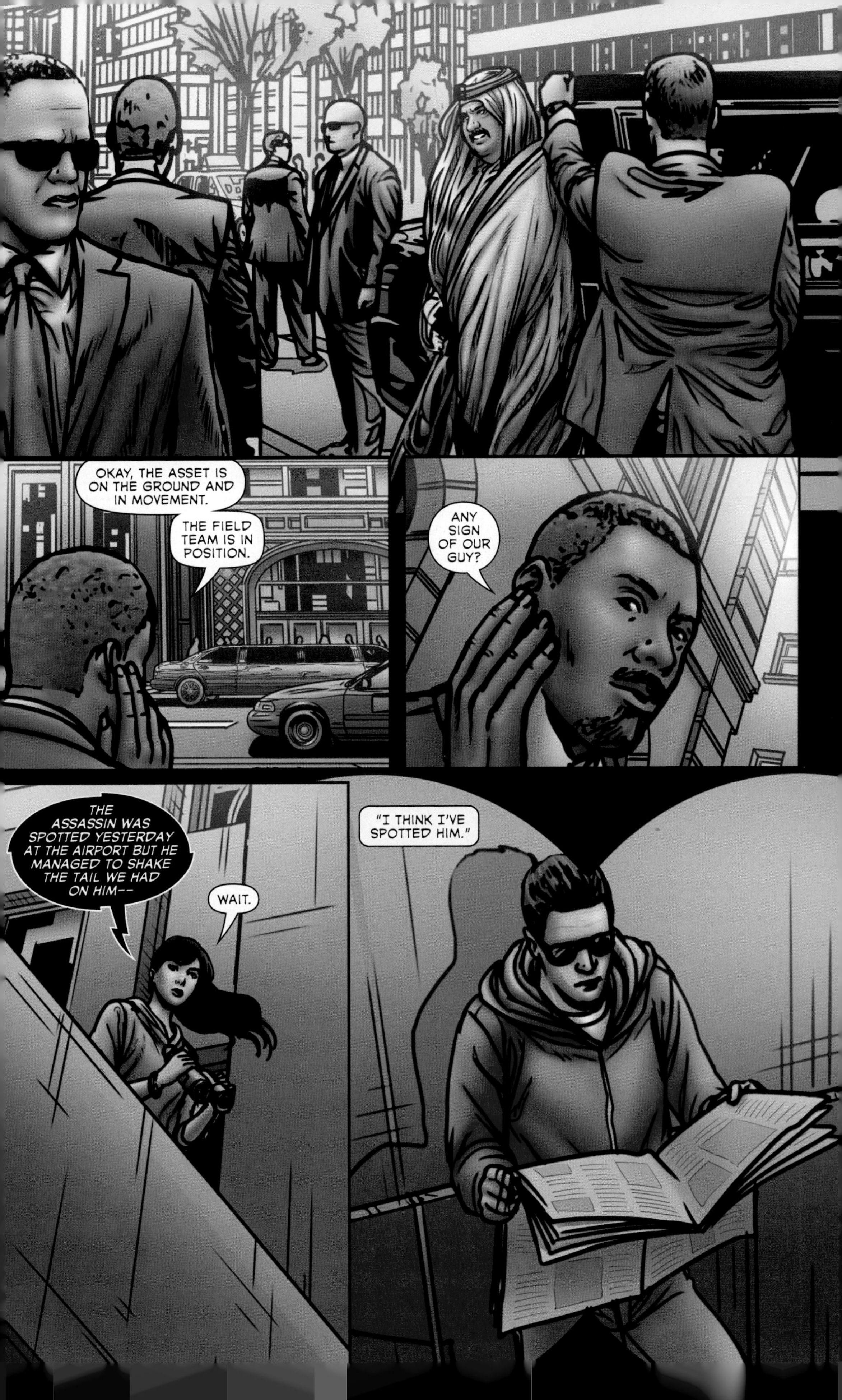

OKAY, THE ASSET IS ON THE GROUND AND IN MOVEMENT.
THE FIELD TEAM IS IN POSITION.
ANY SIGN OF OUR GUY?
THE ASSASSIN WAS SPOTTED YESTERDAY AT THE AIRPORT BUT HE MANAGED TO SHAKE THE TAIL WE HAD ON HIM--
WAIT.
"I THINK I'VE SPOTTED HIM."

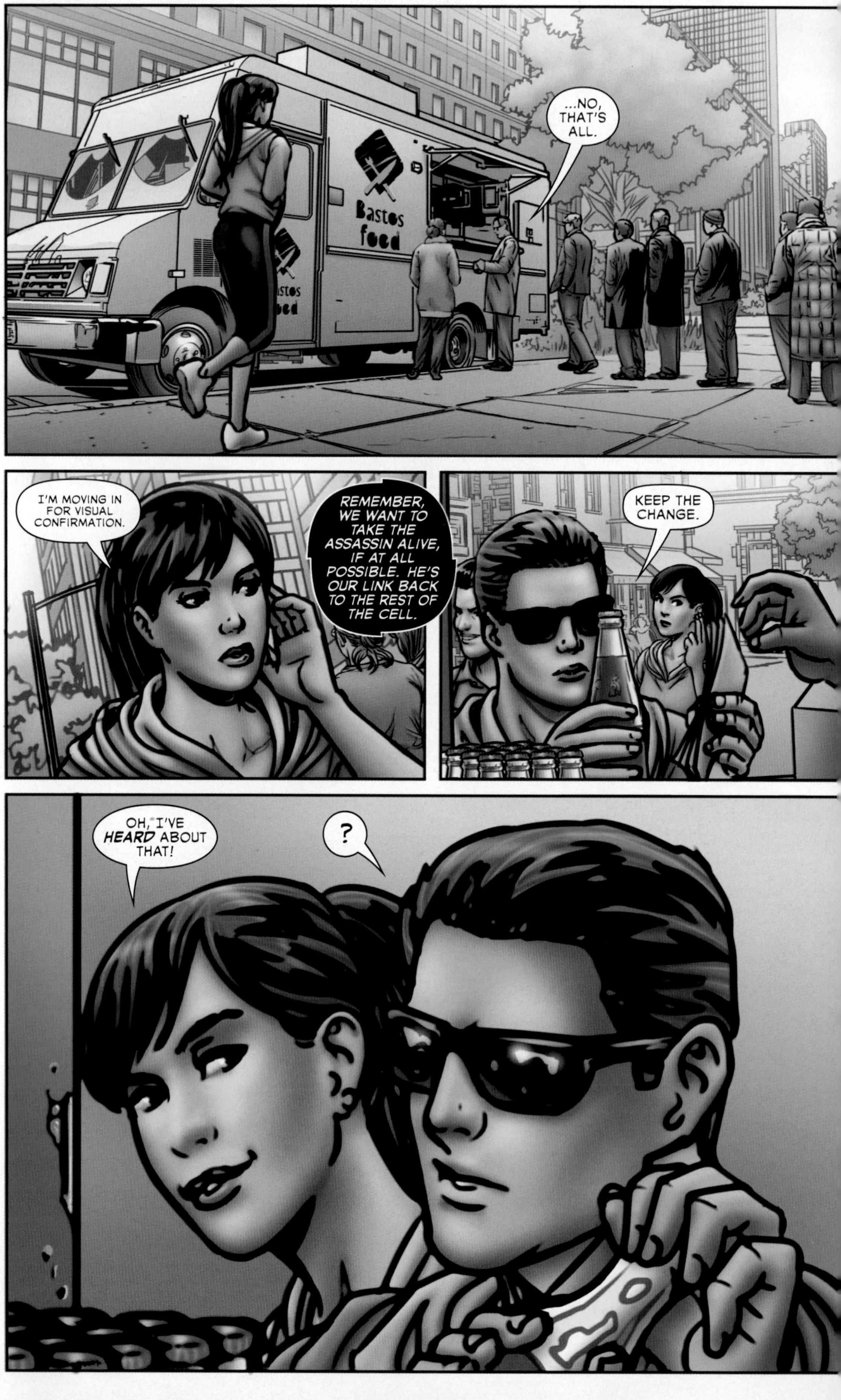
...NO, THAT'S ALL.
Bastos food
I'M MOVING IN FOR VISUAL CONFIRMATION.
REMEMBER, WE WANT TO TAKE THE ASSASSIN ALIVE, IF AT ALL POSSIBLE. HE'S OUR LINK BACK TO THE REST OF THE CELL.
KEEP THE CHANGE.
OH, I'VE *HEARD* ABOUT THAT!
?

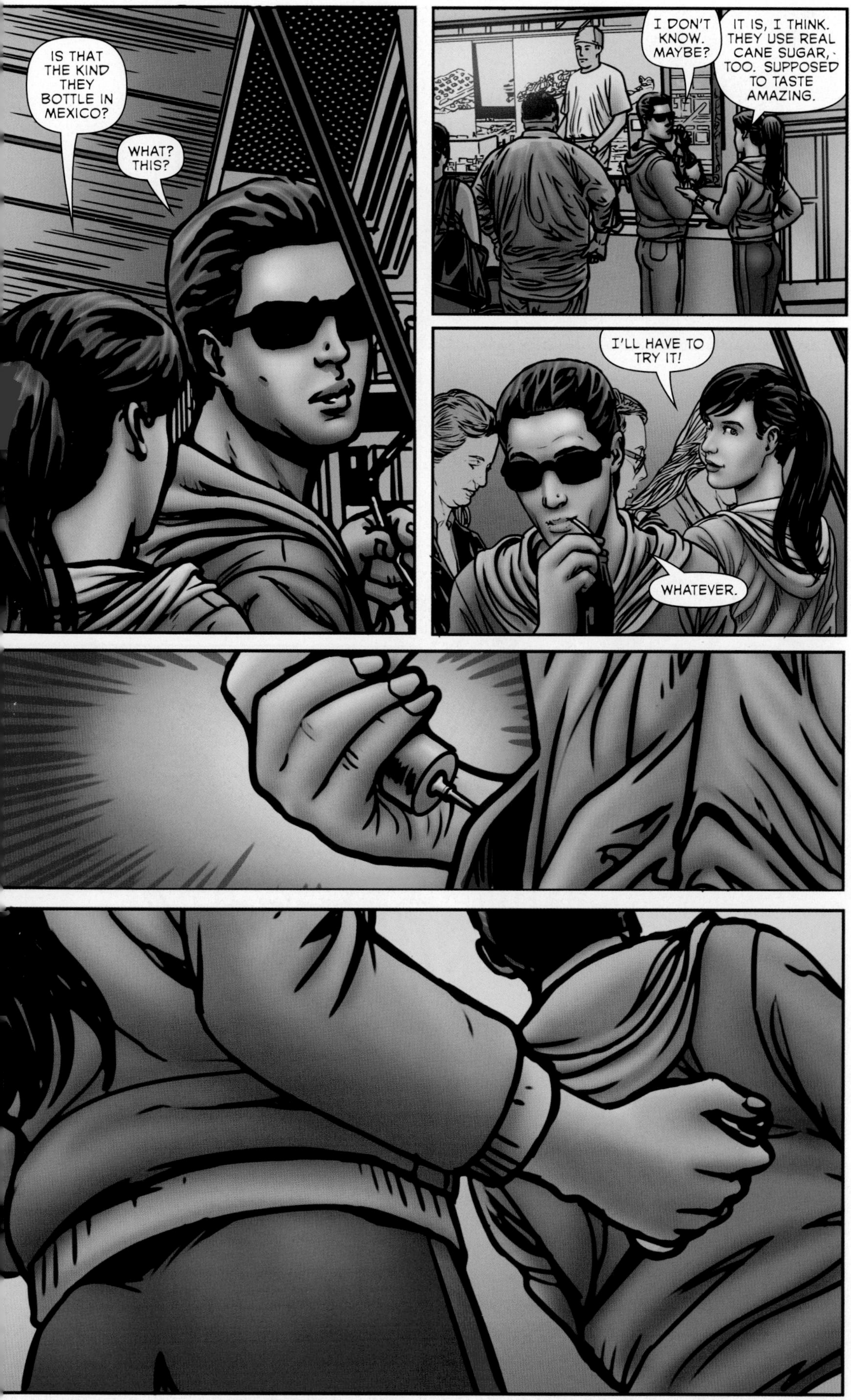
IS THAT THE KIND THEY BOTTLE IN MEXICO?
WHAT? THIS?
I DON'T KNOW. MAYBE?
IT IS, I THINK. THEY USE REAL CANE SUGAR, TOO. SUPPOSED TO TASTE AMAZING.
I'LL HAVE TO TRY IT!
WHATEVER.

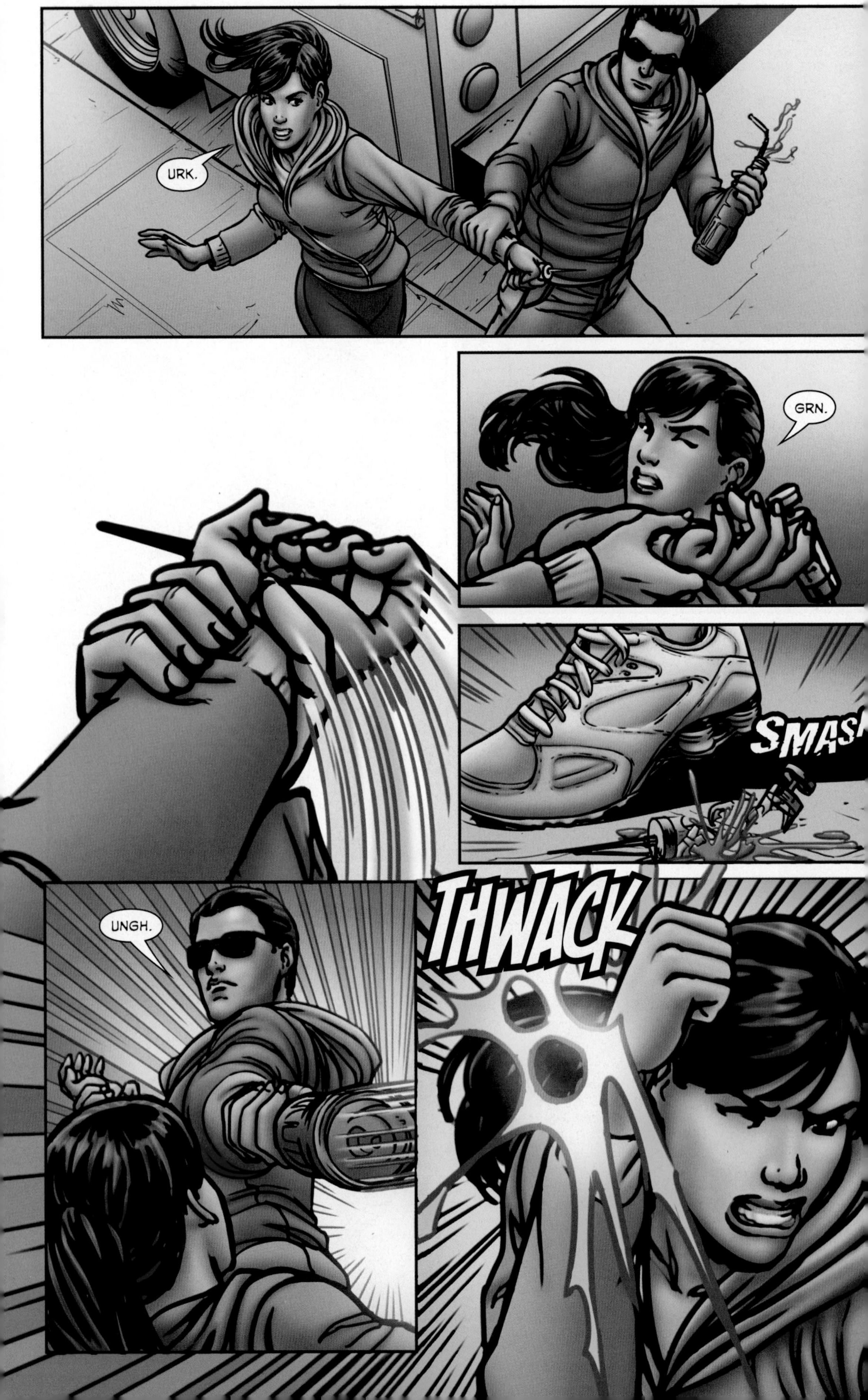
URK.
GRN.
SMASH
UNGH.
THWACK

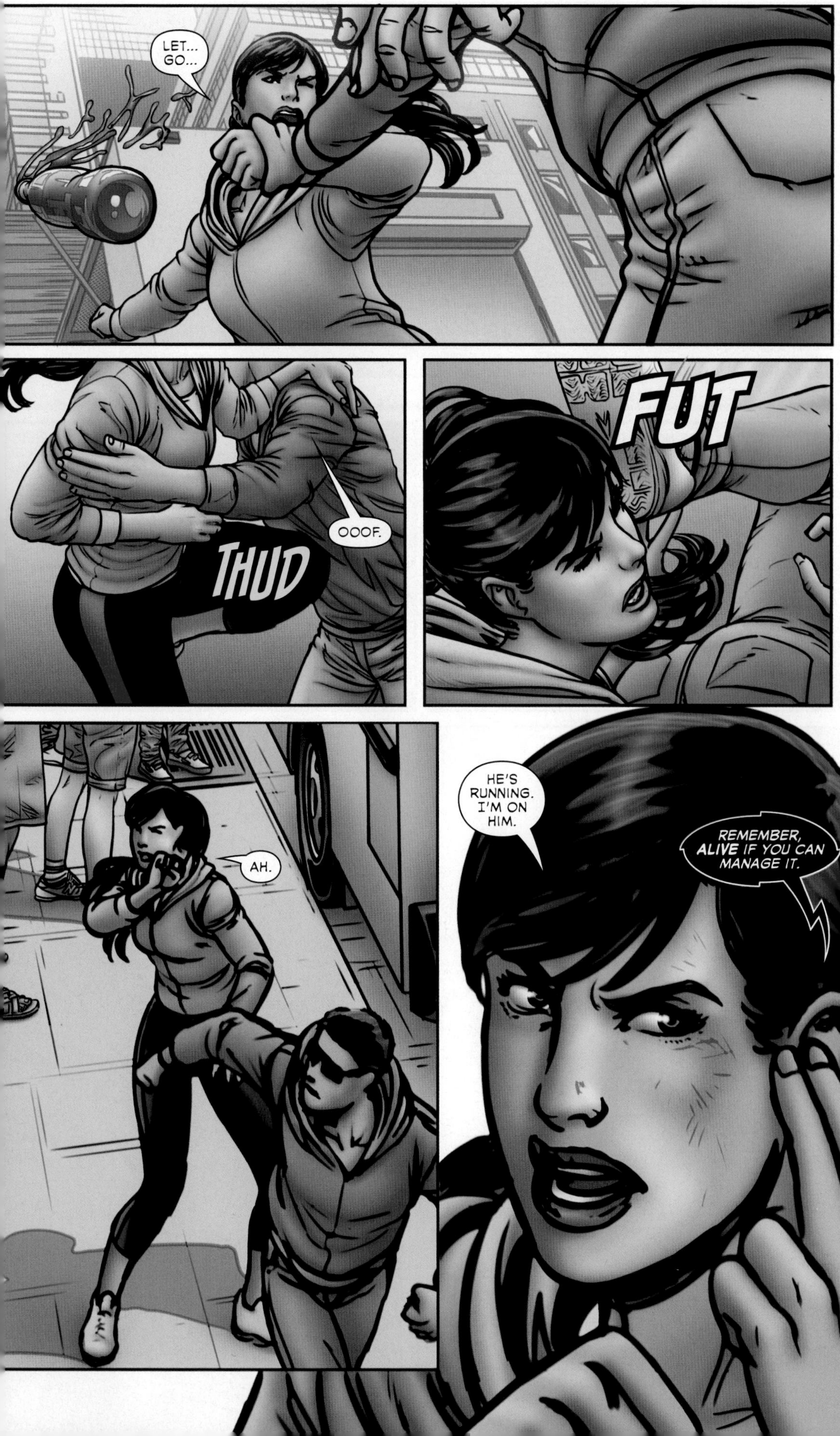
LET... GO...
OOOF.
THUD
FUT
AH.
HE'S RUNNING. I'M ON HIM.
REMEMBER, ALIVE IF YOU CAN MANAGE IT.

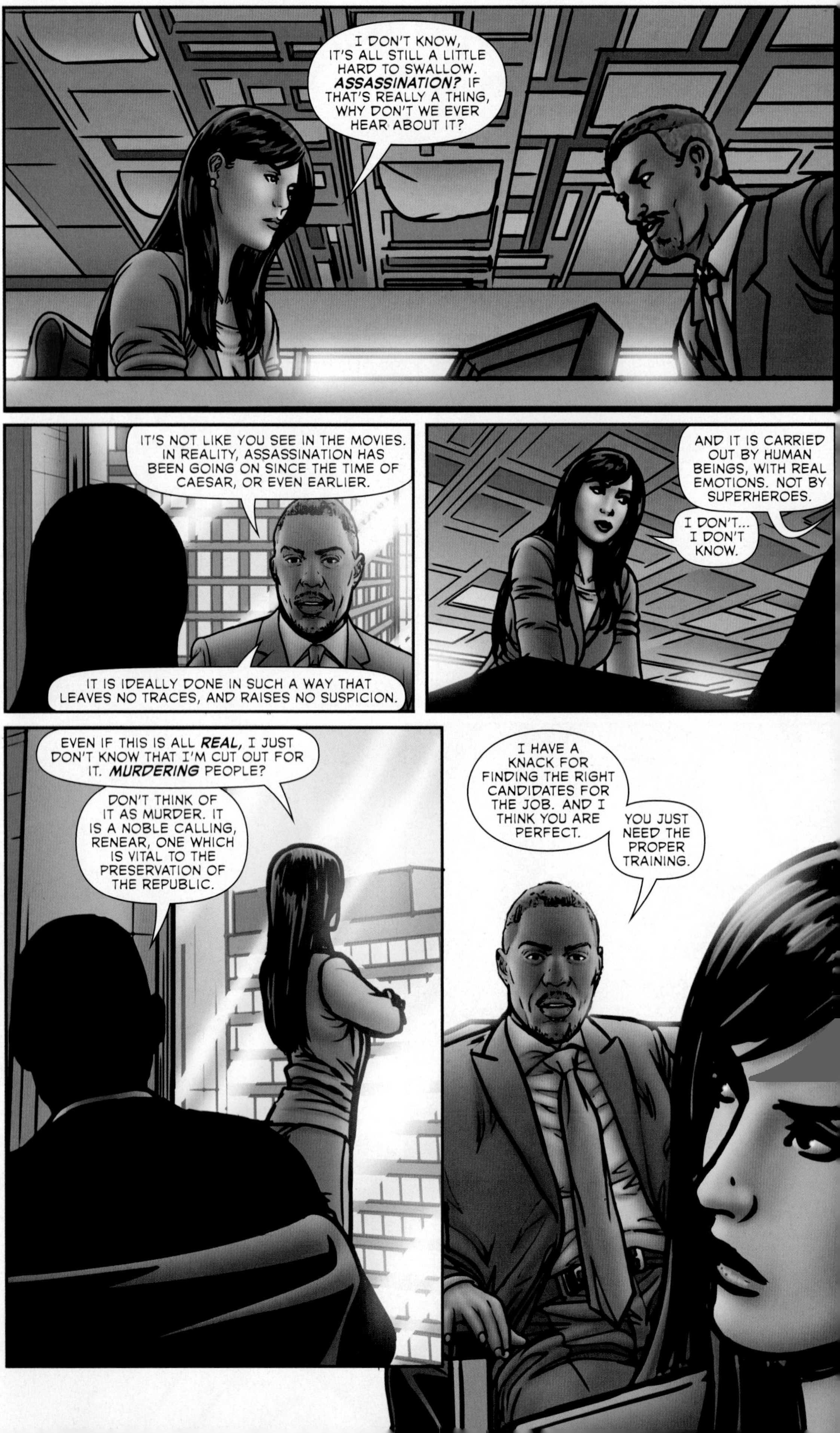
I DON'T KNOW, IT'S ALL STILL A LITTLE HARD TO SWALLOW. ASSASSINATION? IF THAT'S REALLY A THING, WHY DON'T WE EVER HEAR ABOUT IT?
IT'S NOT LIKE YOU SEE IN THE MOVIES. IN REALITY, ASSASSINATION HAS BEEN GOING ON SINCE THE TIME OF CAESAR, OR EVEN EARLIER.
IT IS IDEALLY DONE IN SUCH A WAY THAT LEAVES NO TRACES, AND RAISES NO SUSPICION.
AND IT IS CARRIED OUT BY HUMAN BEINGS, WITH REAL EMOTIONS. NOT BY SUPERHEROES.
I DON'T... I DON'T KNOW.
EVEN IF THIS IS ALL REAL, I JUST DON'T KNOW THAT I'M CUT OUT FOR IT. MURDERING PEOPLE?
DON'T THINK OF IT AS MURDER. IT IS A NOBLE CALLING, RENEAR, ONE WHICH IS VITAL TO THE PRESERVATION OF THE REPUBLIC.
I HAVE A KNACK FOR FINDING THE RIGHT CANDIDATES FOR THE JOB. AND I THINK YOU ARE PERFECT.
YOU JUST NEED THE PROPER TRAINING.

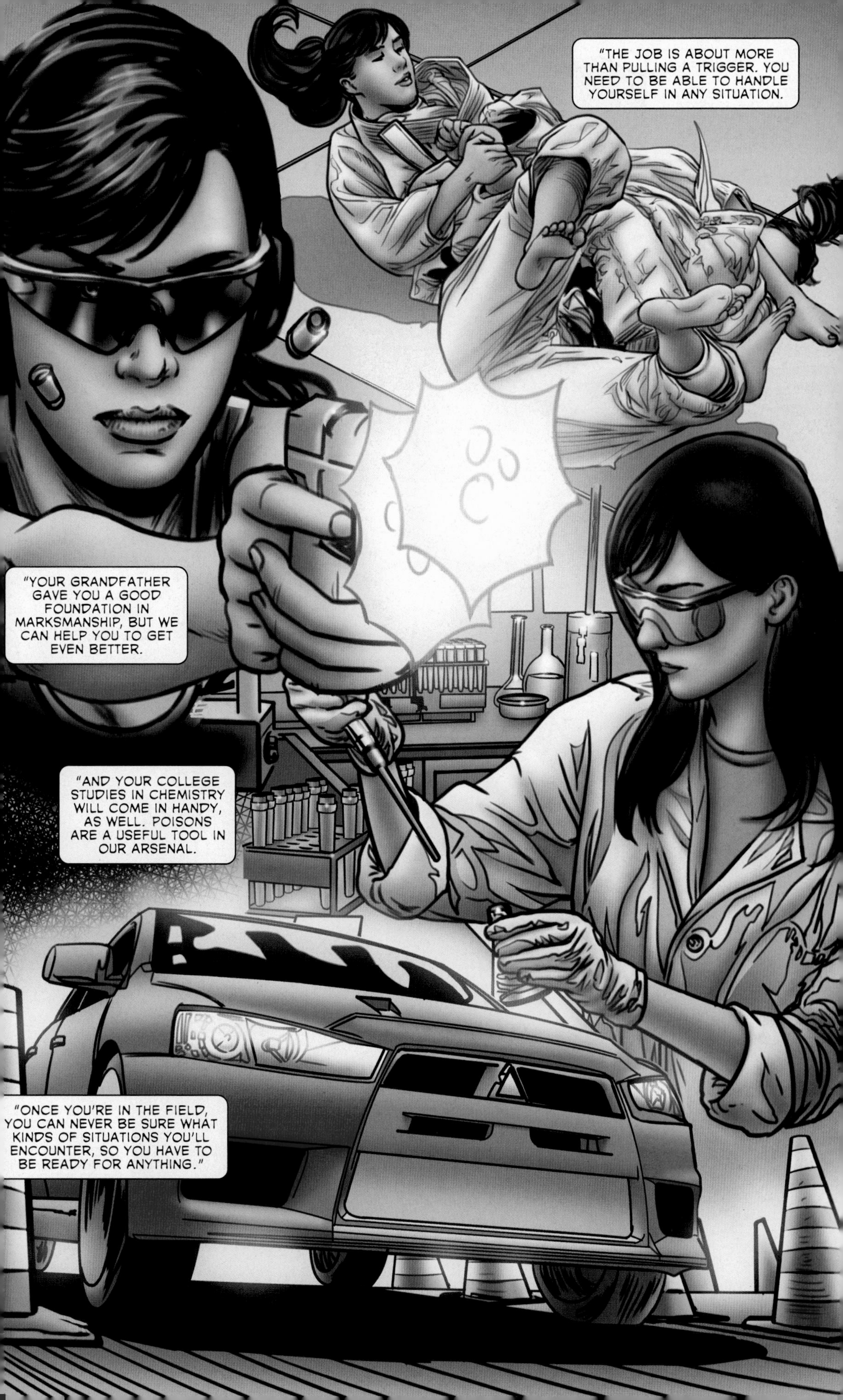
"THE JOB IS ABOUT MORE THAN PULLING A TRIGGER. YOU NEED TO BE ABLE TO HANDLE YOURSELF IN ANY SITUATION.
"YOUR GRANDFATHER GAVE YOU A GOOD FOUNDATION IN MARKSMANSHIP, BUT WE CAN HELP YOU TO GET EVEN BETTER.
"AND YOUR COLLEGE STUDIES IN CHEMISTRY WILL COME IN HANDY, AS WELL. POISONS ARE A USEFUL TOOL IN OUR ARSENAL.
"ONCE YOU'RE IN THE FIELD, YOU CAN NEVER BE SURE WHAT KINDS OF SITUATIONS YOU'LL ENCOUNTER, SO YOU HAVE TO BE READY FOR ANYTHING."

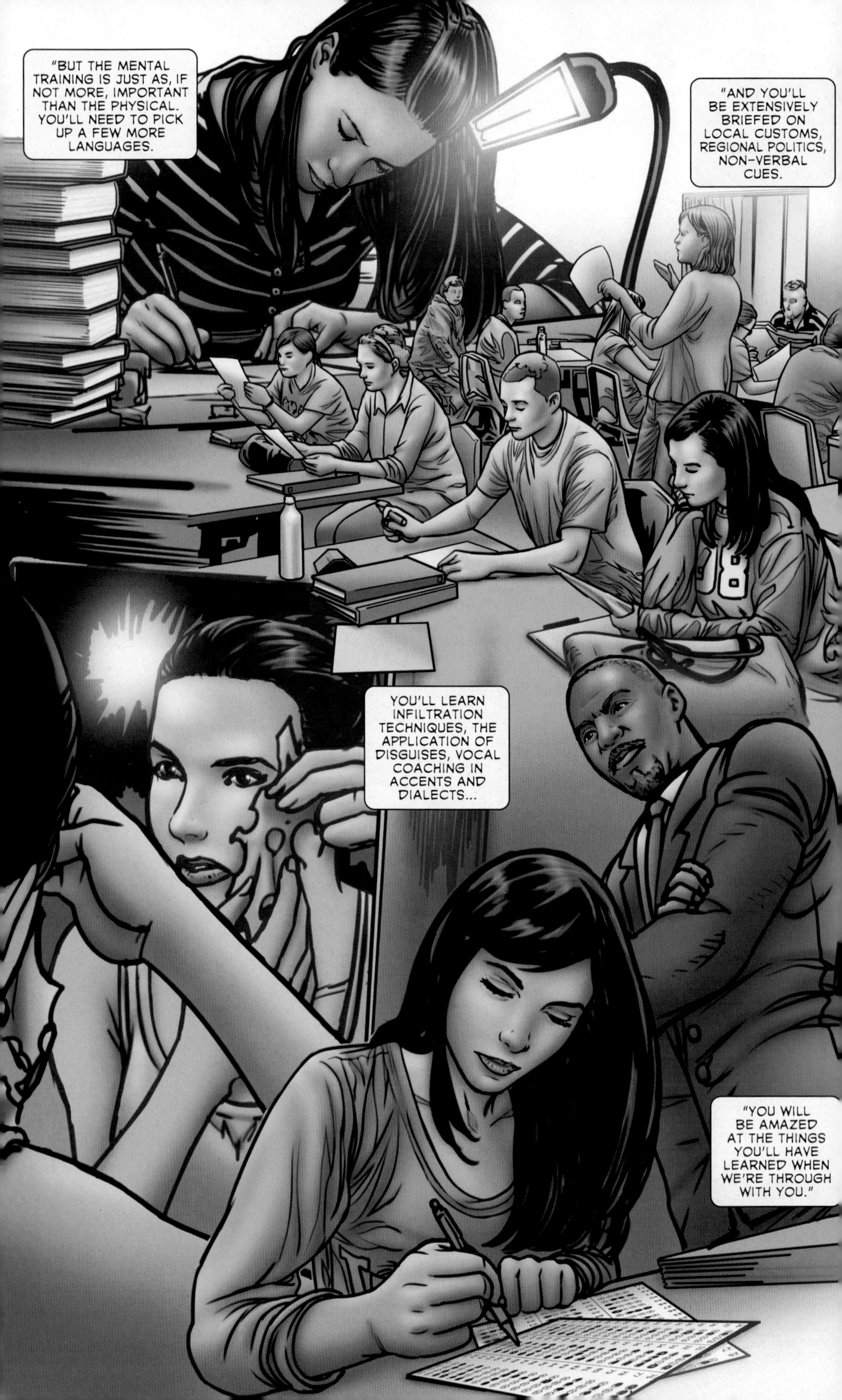
"BUT THE MENTAL TRAINING IS JUST AS, IF NOT MORE, IMPORTANT THAN THE PHYSICAL. YOU'LL NEED TO PICK UP A FEW MORE LANGUAGES.
"AND YOU'LL BE EXTENSIVELY BRIEFED ON LOCAL CUSTOMS, REGIONAL POLITICS, NON-VERBAL CUES.
YOU'LL LEARN INFILTRATION TECHNIQUES, THE APPLICATION OF DISGUISES, VOCAL COACHING IN ACCENTS AND DIALECTS...
"YOU WILL BE AMAZED AT THE THINGS YOU'LL HAVE LEARNED WHEN WE'RE THROUGH WITH YOU."

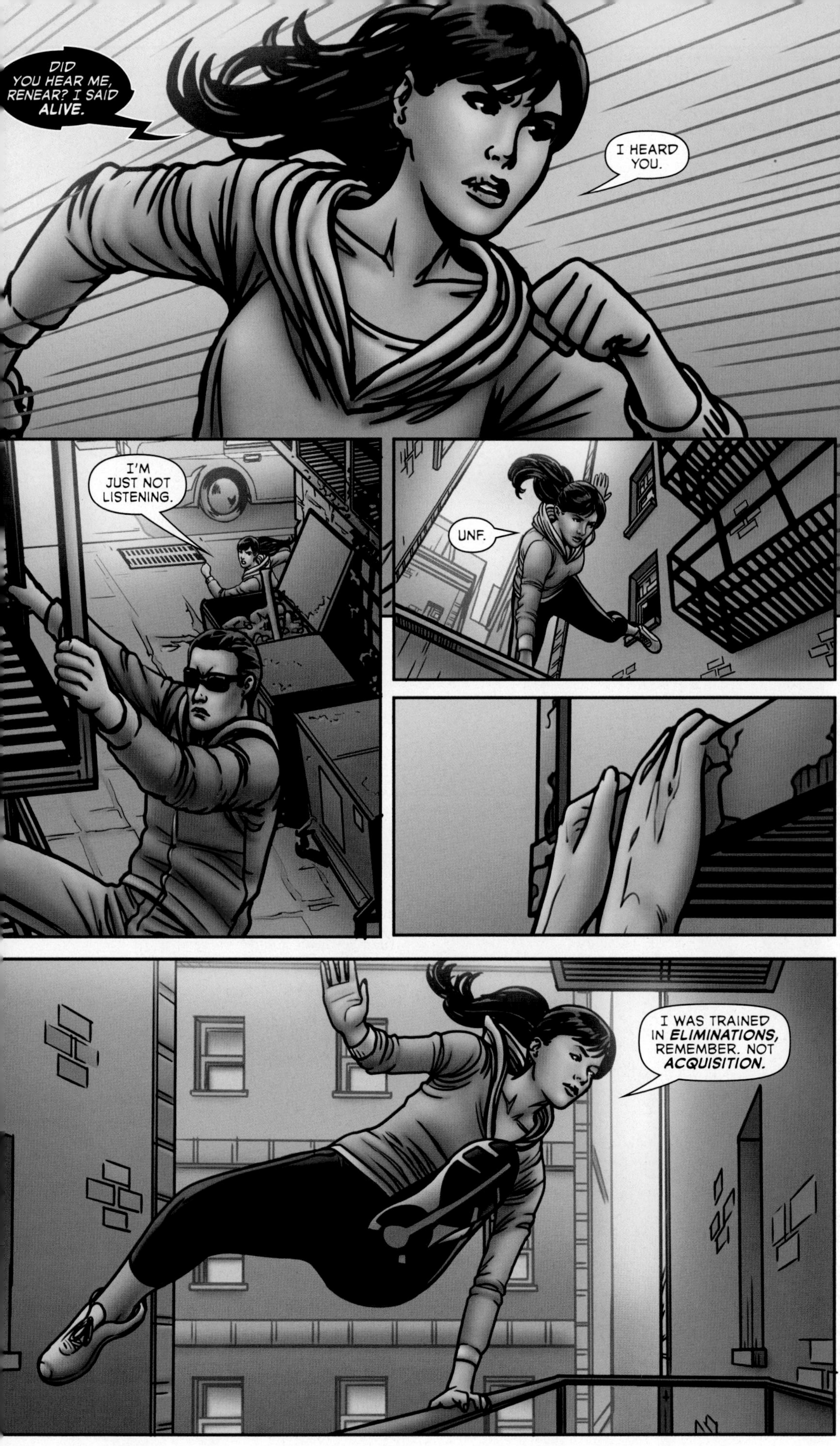
DID YOU HEAR ME, RENEAR? I SAID ALIVE.
I HEARD YOU.
I'M JUST NOT LISTENING.
UNF.
I WAS TRAINED IN ELIMINATIONS, REMEMBER. NOT ACQUISITION.

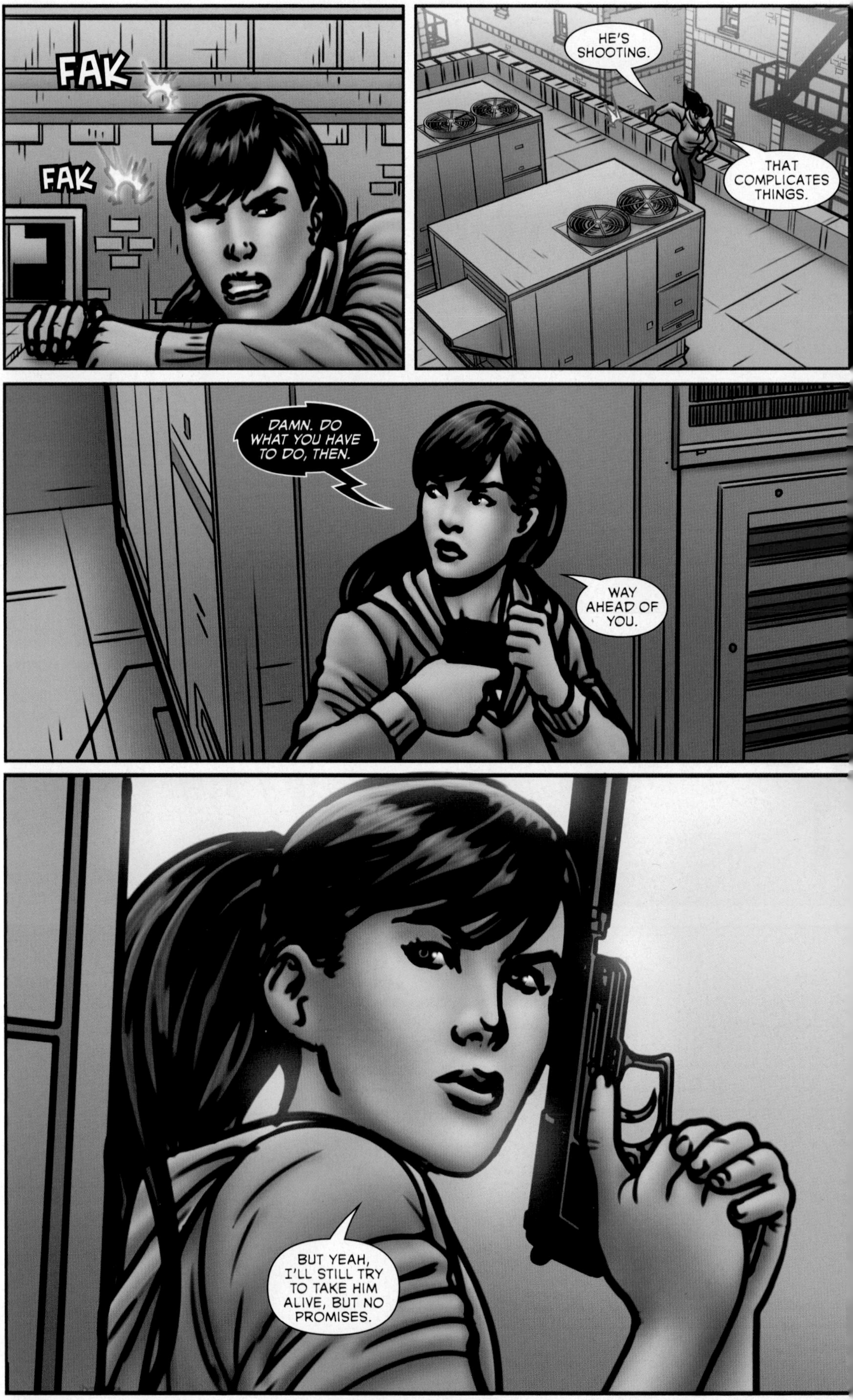
FAK
FAK
HE'S SHOOTING.
THAT COMPLICATES THINGS.
DAMN. DO WHAT YOU HAVE TO DO, THEN.
WAY AHEAD OF YOU.
BUT YEAH, I'LL STILL TRY TO TAKE HIM ALIVE, BUT NO PROMISES.

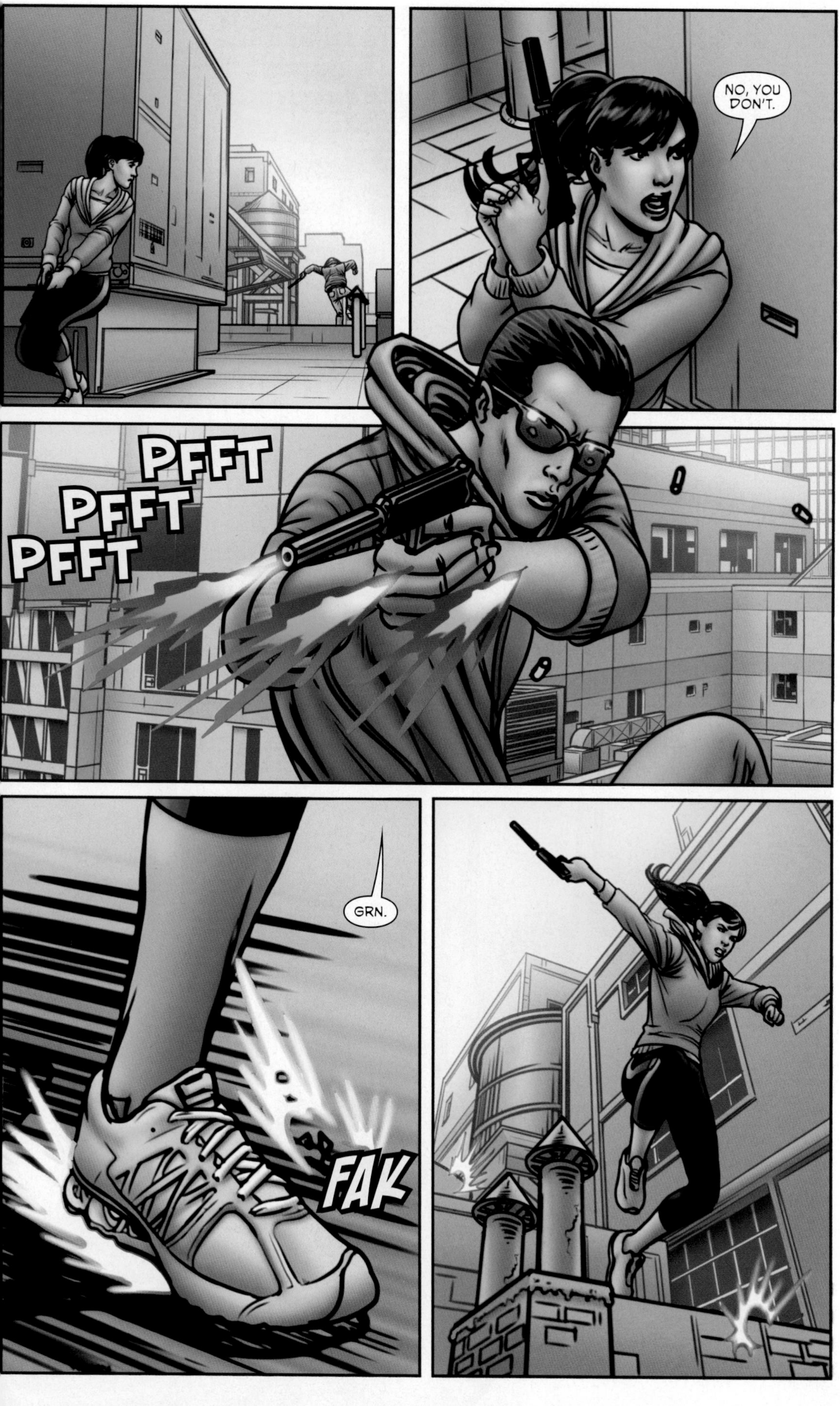
NO, YOU DON'T.
PFFT
PFFT
PFFT
GRN.
FAK

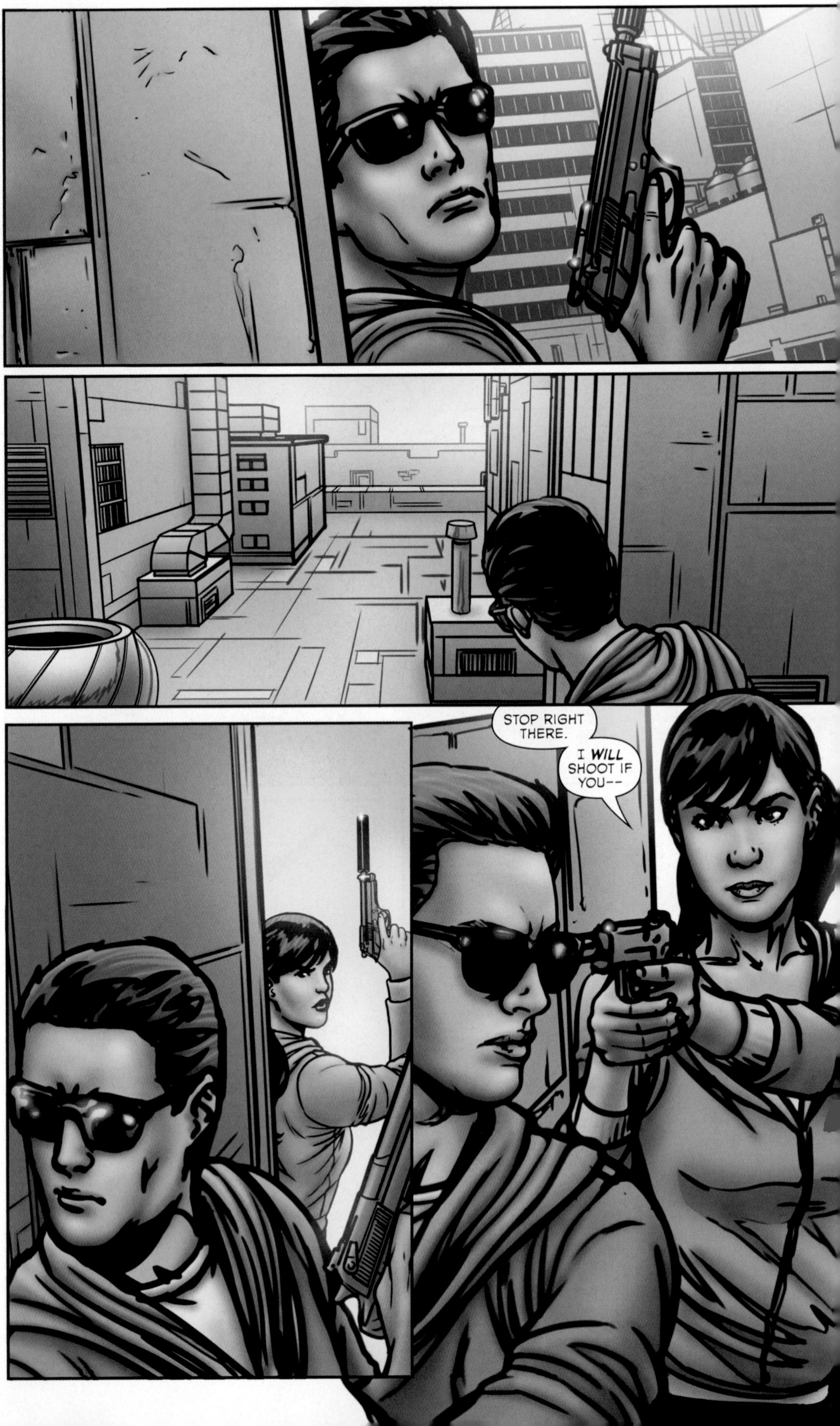
STOP RIGHT THERE.
I WILL SHOOT IF YOU--

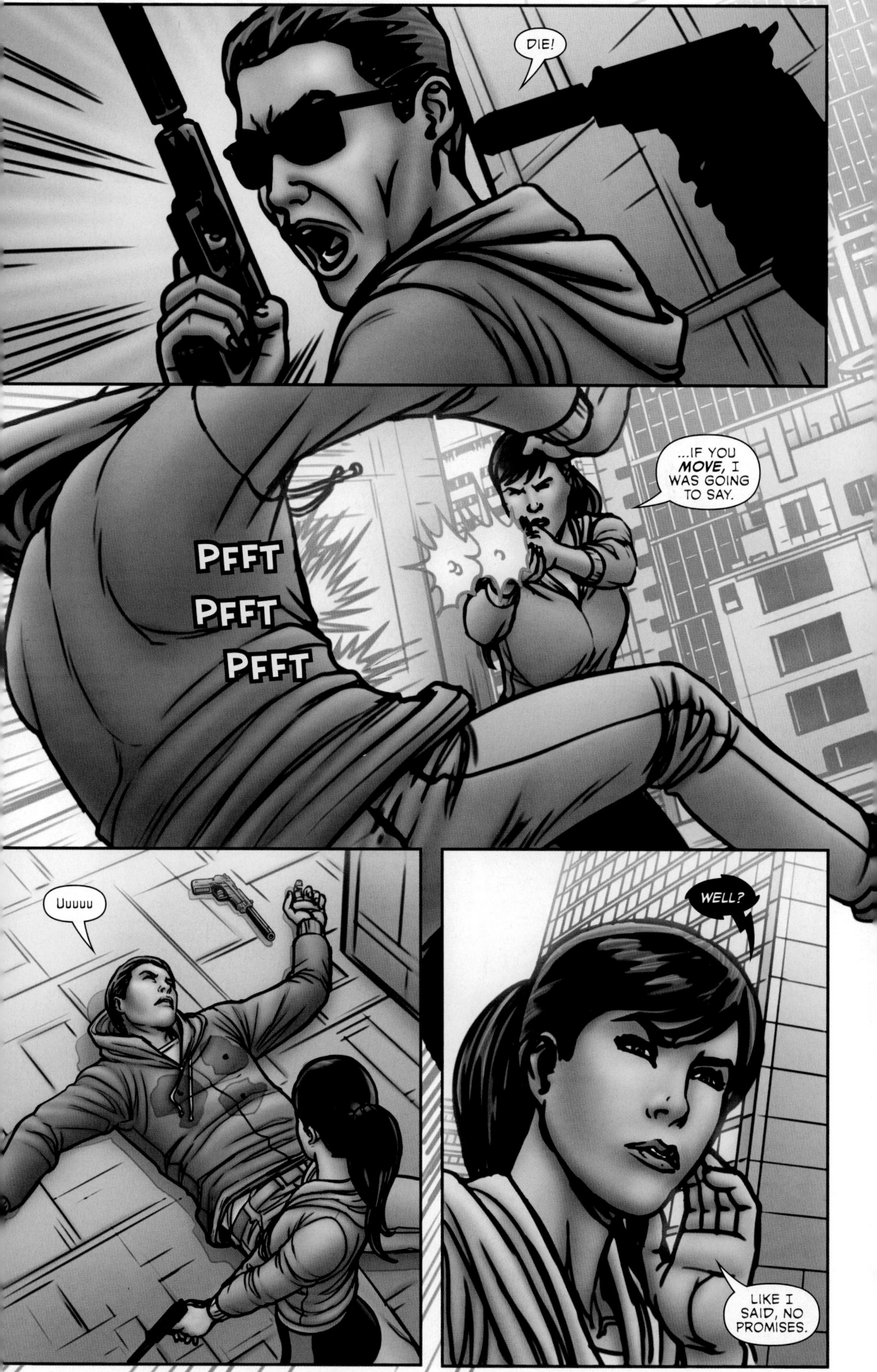
DIE!
...IF YOU MOVE, I WAS GOING TO SAY.
PFFT
PFFT
PFFT
Uuuuu
WELL?
LIKE I SAID, NO PROMISES.

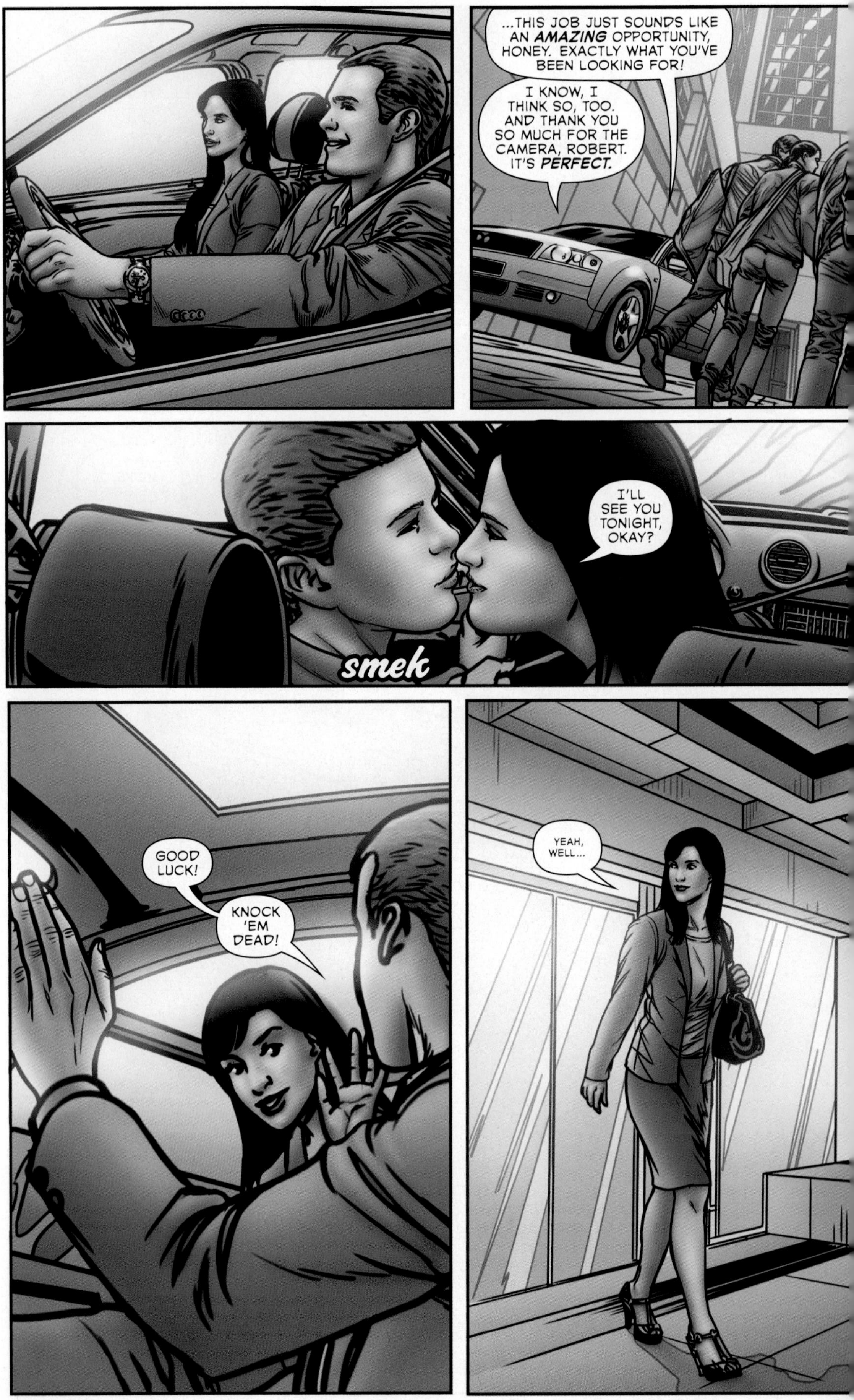
...THIS JOB JUST SOUNDS LIKE AN *AMAZING* OPPORTUNITY, HONEY. EXACTLY WHAT YOU'VE BEEN LOOKING FOR!
I KNOW, I THINK SO, TOO. AND THANK YOU SO MUCH FOR THE CAMERA, ROBERT. IT'S *PERFECT.*
I'LL SEE YOU TONIGHT, OKAY?
smek
GOOD LUCK!
KNOCK 'EM DEAD!
YEAH, WELL...

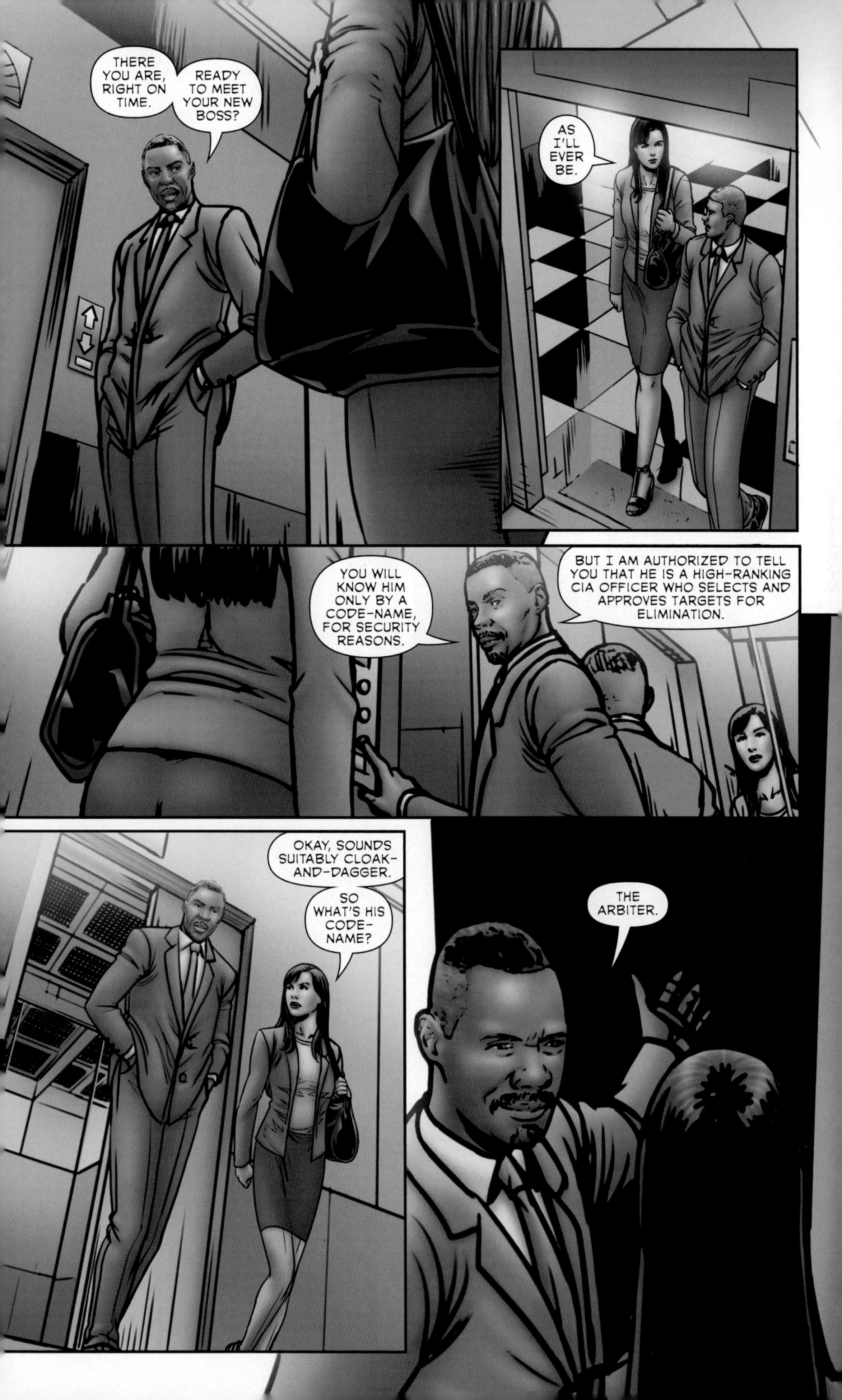
THERE YOU ARE, RIGHT ON TIME.
READY TO MEET YOUR NEW BOSS?
AS I'LL EVER BE.
YOU WILL KNOW HIM ONLY BY A CODE-NAME, FOR SECURITY REASONS.
BUT I AM AUTHORIZED TO TELL YOU THAT HE IS A HIGH-RANKING CIA OFFICER WHO SELECTS AND APPROVES TARGETS FOR ELIMINATION.
OKAY, SOUNDS SUITABLY CLOAK-AND-DAGGER.
SO WHAT'S HIS CODE-NAME?
THE ARBITER.

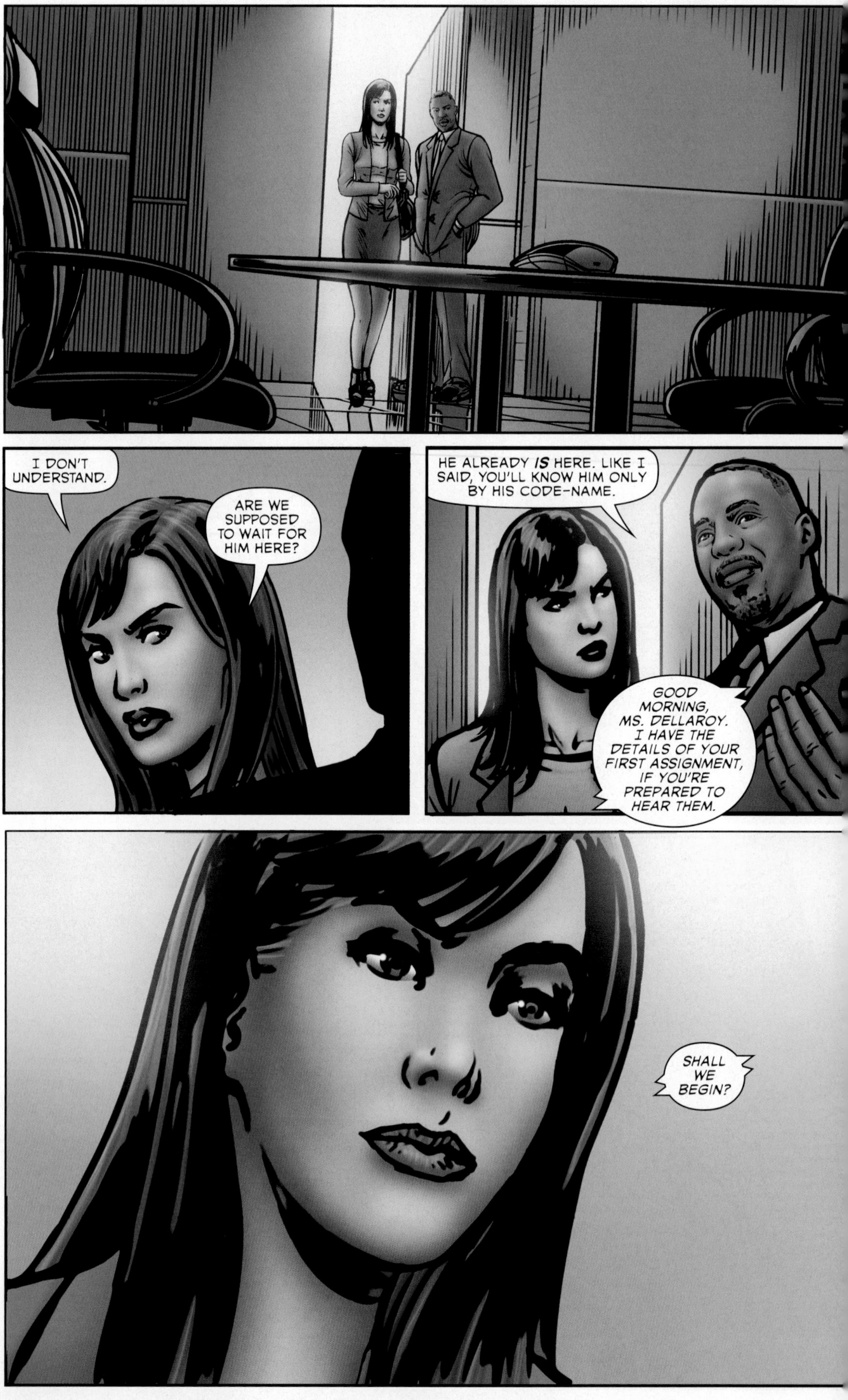
I DON'T UNDERSTAND.
ARE WE SUPPOSED TO WAIT FOR HIM HERE?
HE ALREADY *IS* HERE. LIKE I SAID, YOU'LL KNOW HIM ONLY BY HIS CODE-NAME.
GOOD MORNING, MS. DELLAROY. I HAVE THE DETAILS OF YOUR FIRST ASSIGNMENT, IF YOU'RE PREPARED TO HEAR THEM.
SHALL WE BEGIN?

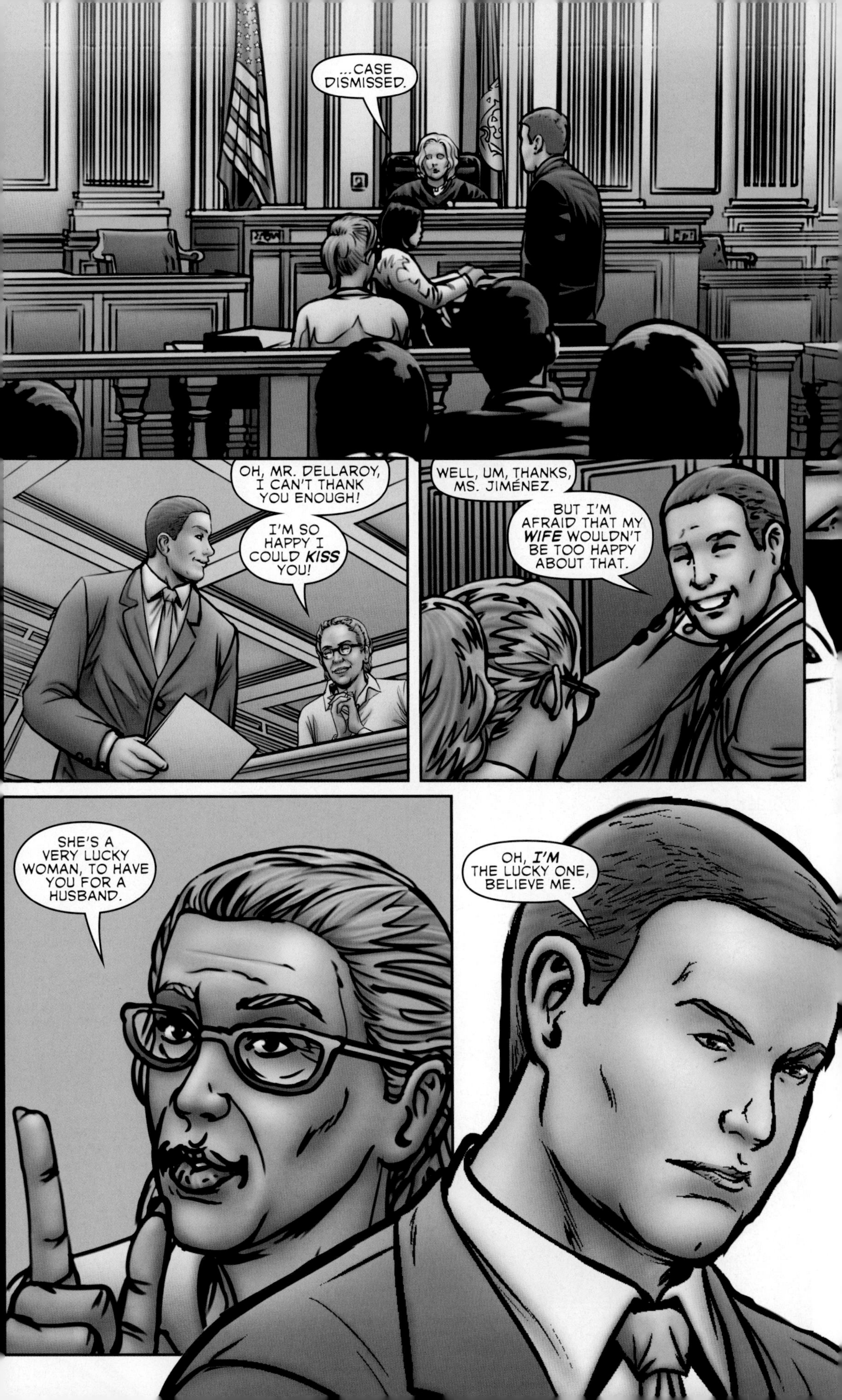
...CASE DISMISSED.
OH, MR. DELLAROY, I CAN'T THANK YOU ENOUGH!
I'M SO HAPPY I COULD KISS YOU!
WELL, UM, THANKS, MS. JIMÉNEZ.
BUT I'M AFRAID THAT MY WIFE WOULDN'T BE TOO HAPPY ABOUT THAT.
SHE'S A VERY LUCKY WOMAN, TO HAVE YOU FOR A HUSBAND.
OH, I'M THE LUCKY ONE, BELIEVE ME.

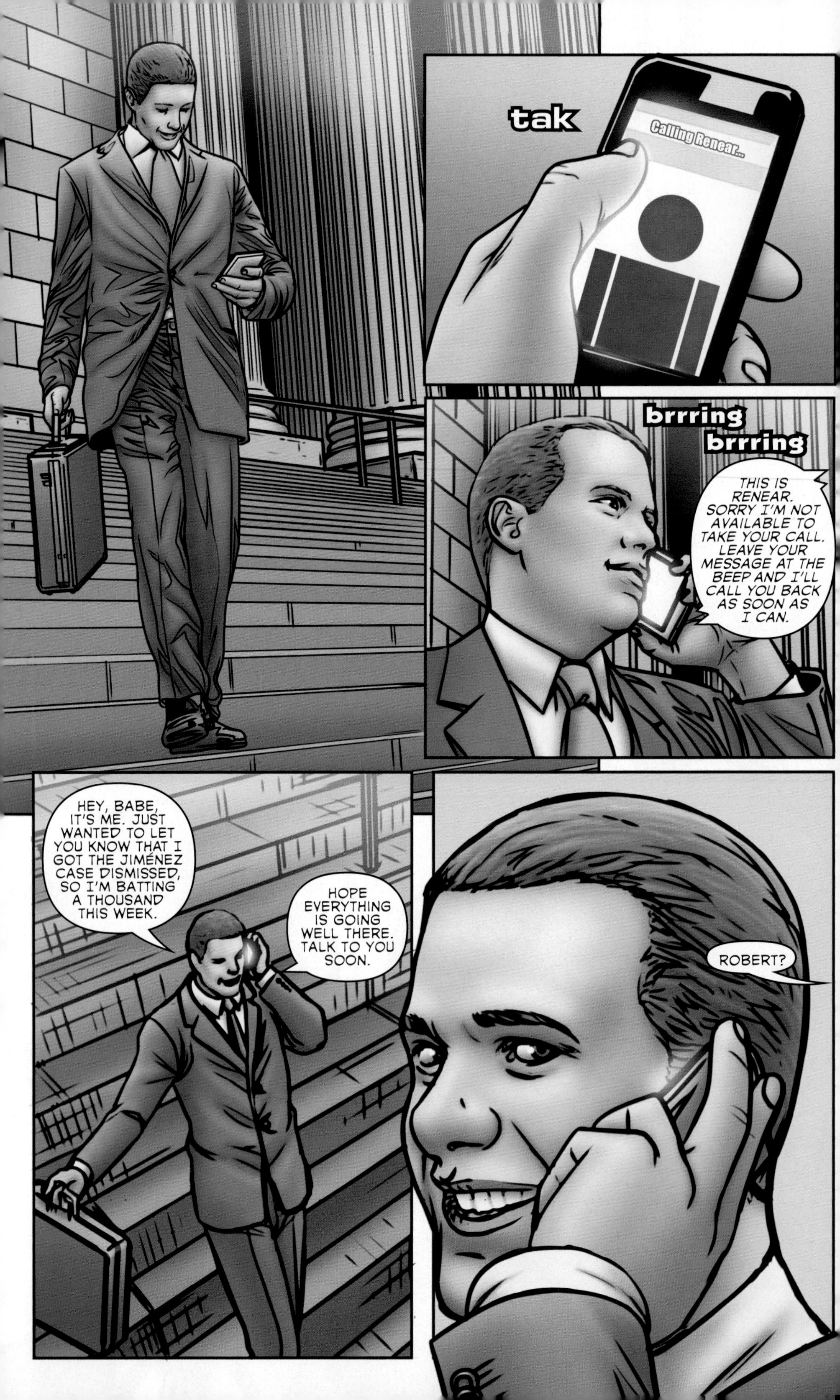
tak
Calling Renear...
brrring
brrring
THIS IS RENEAR. SORRY I'M NOT AVAILABLE TO TAKE YOUR CALL. LEAVE YOUR MESSAGE AT THE BEEP AND I'LL CALL YOU BACK AS SOON AS I CAN.
HEY, BABE, IT'S ME. JUST WANTED TO LET YOU KNOW THAT I GOT THE JIMÉNEZ CASE DISMISSED, SO I'M BATTING A THOUSAND THIS WEEK.
HOPE EVERYTHING IS GOING WELL THERE. TALK TO YOU SOON.
ROBERT?

HI! HOW ARE YOU?

IT'S BEEN *AGES*.

OH, HEY, STEPHANIE. GOOD TO SEE YOU.

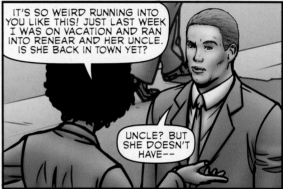

IT'S SO WEIRD RUNNING INTO YOU LIKE THIS! JUST LAST WEEK I WAS ON VACATION AND RAN INTO RENEAR AND HER UNCLE. IS SHE BACK IN TOWN YET?

UNCLE? BUT SHE DOESN'T HAVE--

OH, MY GOD! I... I JUST... I GUESS I MUST HAVE *MISHEARD* HER?

I THOUGHT SHE SAID... BUT SHE MUST HAVE MEANT...

NEVER MIND. I'M SURE IT'S JUST A MISCOMMUNICATION. RIGHT? SO... IS SHE BACK IN TOWN?

NO. I MEAN, SHE *CAME* BACK LAST WEEK, BUT NOW SHE'S HAD TO LEAVE AGAIN.

WELL, *erm*, GIVE HER MY LOVE, OKAY? IT WAS... GREAT RUNNING INTO YOU.

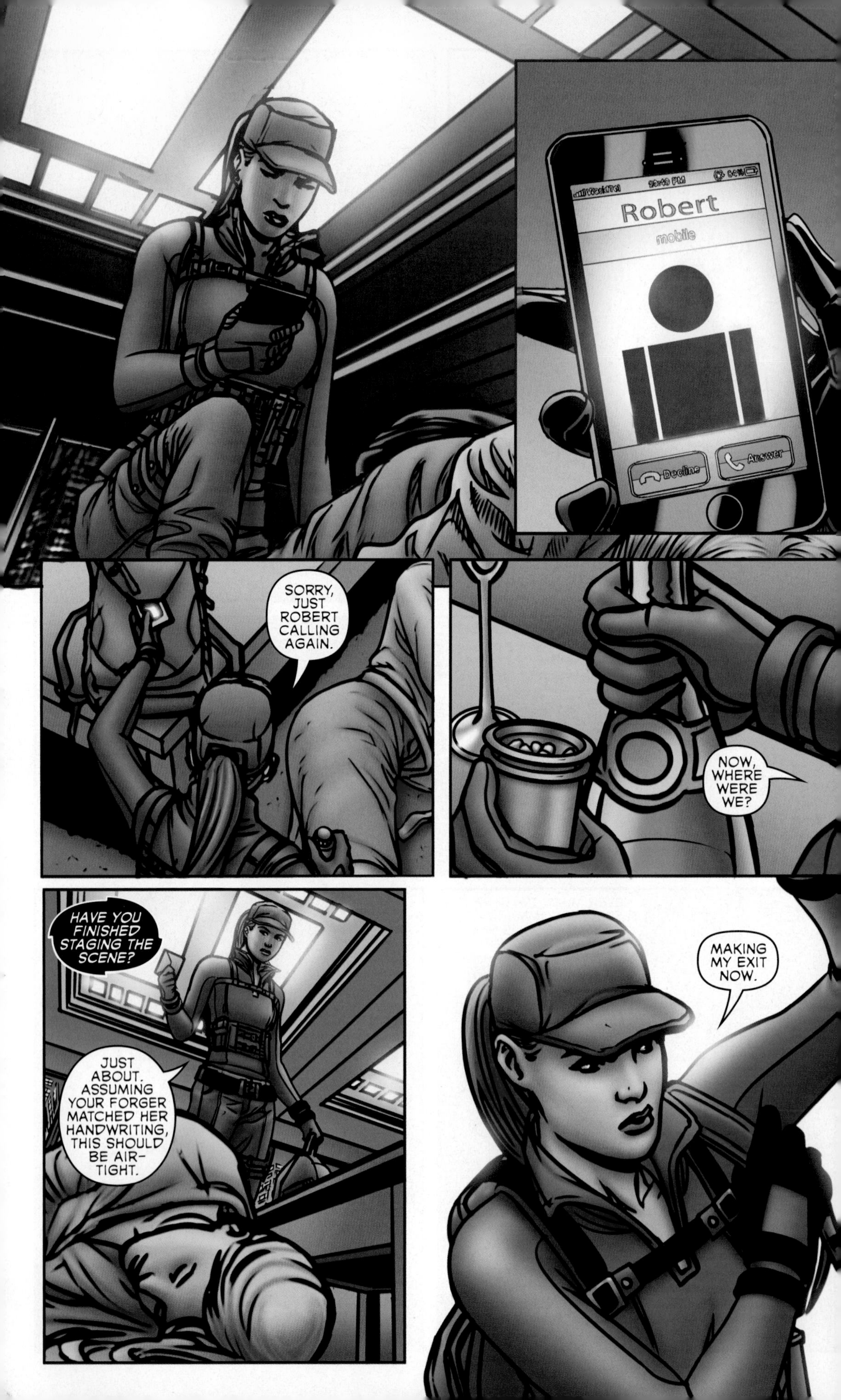
Robert
mobile
Decline
Answer
SORRY, JUST ROBERT CALLING AGAIN.
NOW, WHERE WERE WE?
HAVE YOU FINISHED STAGING THE SCENE?
JUST ABOUT. ASSUMING YOUR FORGER MATCHED HER HANDWRITING, THIS SHOULD BE AIR-TIGHT.
MAKING MY EXIT NOW.

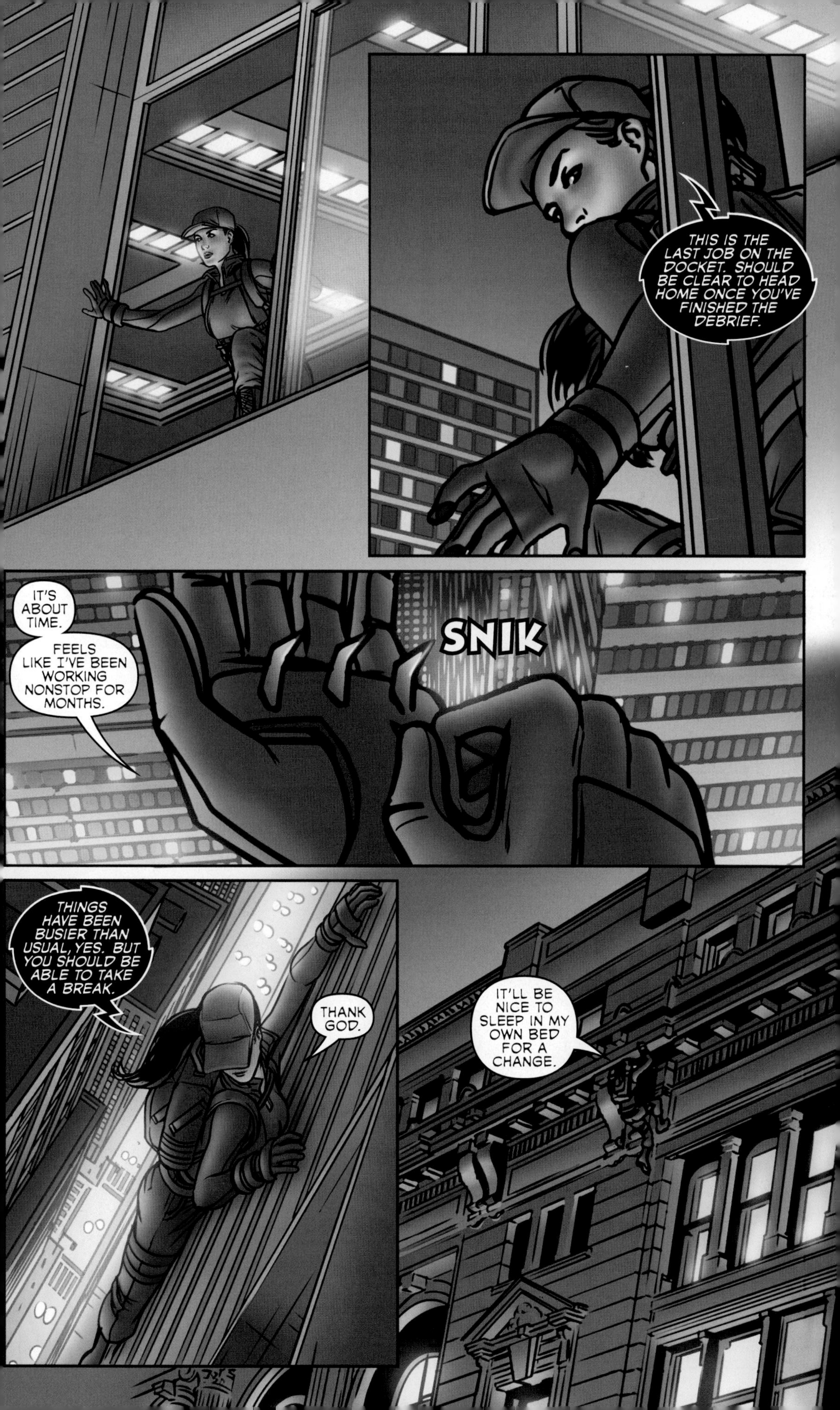
THIS IS THE LAST JOB ON THE DOCKET. SHOULD BE CLEAR TO HEAD HOME ONCE YOU'VE FINISHED THE DEBRIEF.
IT'S ABOUT TIME.
FEELS LIKE I'VE BEEN WORKING NONSTOP FOR MONTHS.
SNIK
THINGS HAVE BEEN BUSIER THAN USUAL, YES. BUT YOU SHOULD BE ABLE TO TAKE A BREAK.
THANK GOD.
IT'LL BE NICE TO SLEEP IN MY OWN BED FOR A CHANGE.

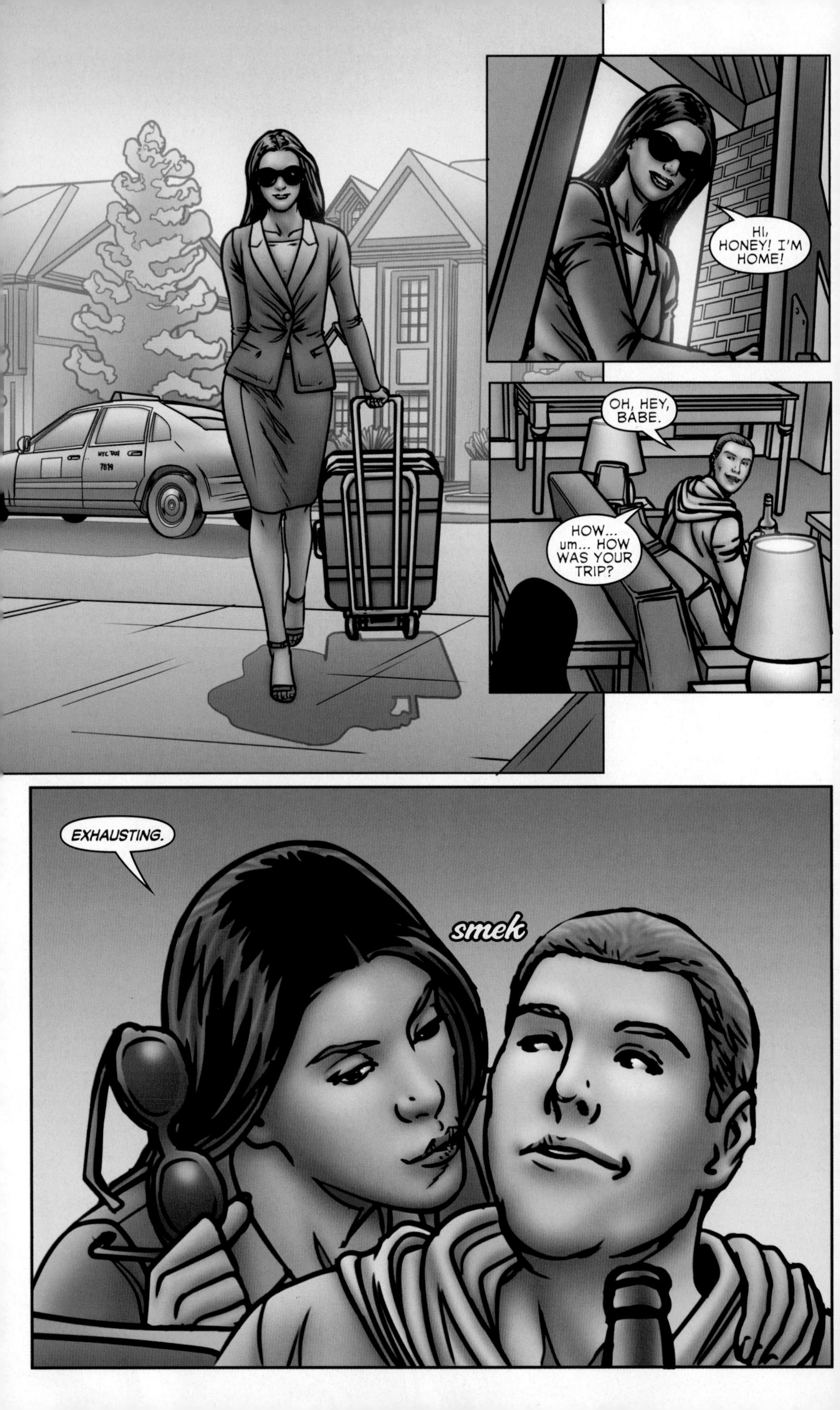
HI, HONEY! I'M HOME!
OH, HEY, BABE.
HOW... um... HOW WAS YOUR TRIP?
EXHAUSTING.
smek

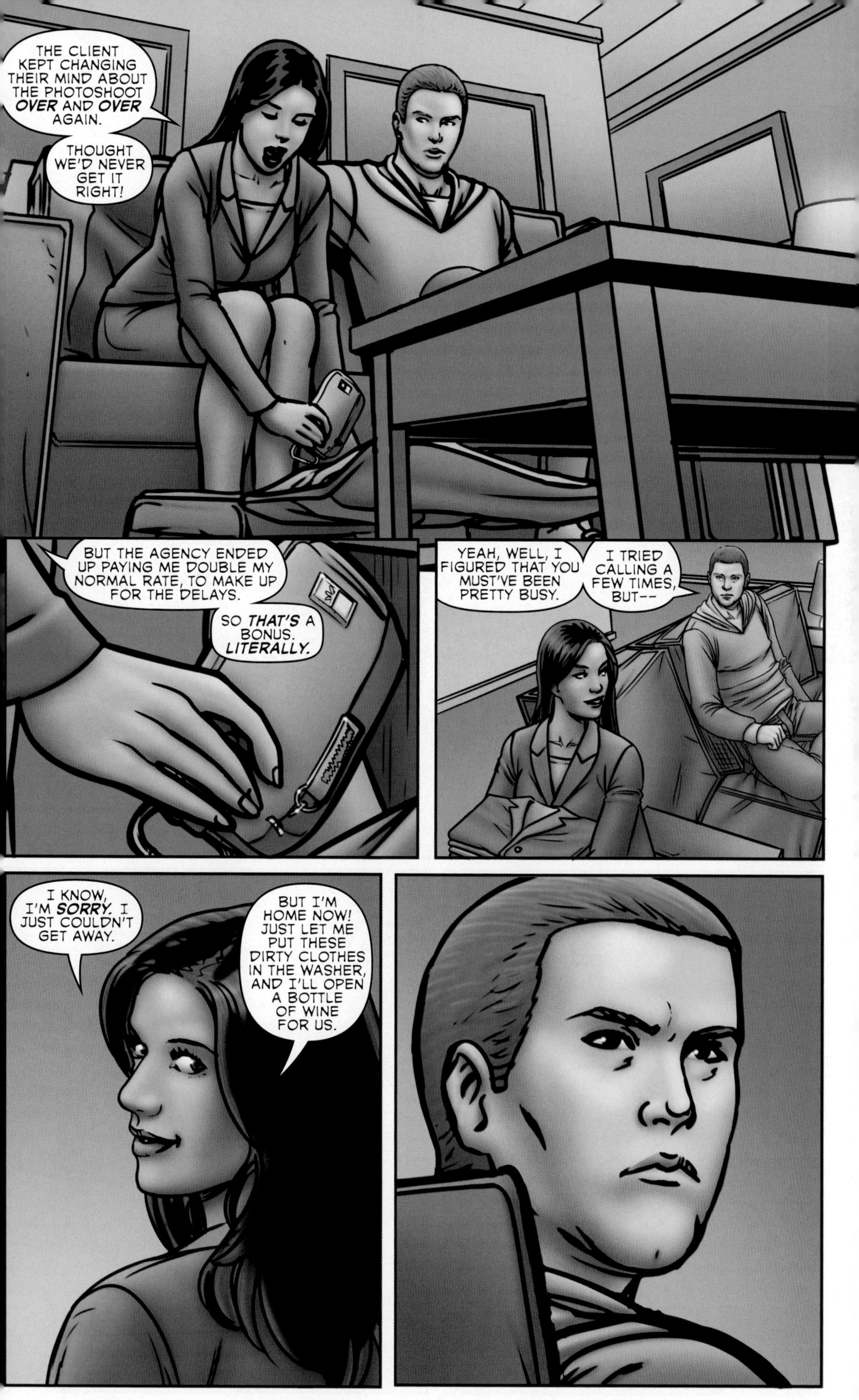
THE CLIENT KEPT CHANGING THEIR MIND ABOUT THE PHOTOSHOOT *OVER* AND *OVER* AGAIN.
THOUGHT WE'D NEVER GET IT RIGHT!
BUT THE AGENCY ENDED UP PAYING ME DOUBLE MY NORMAL RATE, TO MAKE UP FOR THE DELAYS.
SO *THAT'S* A BONUS. *LITERALLY.*
I TRIED CALLING A FEW TIMES, BUT--
YEAH, WELL, I FIGURED THAT YOU MUST'VE BEEN PRETTY BUSY.
I KNOW, I'M *SORRY.* I JUST COULDN'T GET AWAY.
BUT I'M HOME NOW! JUST LET ME PUT THESE DIRTY CLOTHES IN THE WASHER, AND I'LL OPEN A BOTTLE OF WINE FOR US.

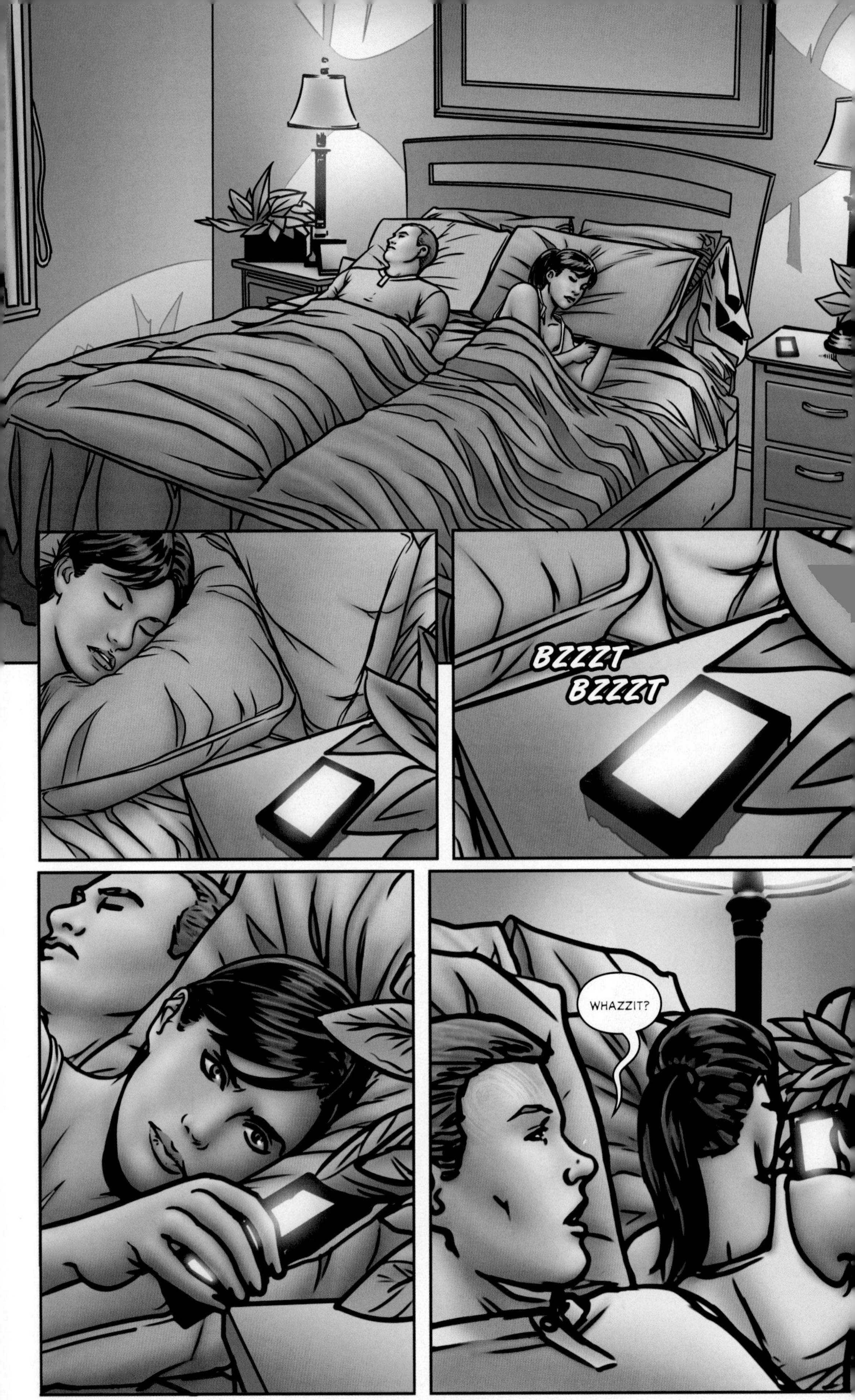
BZZZT
BZZZT
WHAZZIT?

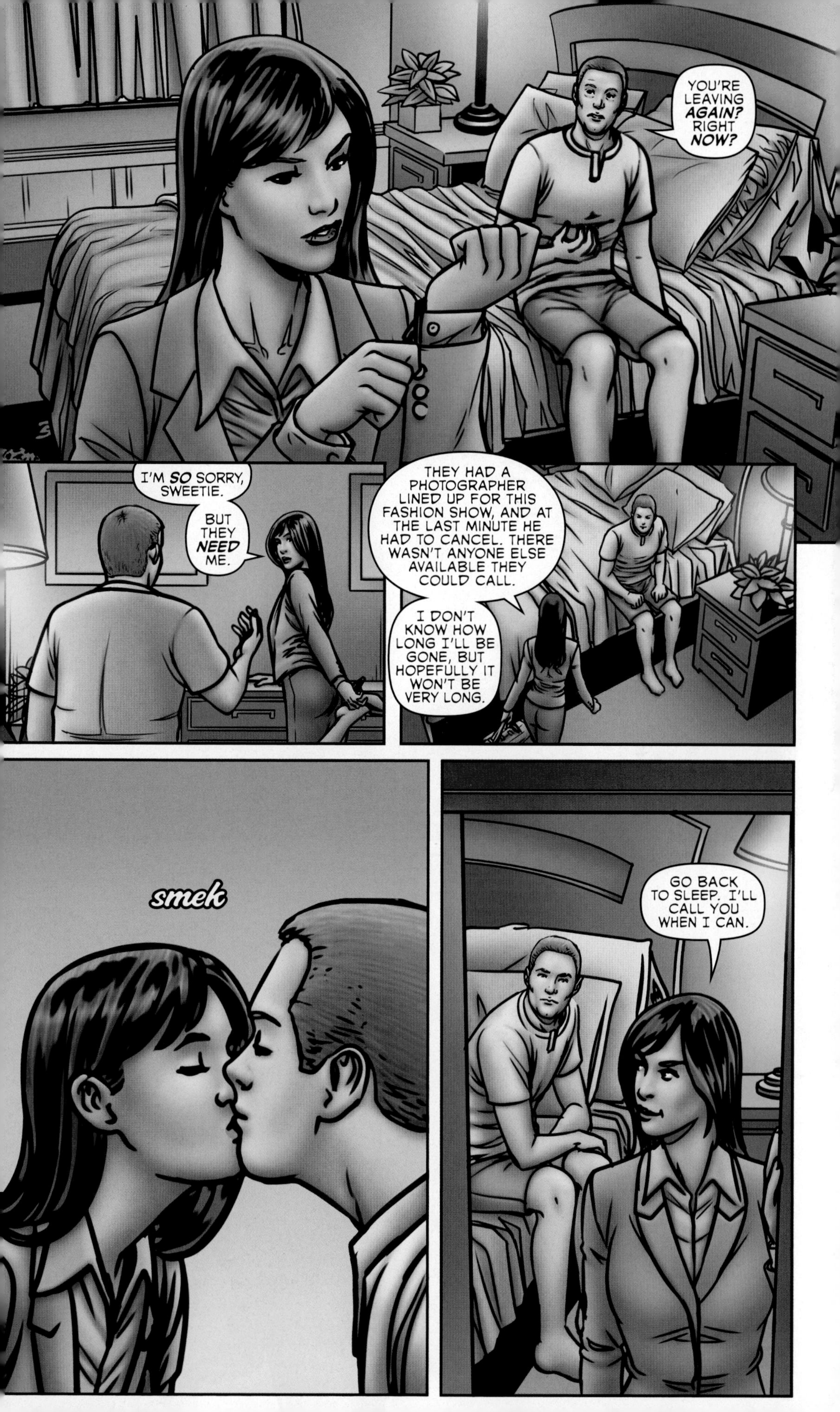
YOU'RE LEAVING *AGAIN?* RIGHT *NOW?*
I'M *SO* SORRY, SWEETIE.
BUT THEY *NEED* ME.
THEY HAD A PHOTOGRAPHER LINED UP FOR THIS FASHION SHOW, AND AT THE LAST MINUTE HE HAD TO CANCEL. THERE WASN'T ANYONE ELSE AVAILABLE THEY COULD CALL.
I DON'T KNOW HOW LONG I'LL BE GONE, BUT HOPEFULLY IT WON'T BE VERY LONG.
smek
GO BACK TO SLEEP. I'LL CALL YOU WHEN I CAN.

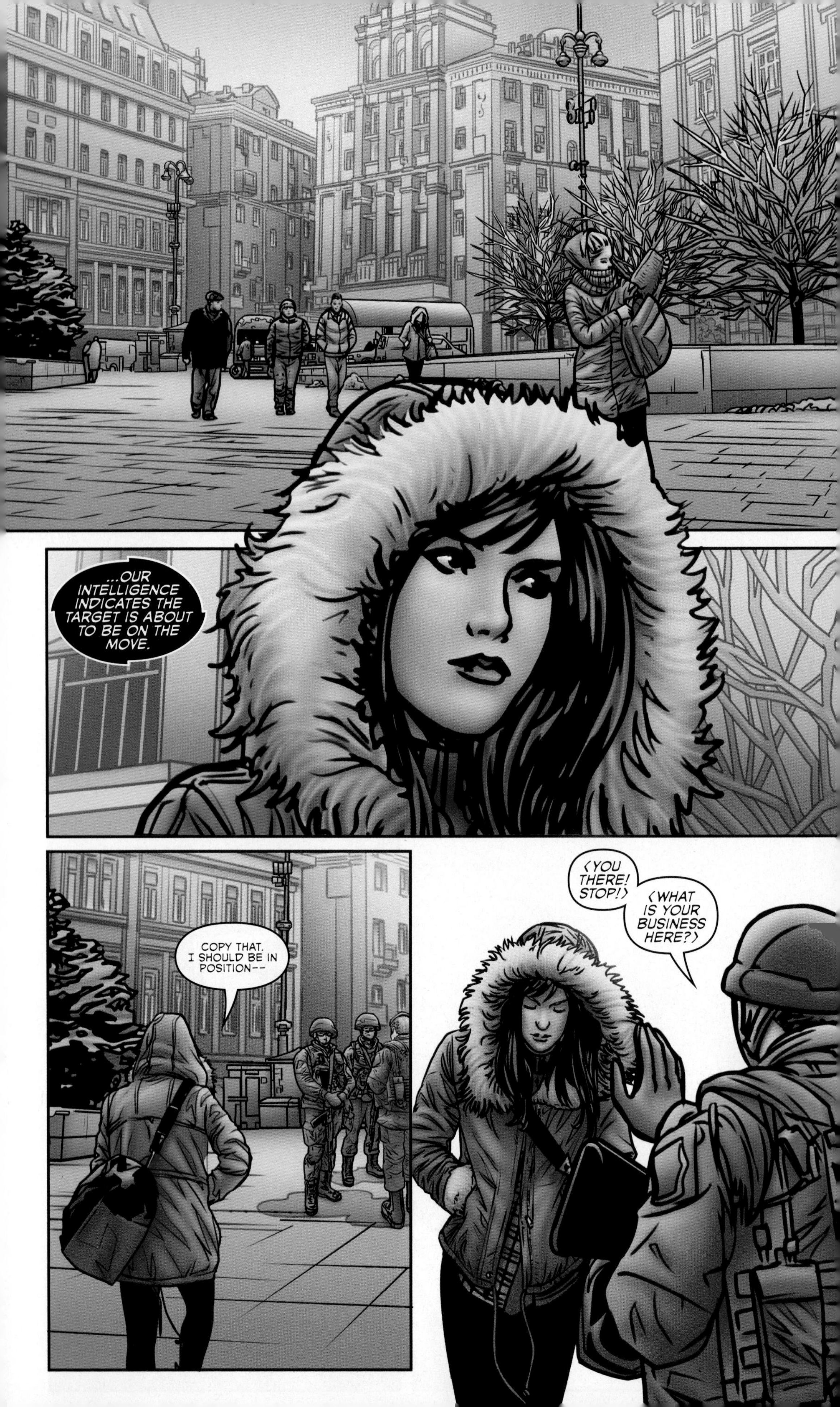
...OUR INTELLIGENCE INDICATES THE TARGET IS ABOUT TO BE ON THE MOVE.
COPY THAT. I SHOULD BE IN POSITION--
‹YOU THERE! STOP!›
‹WHAT IS YOUR BUSINESS HERE?›

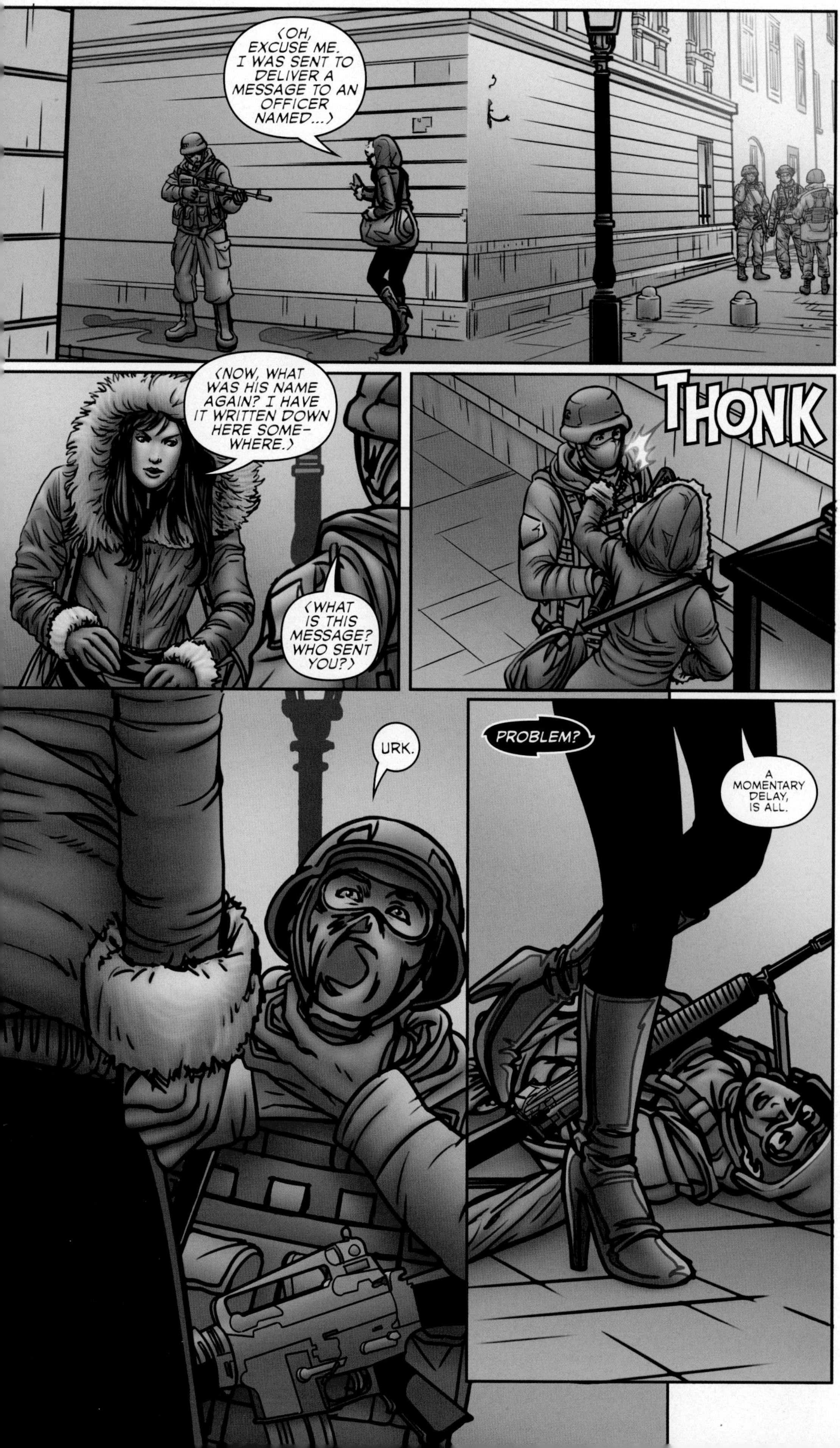

‹OH, EXCUSE ME. I WAS SENT TO DELIVER A MESSAGE TO AN OFFICER NAMED...›
‹NOW, WHAT WAS HIS NAME AGAIN? I HAVE IT WRITTEN DOWN HERE SOME-WHERE.›
‹WHAT IS THIS MESSAGE? WHO SENT YOU?›
THONK
URK.
PROBLEM?
A MOMENTARY DELAY, IS ALL.

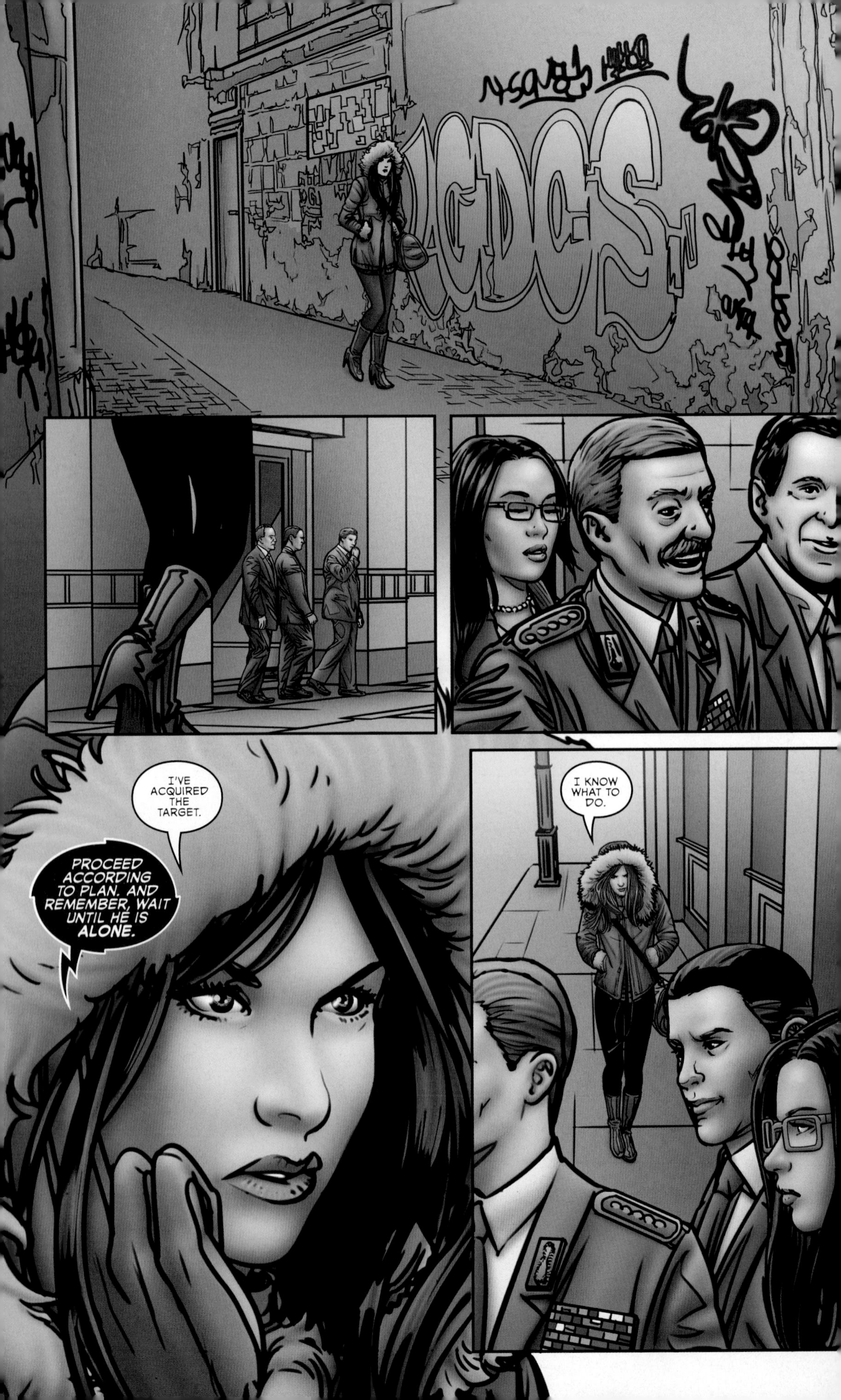

I'VE ACQUIRED THE TARGET.
PROCEED ACCORDING TO PLAN. AND REMEMBER, WAIT UNTIL HE IS ALONE.
I KNOW WHAT TO DO.

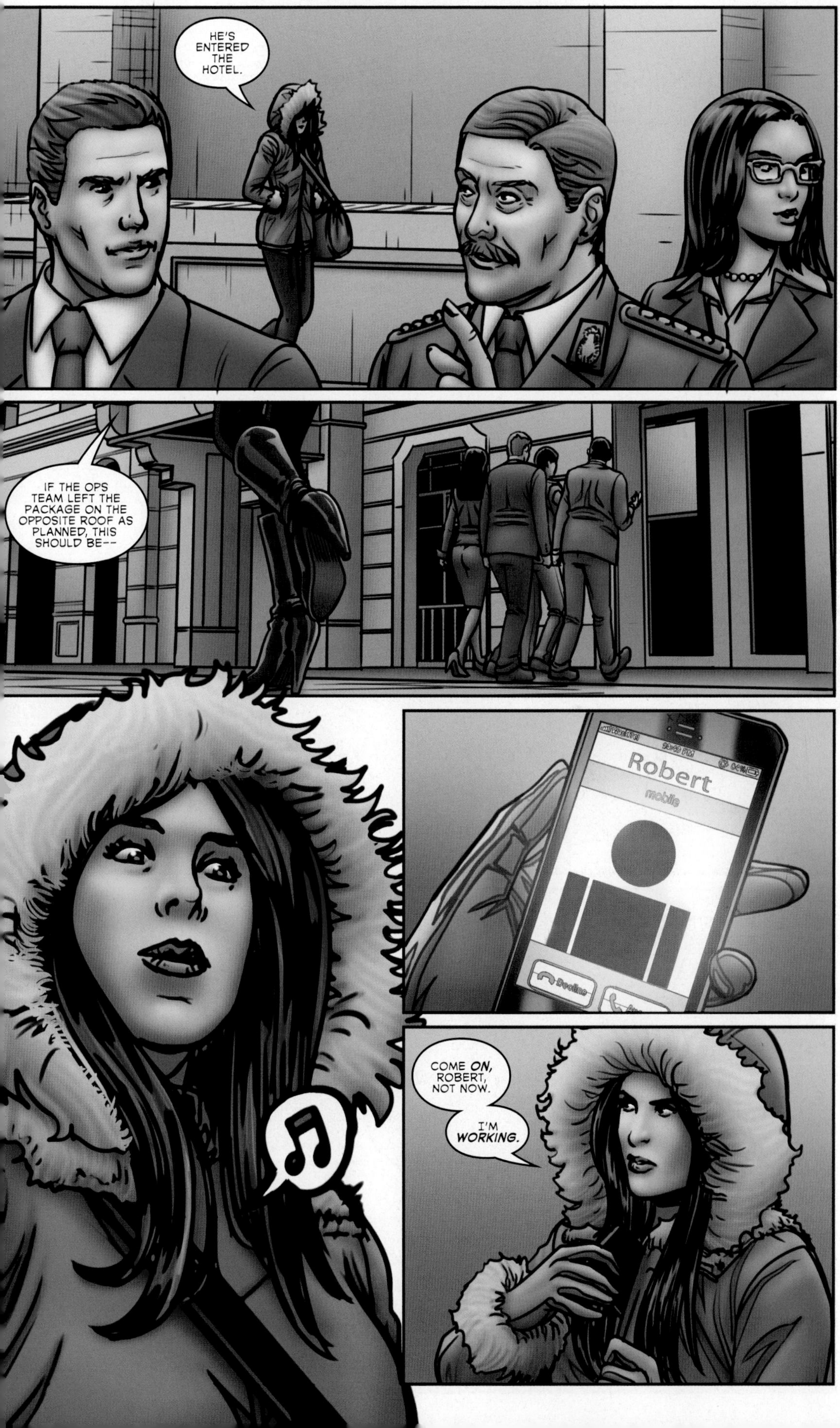
HE'S ENTERED THE HOTEL.
IF THE OPS TEAM LEFT THE PACKAGE ON THE OPPOSITE ROOF AS PLANNED, THIS SHOULD BE--
Robert
mobile
COME *ON*, ROBERT, NOT NOW.
I'M *WORKING.*

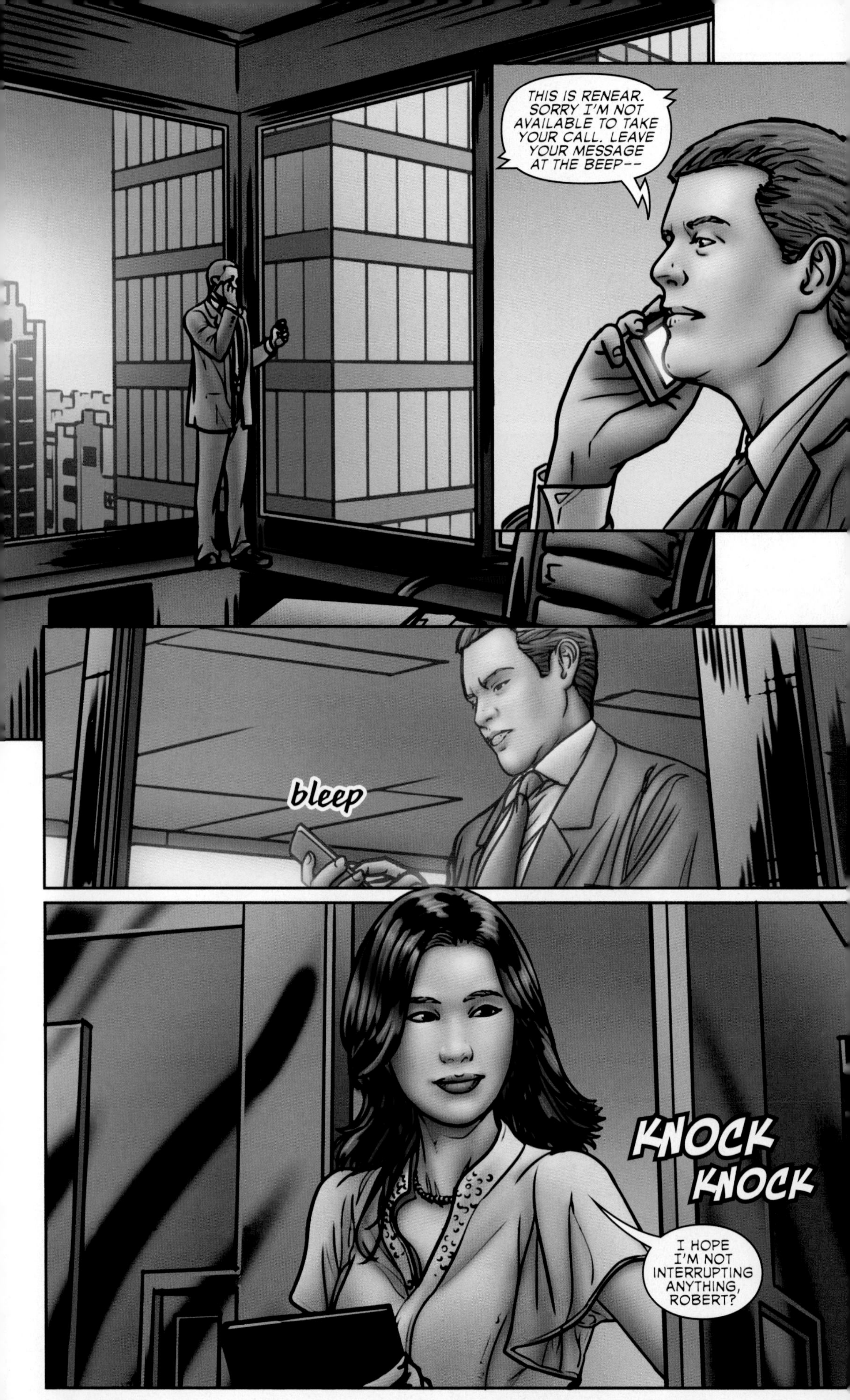
THIS IS RENEAR. SORRY I'M NOT AVAILABLE TO TAKE YOUR CALL. LEAVE YOUR MESSAGE AT THE BEEP--
bleep
KNOCK KNOCK
I HOPE I'M NOT INTERRUPTING ANYTHING, ROBERT?

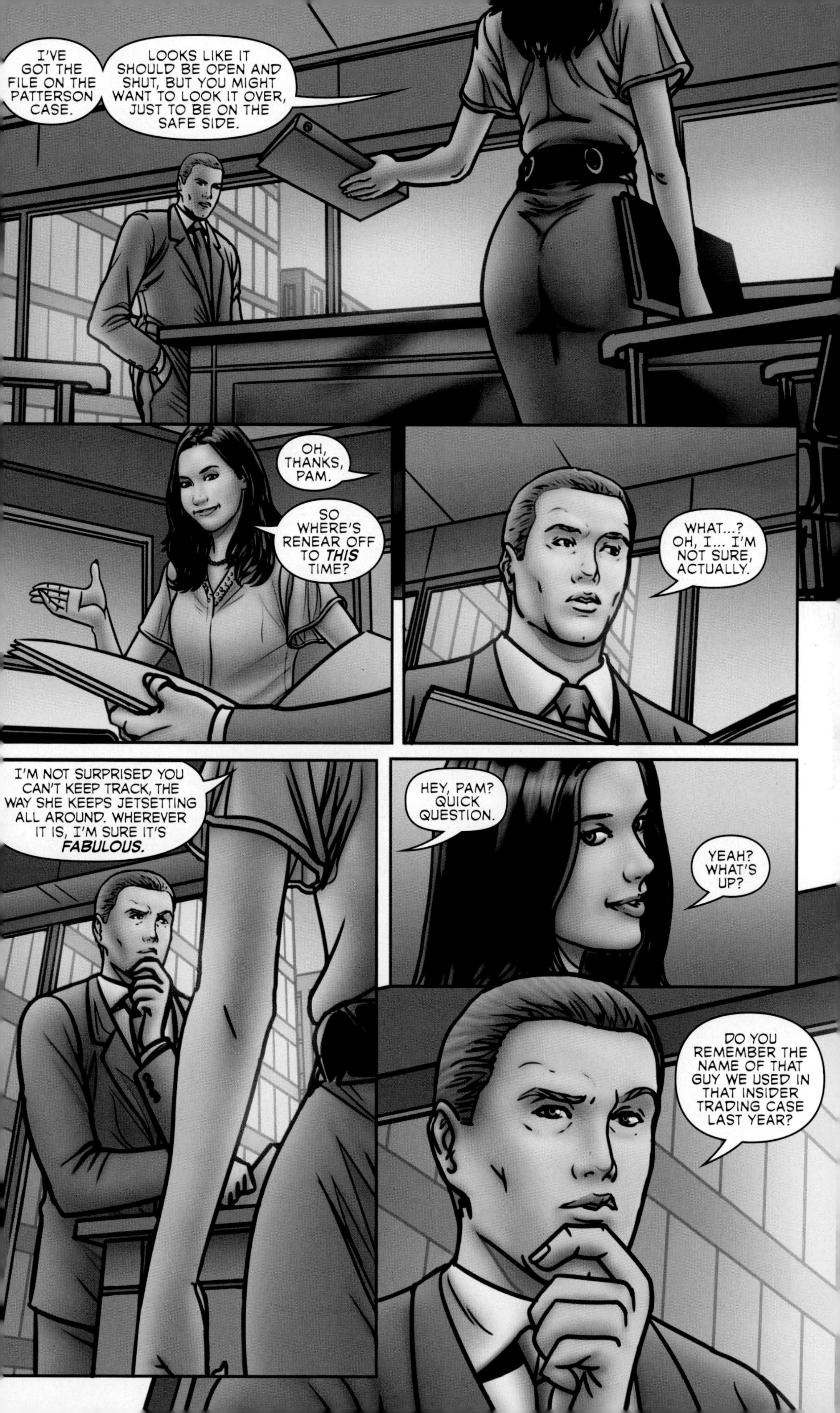

I'VE GOT THE FILE ON THE PATTERSON CASE.
LOOKS LIKE IT SHOULD BE OPEN AND SHUT, BUT YOU MIGHT WANT TO LOOK IT OVER, JUST TO BE ON THE SAFE SIDE.
OH, THANKS, PAM.
SO WHERE'S RENEAR OFF TO *THIS* TIME?
WHAT...? OH, I... I'M NOT SURE, ACTUALLY.
I'M NOT SURPRISED YOU CAN'T KEEP TRACK, THE WAY SHE KEEPS JETSETTING ALL AROUND. WHEREVER IT IS, I'M SURE IT'S ***FABULOUS.***
HEY, PAM? QUICK QUESTION.
YEAH? WHAT'S UP?
DO YOU REMEMBER THE NAME OF THAT GUY WE USED IN THAT INSIDER TRADING CASE LAST YEAR?

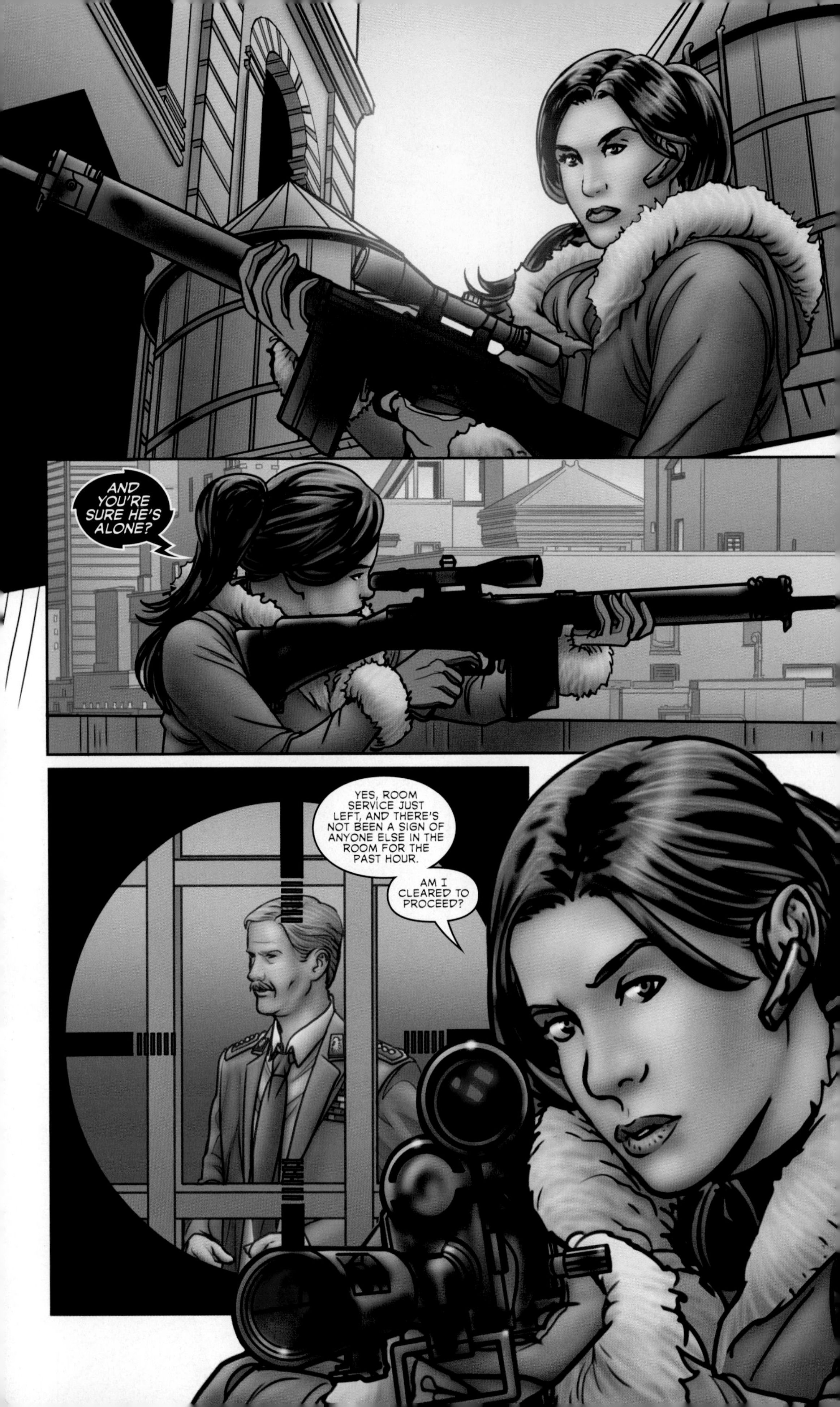
AND YOU'RE SURE HE'S ALONE?
YES, ROOM SERVICE JUST LEFT, AND THERE'S NOT BEEN A SIGN OF ANYONE ELSE IN THE ROOM FOR THE PAST HOUR.
AM I CLEARED TO PROCEED?

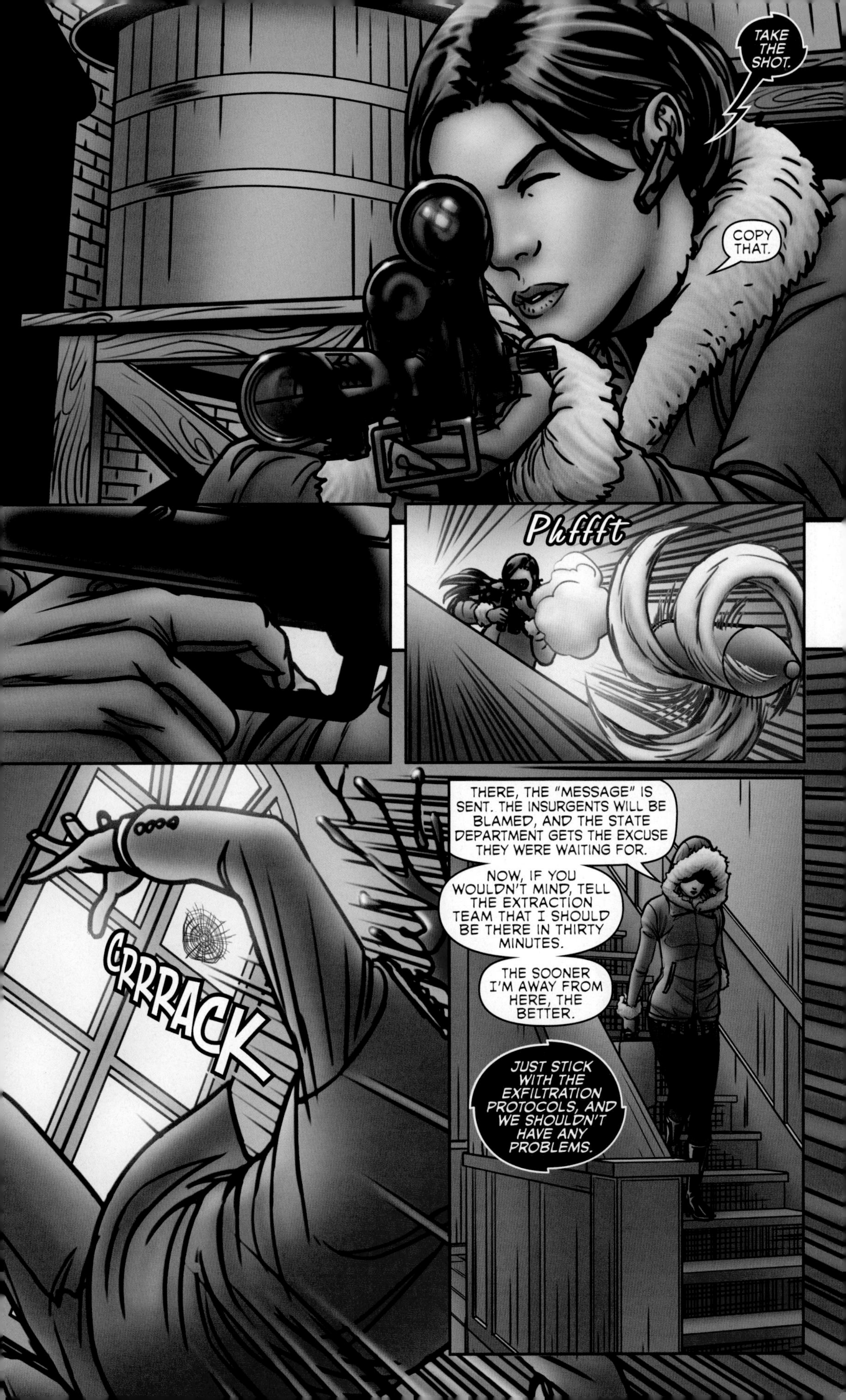

TAKE THE SHOT.
COPY THAT.
Phffft
CRRRACK
THERE, THE "MESSAGE" IS SENT. THE INSURGENTS WILL BE BLAMED, AND THE STATE DEPARTMENT GETS THE EXCUSE THEY WERE WAITING FOR.
NOW, IF YOU WOULDN'T MIND, TELL THE EXTRACTION TEAM THAT I SHOULD BE THERE IN THIRTY MINUTES.
THE SOONER I'M AWAY FROM HERE, THE BETTER.
JUST STICK WITH THE EXFILTRATION PROTOCOLS, AND WE SHOULDN'T HAVE ANY PROBLEMS.

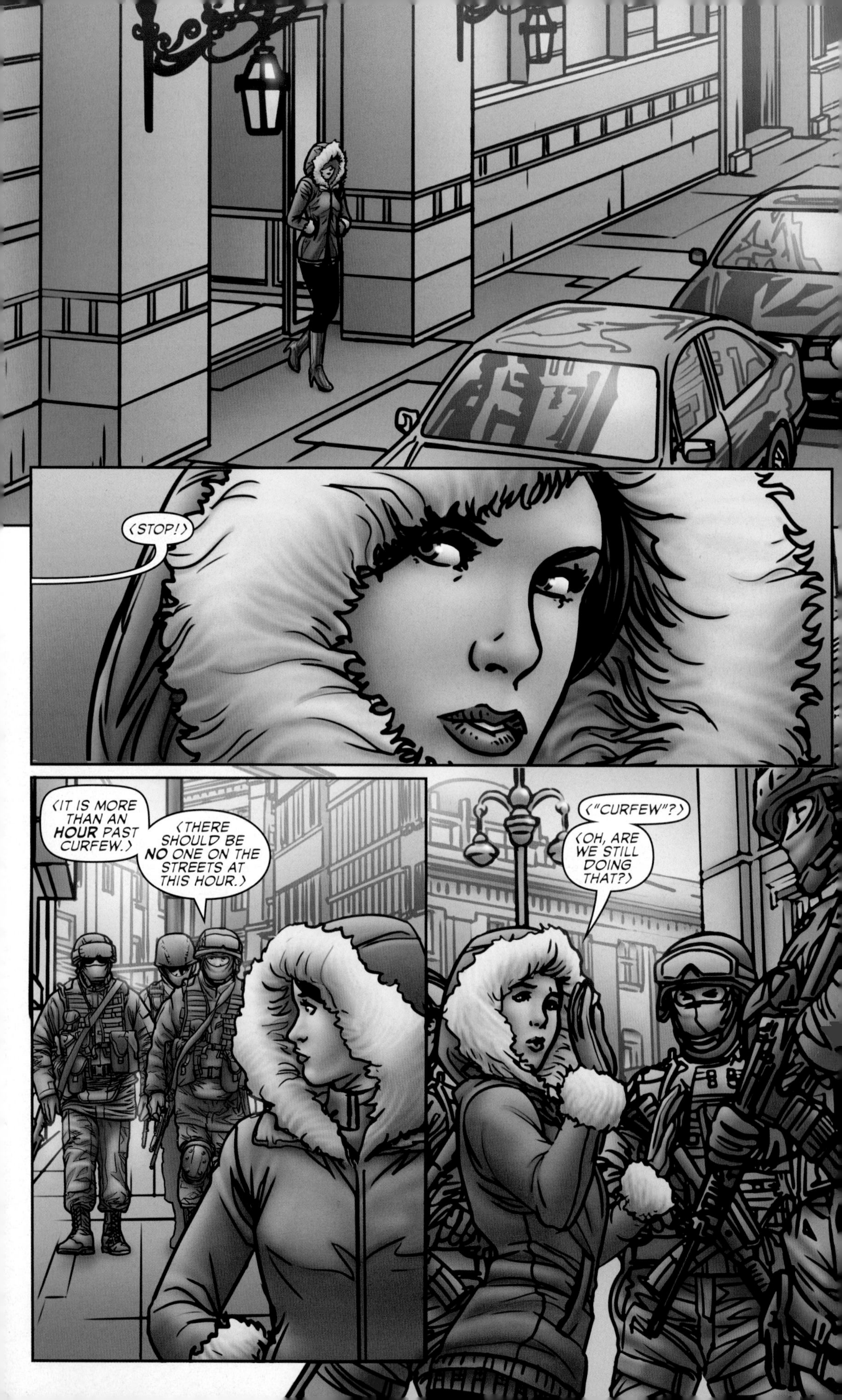

‹STOP!›
‹IT IS MORE THAN AN HOUR PAST CURFEW.›
‹THERE SHOULD BE NO ONE ON THE STREETS AT THIS HOUR.›
‹"CURFEW"?›
‹OH, ARE WE STILL DOING THAT?›

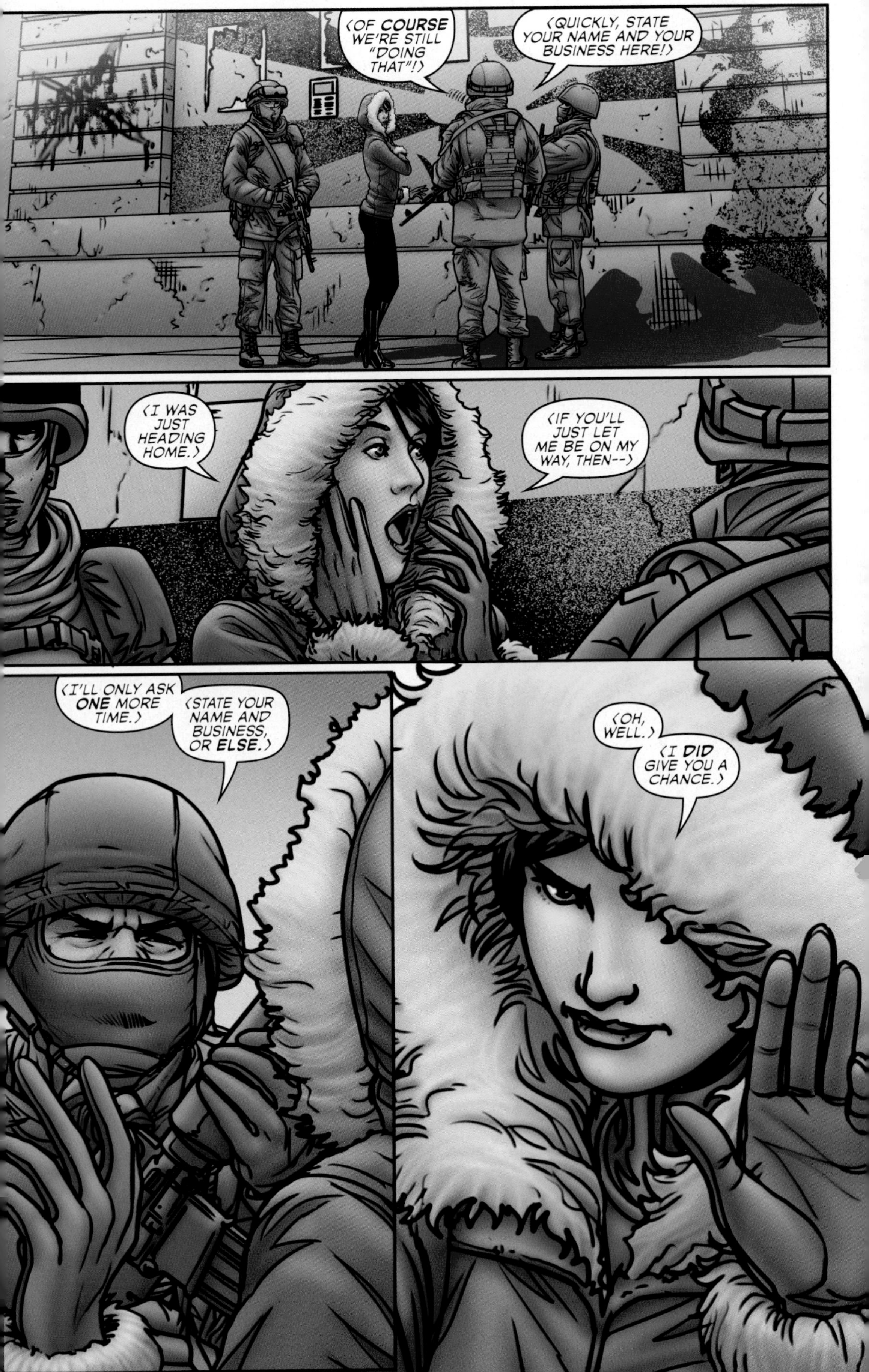

‹OF COURSE WE'RE STILL "DOING THAT"!›
‹QUICKLY, STATE YOUR NAME AND YOUR BUSINESS HERE!›
‹I WAS JUST HEADING HOME.›
‹IF YOU'LL JUST LET ME BE ON MY WAY, THEN--›
‹I'LL ONLY ASK ONE MORE TIME.›
‹STATE YOUR NAME AND BUSINESS, OR ELSE.›
‹OH, WELL.›
‹I DID GIVE YOU A CHANCE.›

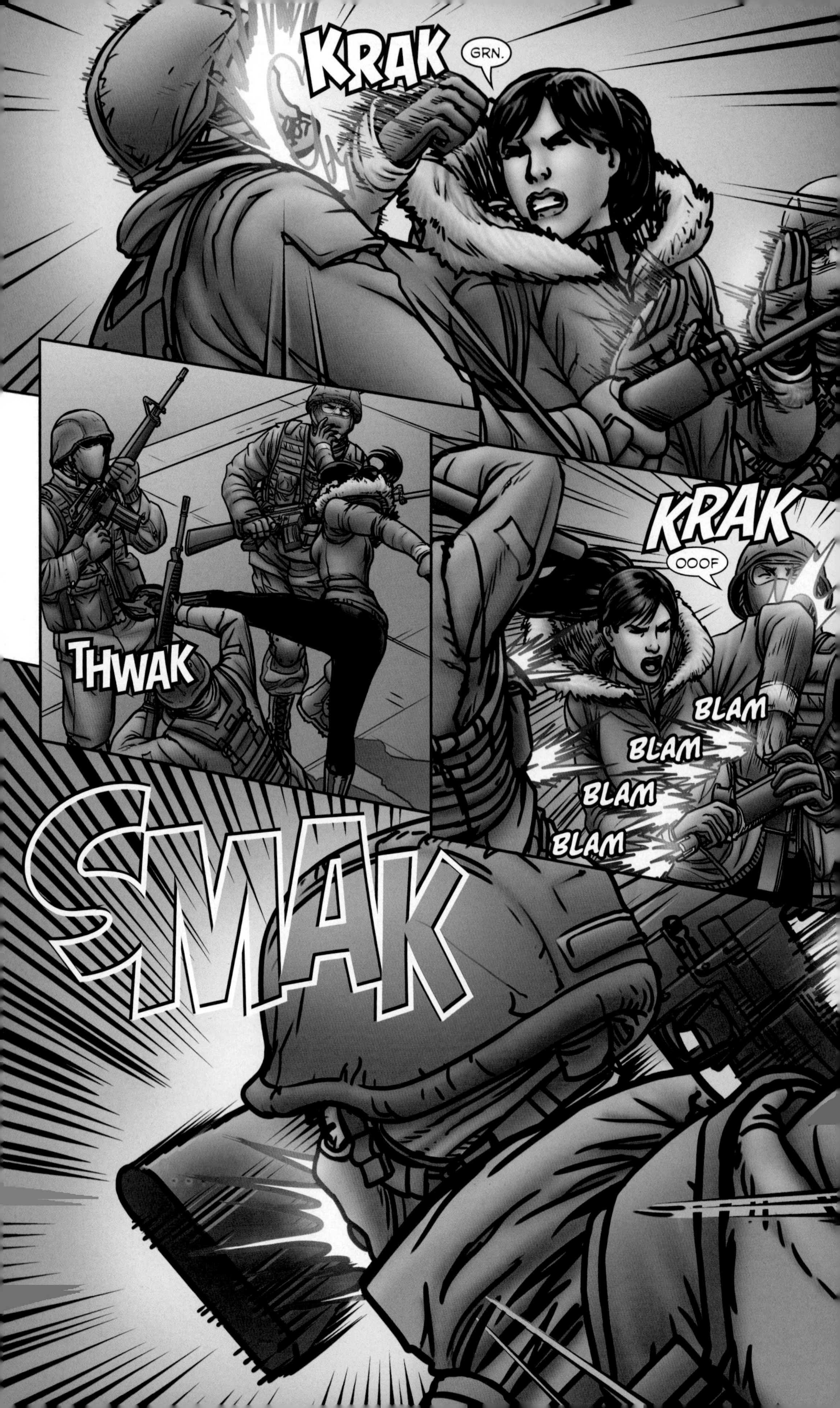
KRAK
GRN.
THWAK
KRAK
OOOF
BLAM
BLAM
BLAM
BLAM
SMAK

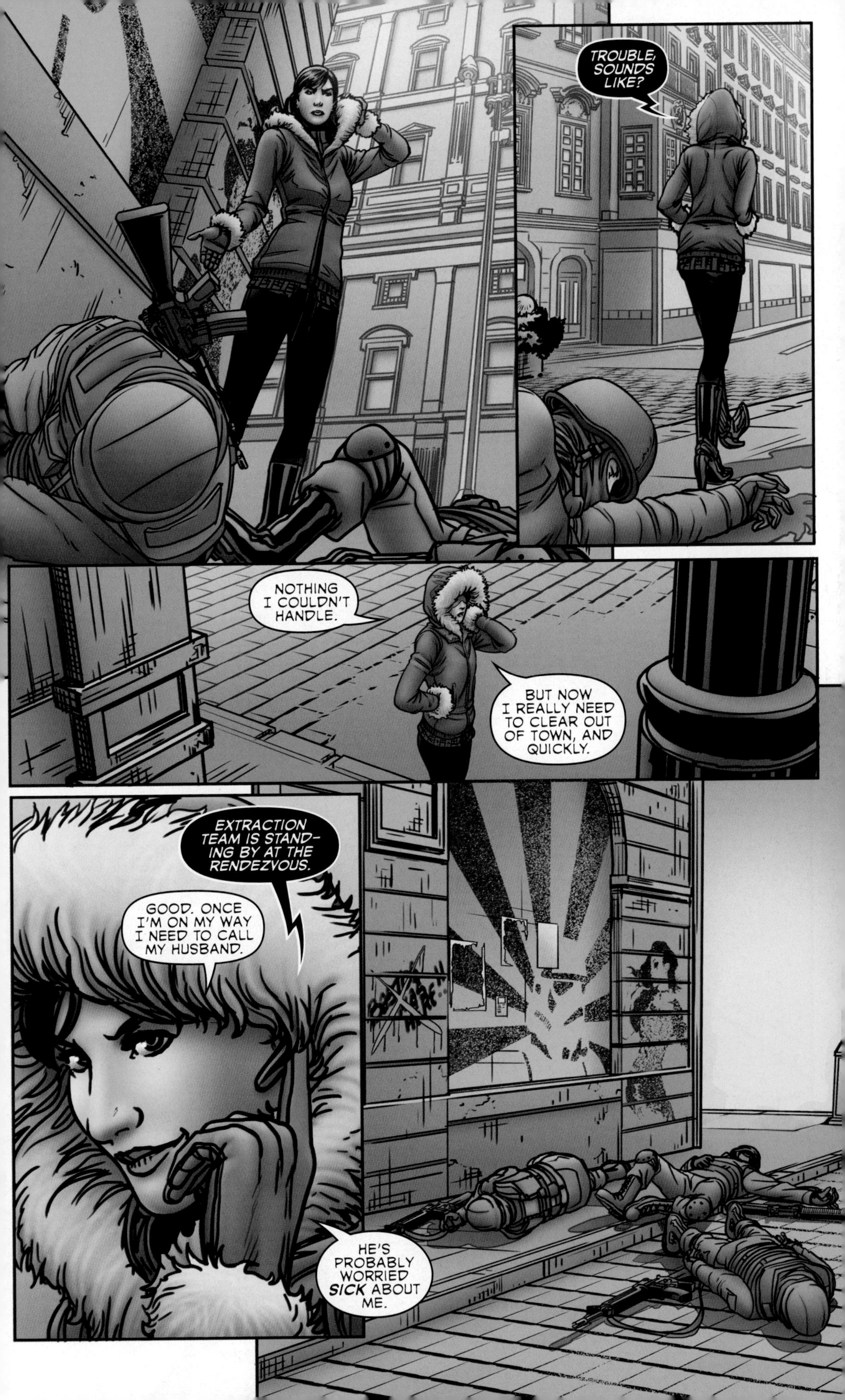
TROUBLE, SOUNDS LIKE?
NOTHING I COULDN'T HANDLE.
BUT NOW I REALLY NEED TO CLEAR OUT OF TOWN, AND QUICKLY.
EXTRACTION TEAM IS STANDING BY AT THE RENDEZVOUS.
GOOD. ONCE I'M ON MY WAY I NEED TO CALL MY HUSBAND.
HE'S PROBABLY WORRIED SICK ABOUT ME.

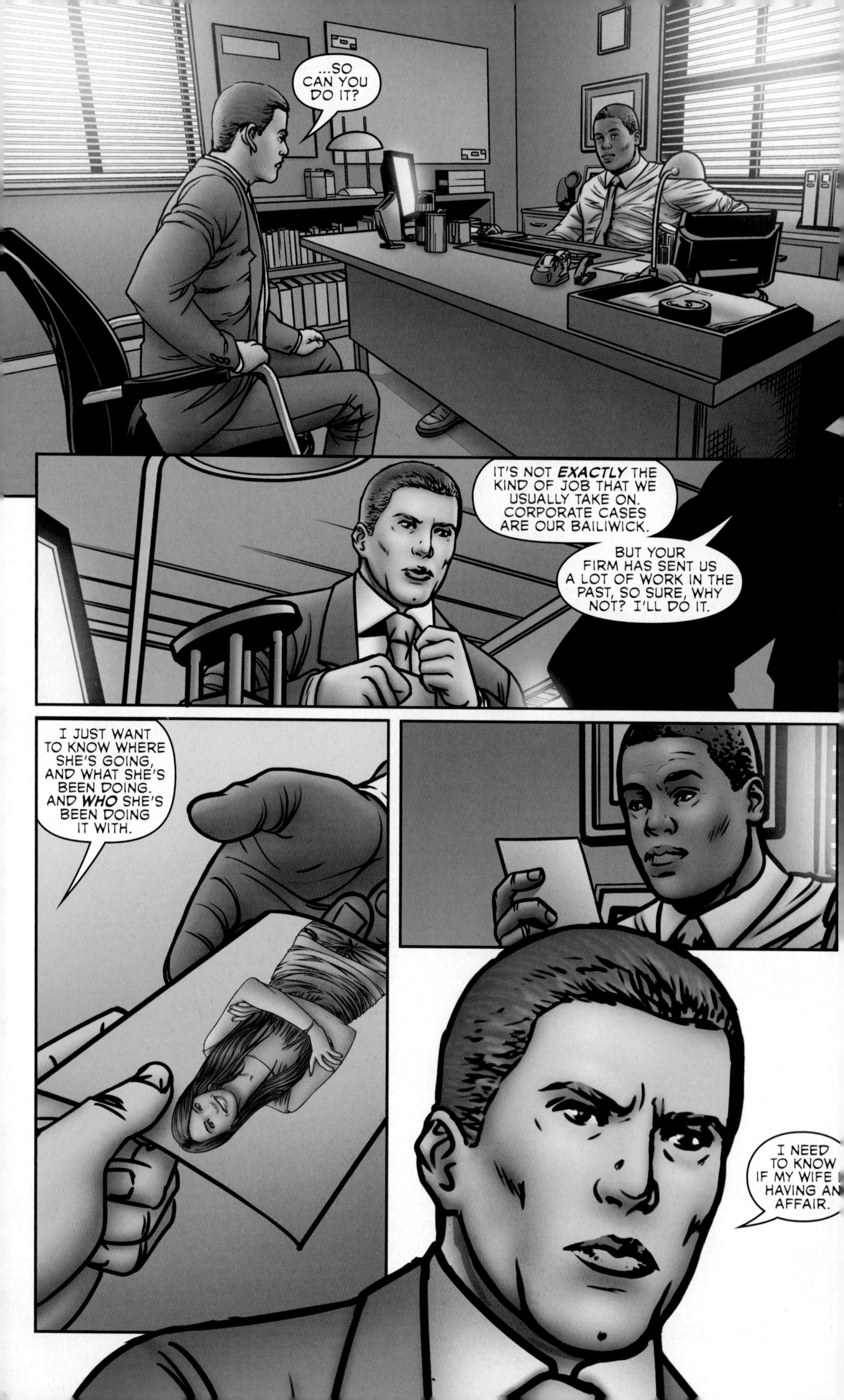
...SO CAN YOU DO IT?
IT'S NOT EXACTLY THE KIND OF JOB THAT WE USUALLY TAKE ON. CORPORATE CASES ARE OUR BAILIWICK.
BUT YOUR FIRM HAS SENT US A LOT OF WORK IN THE PAST, SO SURE, WHY NOT? I'LL DO IT.
I JUST WANT TO KNOW WHERE SHE'S GOING, AND WHAT SHE'S BEEN DOING. AND WHO SHE'S BEEN DOING IT WITH.
I NEED TO KNOW IF MY WIFE

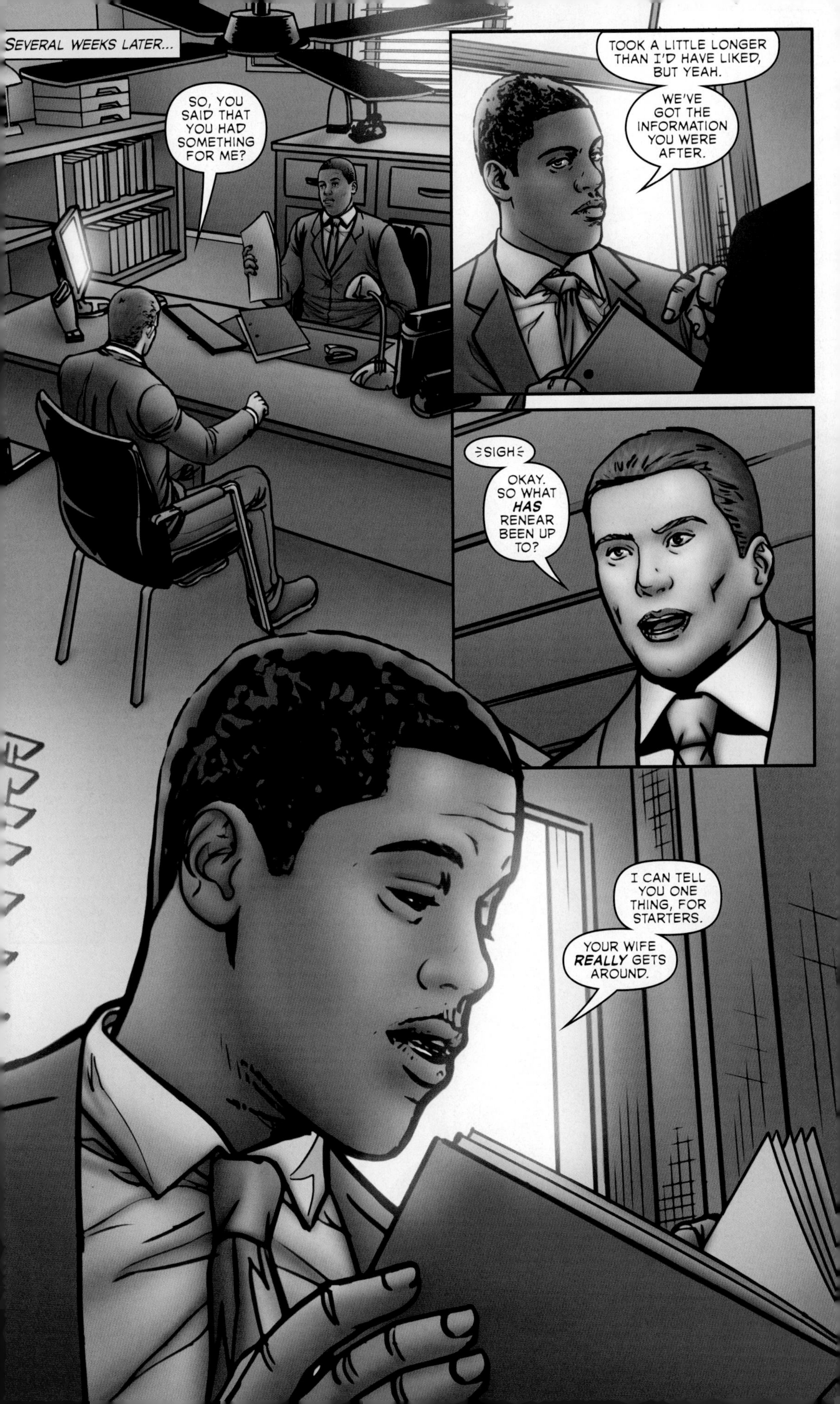
SEVERAL WEEKS LATER...
SO, YOU SAID THAT YOU HAD SOMETHING FOR ME?
TOOK A LITTLE LONGER THAN I'D HAVE LIKED, BUT YEAH.
WE'VE GOT THE INFORMATION YOU WERE AFTER.
SIGH
OKAY. SO WHAT **HAS** RENEAR BEEN UP TO?
I CAN TELL YOU ONE THING, FOR STARTERS.
YOUR WIFE ***REALLY*** GETS AROUND.

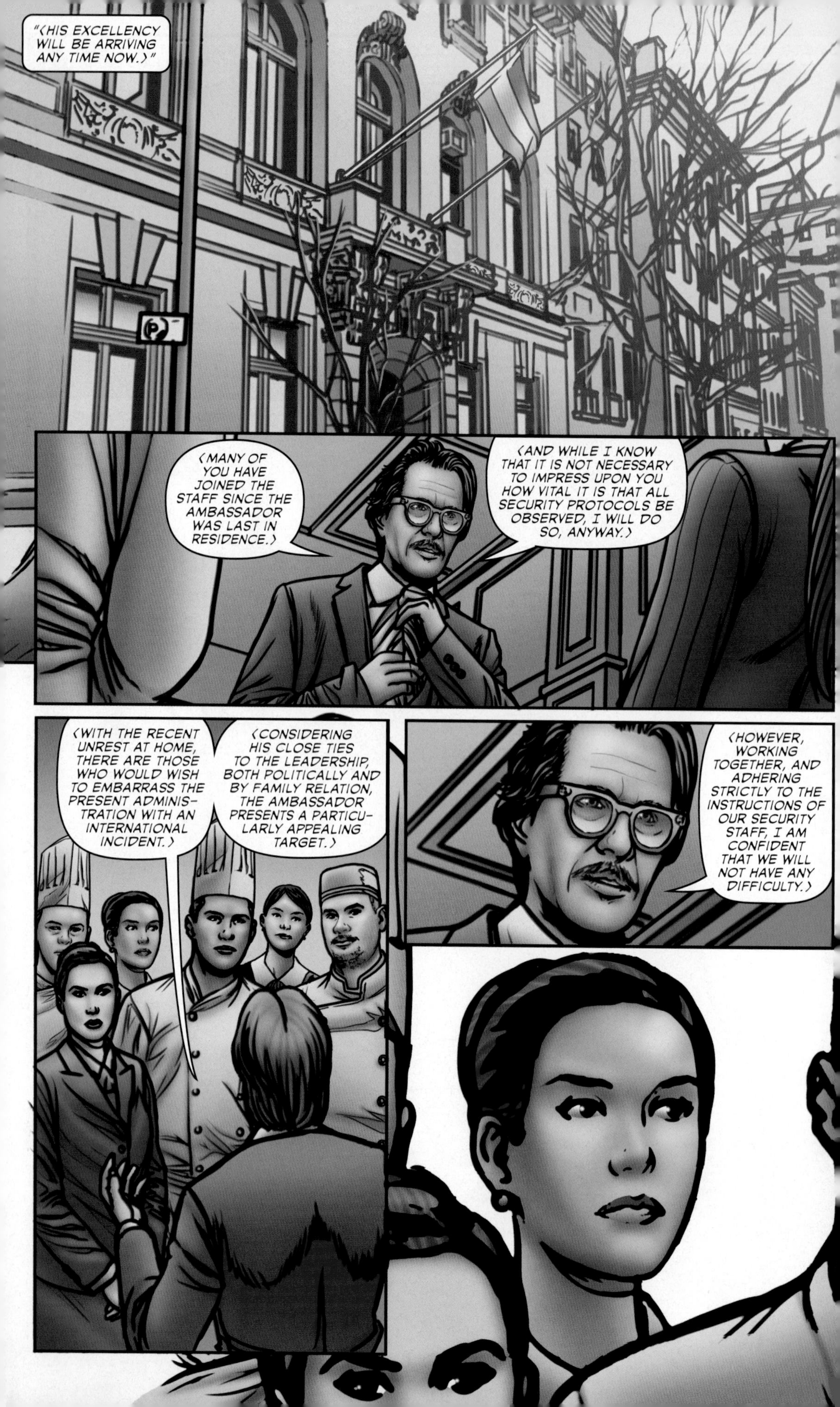
"⟨HIS EXCELLENCY WILL BE ARRIVING ANY TIME NOW.⟩"
⟨MANY OF YOU HAVE JOINED THE STAFF SINCE THE AMBASSADOR WAS LAST IN RESIDENCE.⟩
⟨AND WHILE I KNOW THAT IT IS NOT NECESSARY TO IMPRESS UPON YOU HOW VITAL IT IS THAT ALL SECURITY PROTOCOLS BE OBSERVED, I WILL DO SO, ANYWAY.⟩
⟨WITH THE RECENT UNREST AT HOME, THERE ARE THOSE WHO WOULD WISH TO EMBARRASS THE PRESENT ADMINIS-TRATION WITH AN INTERNATIONAL INCIDENT.⟩
⟨CONSIDERING HIS CLOSE TIES TO THE LEADERSHIP, BOTH POLITICALLY AND BY FAMILY RELATION, THE AMBASSADOR PRESENTS A PARTICU-LARLY APPEALING TARGET.⟩
⟨HOWEVER, WORKING TOGETHER, AND ADHERING STRICTLY TO THE INSTRUCTIONS OF OUR SECURITY STAFF, I AM CONFIDENT THAT WE WILL NOT HAVE ANY DIFFICULTY.⟩

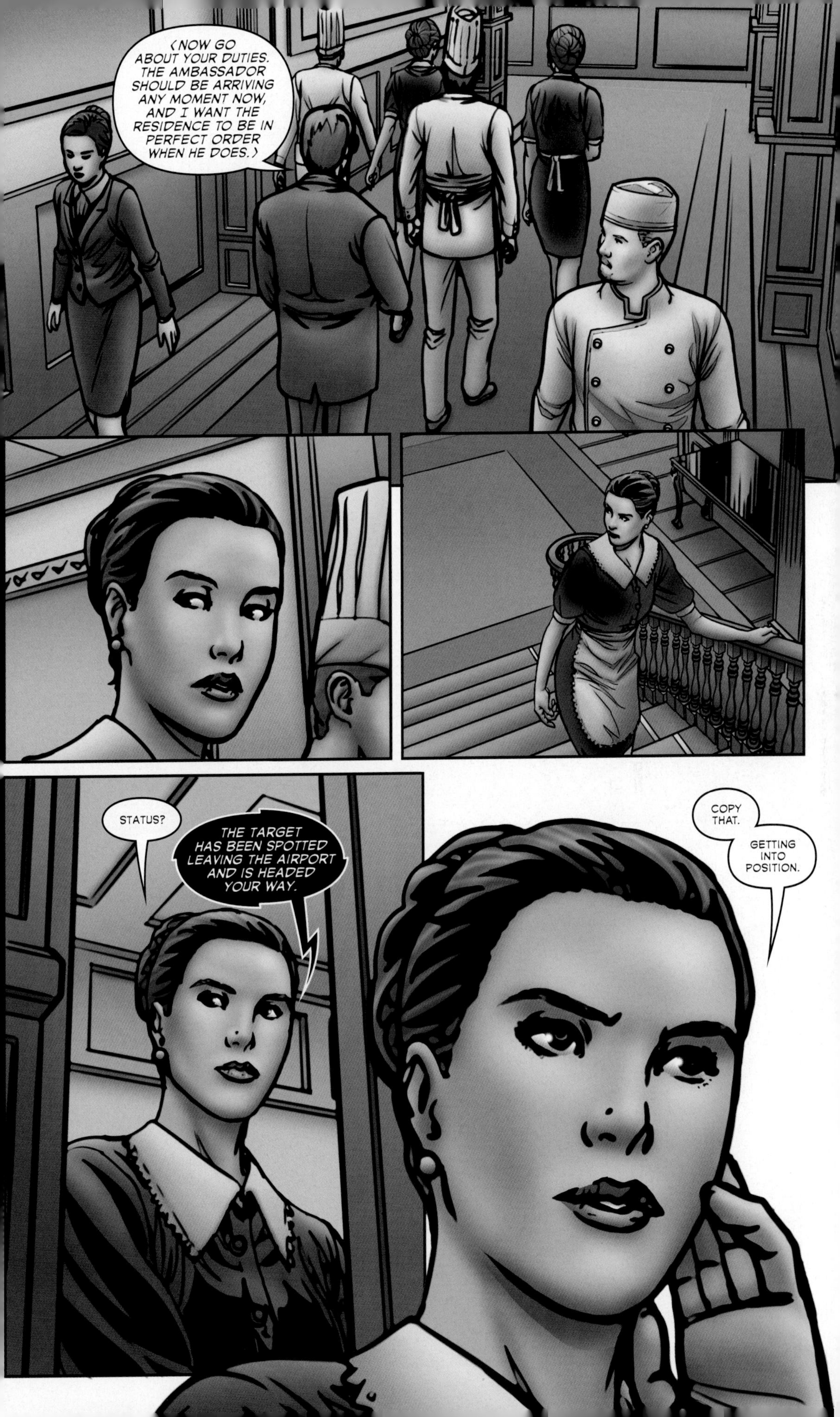
‹NOW GO ABOUT YOUR DUTIES. THE AMBASSADOR SHOULD BE ARRIVING ANY MOMENT NOW, AND I WANT THE RESIDENCE TO BE IN PERFECT ORDER WHEN HE DOES.›
STATUS?
THE TARGET HAS BEEN SPOTTED LEAVING THE AIRPORT AND IS HEADED YOUR WAY.
COPY THAT.
GETTING INTO POSITION.

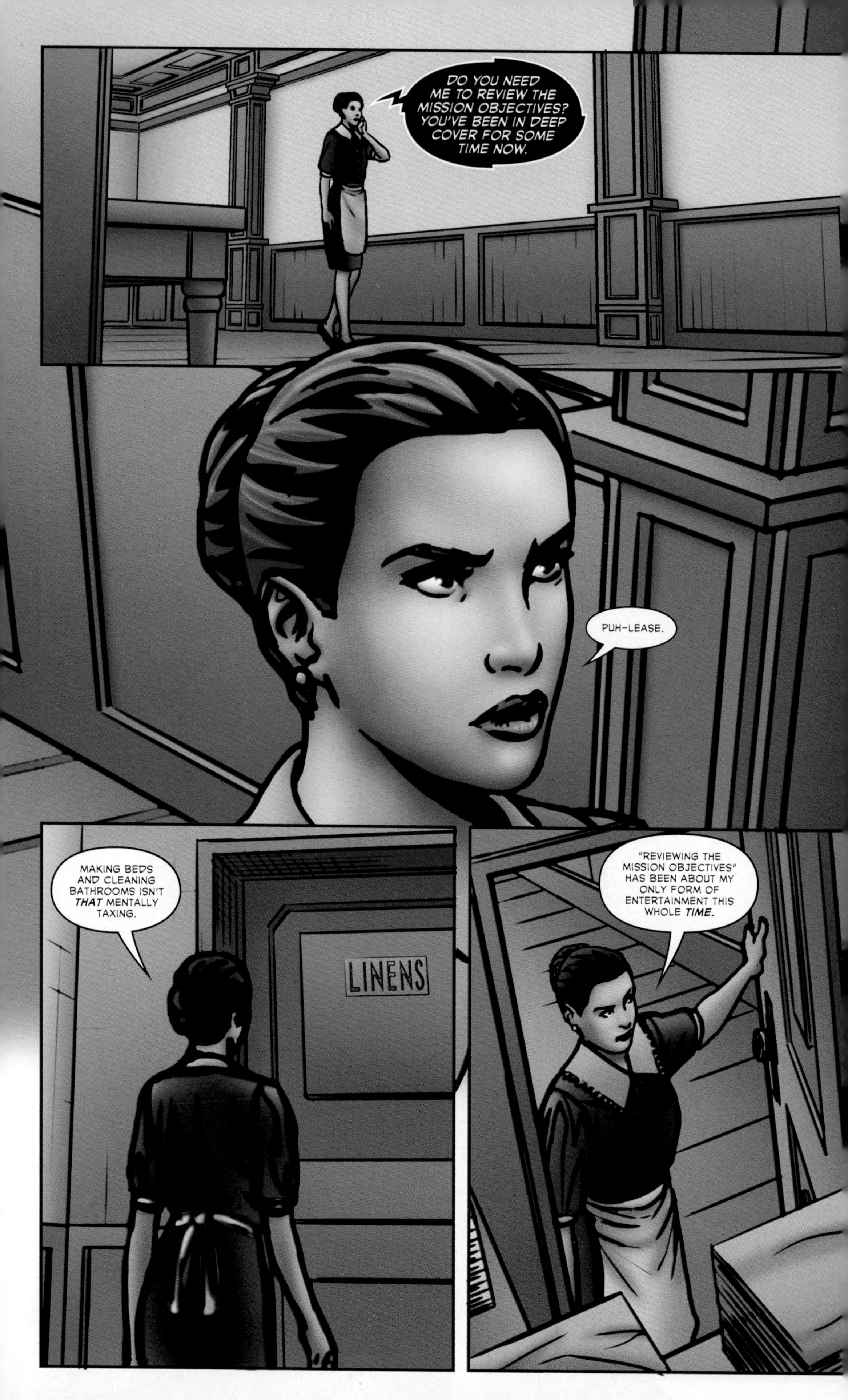
DO YOU NEED ME TO REVIEW THE MISSION OBJECTIVES? YOU'VE BEEN IN DEEP COVER FOR SOME TIME NOW.
PUH-LEASE.
MAKING BEDS AND CLEANING BATHROOMS ISN'T *THAT* MENTALLY TAXING.
LINENS
"REVIEWING THE MISSION OBJECTIVES" HAS BEEN ABOUT MY ONLY FORM OF ENTERTAINMENT THIS WHOLE *TIME.*

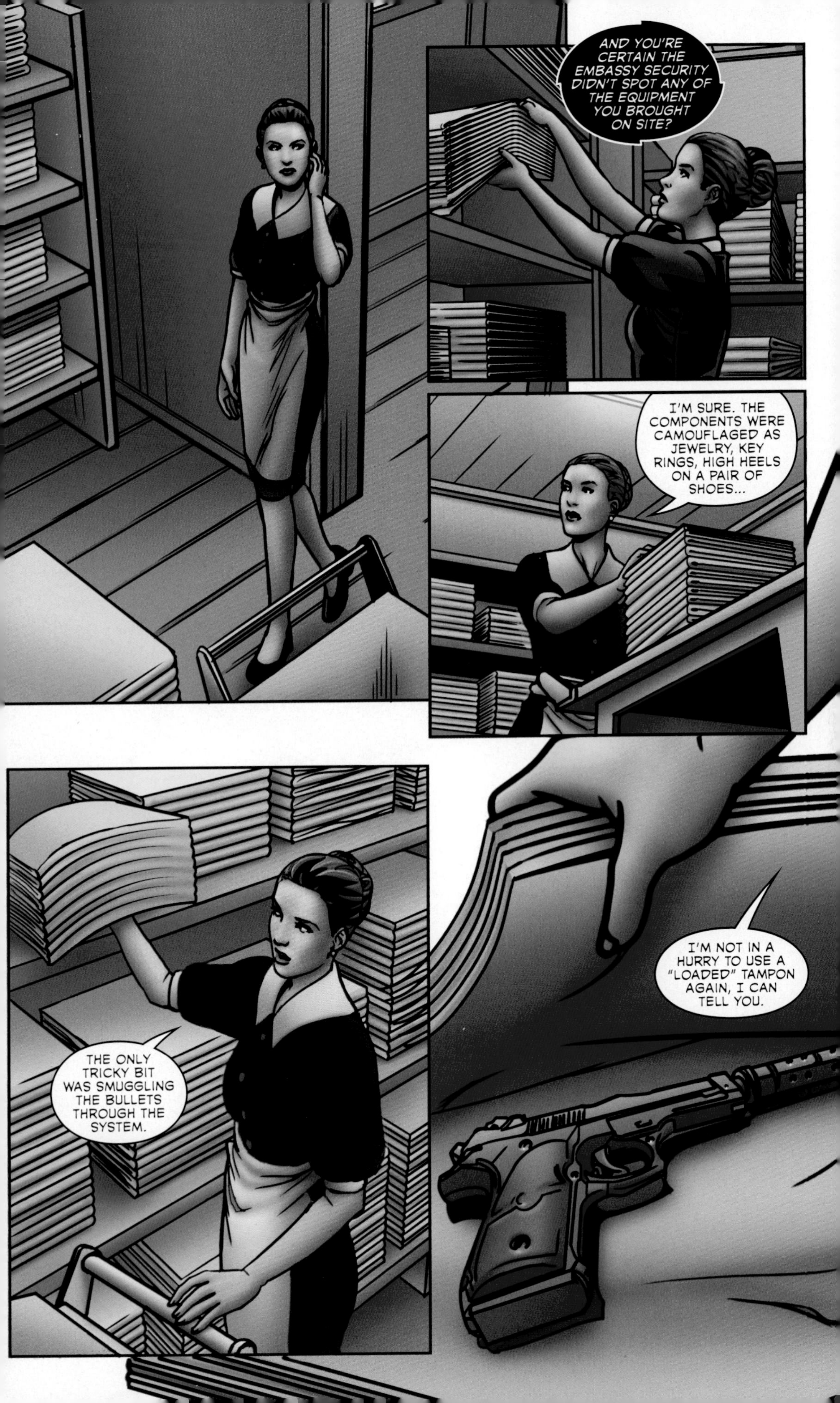
AND YOU'RE CERTAIN THE EMBASSY SECURITY DIDN'T SPOT ANY OF THE EQUIPMENT YOU BROUGHT ON SITE?
I'M SURE. THE COMPONENTS WERE CAMOUFLAGED AS JEWELRY, KEY RINGS, HIGH HEELS ON A PAIR OF SHOES...
THE ONLY TRICKY BIT WAS SMUGGLING THE BULLETS THROUGH THE SYSTEM.
I'M NOT IN A HURRY TO USE A "LOADED" TAMPON AGAIN, I CAN TELL YOU.

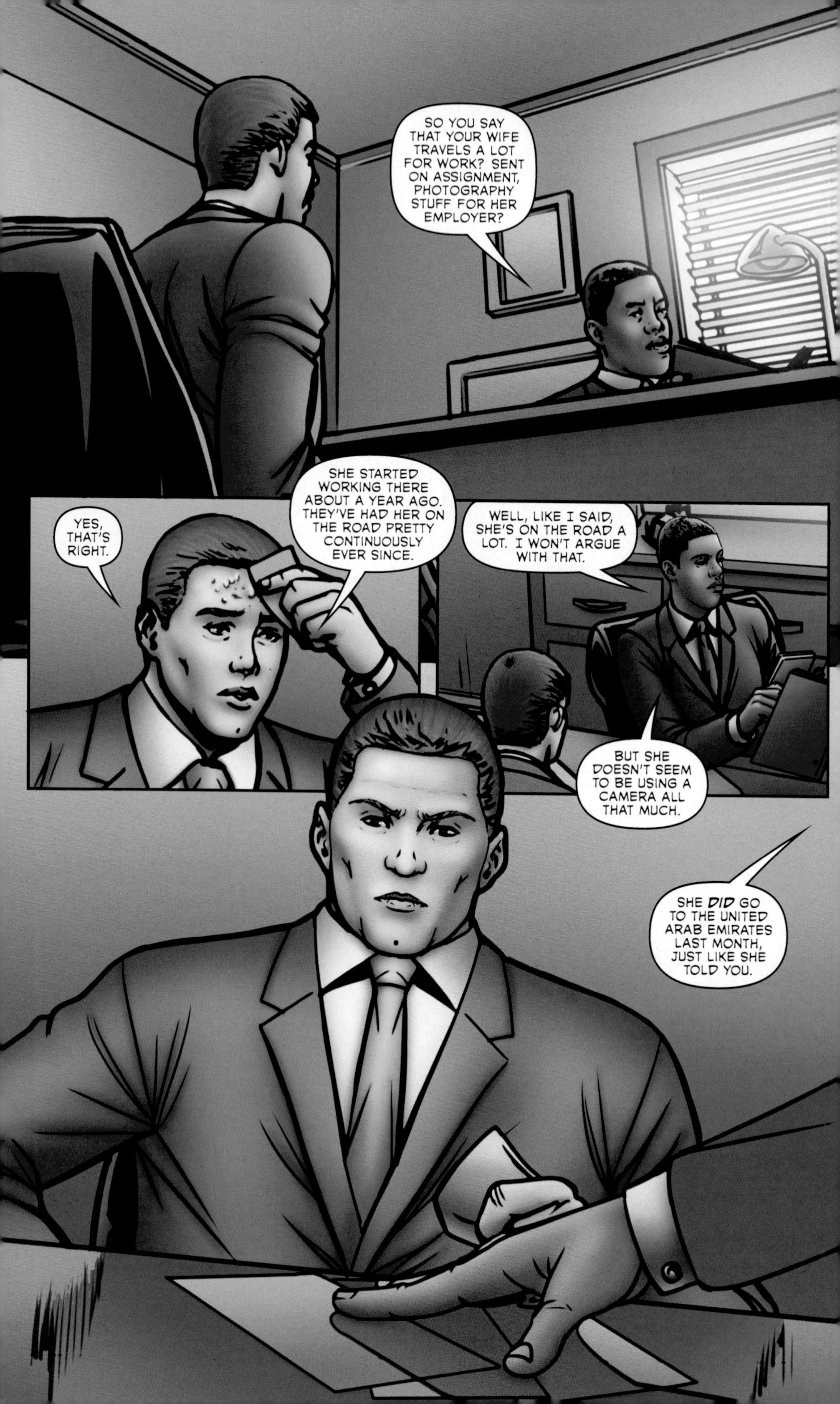

SO YOU SAY THAT YOUR WIFE TRAVELS A LOT FOR WORK? SENT ON ASSIGNMENT, PHOTOGRAPHY STUFF FOR HER EMPLOYER?
YES, THAT'S RIGHT.
SHE STARTED WORKING THERE ABOUT A YEAR AGO. THEY'VE HAD HER ON THE ROAD PRETTY CONTINUOUSLY EVER SINCE.
WELL, LIKE I SAID, SHE'S ON THE ROAD A LOT. I WON'T ARGUE WITH THAT.
BUT SHE DOESN'T SEEM TO BE USING A CAMERA ALL THAT MUCH.
SHE *DID* GO TO THE UNITED ARAB EMIRATES LAST MONTH, JUST LIKE SHE TOLD YOU.

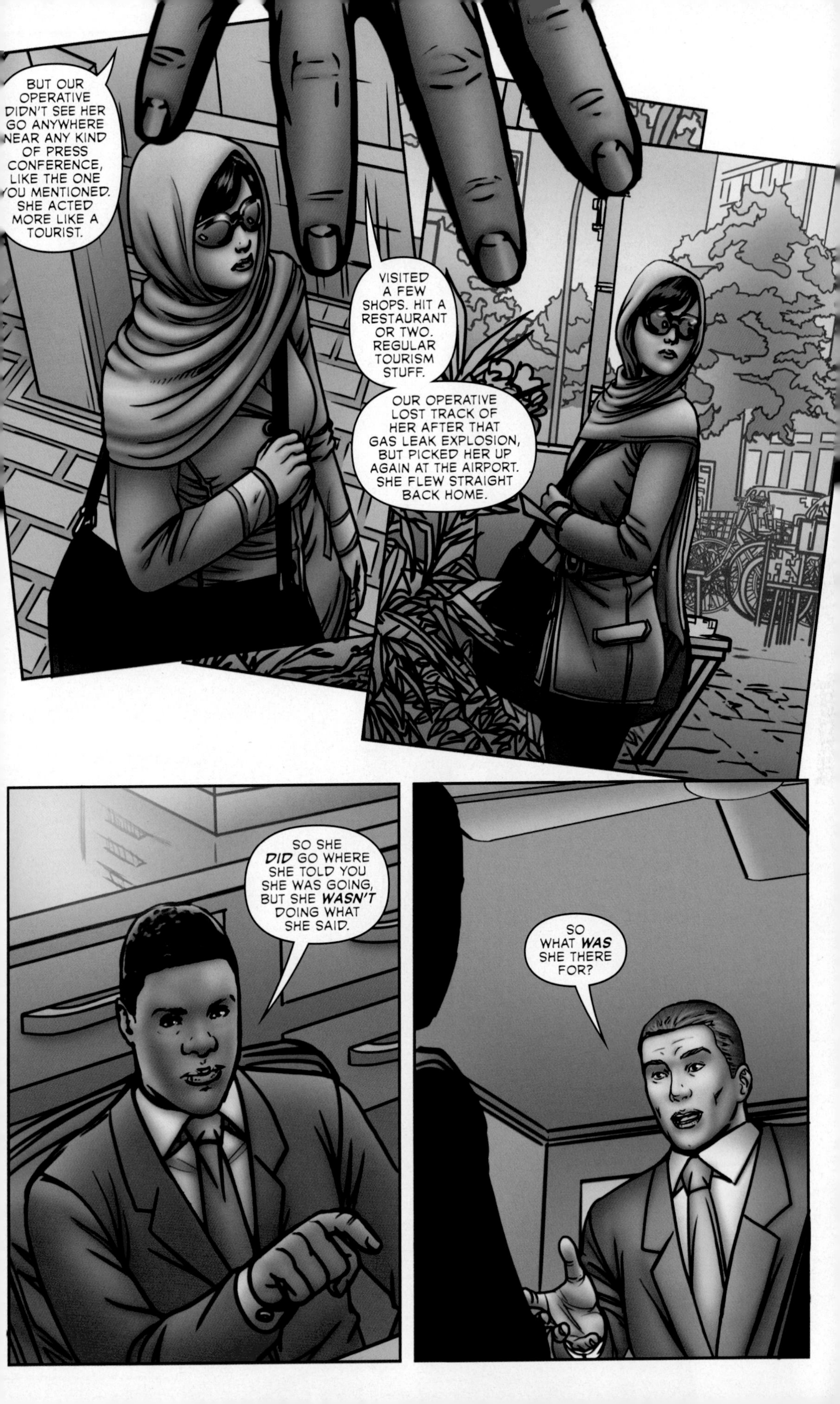
BUT OUR OPERATIVE DIDN'T SEE HER GO ANYWHERE NEAR ANY KIND OF PRESS CONFERENCE, LIKE THE ONE YOU MENTIONED. SHE ACTED MORE LIKE A TOURIST.
VISITED A FEW SHOPS. HIT A RESTAURANT OR TWO. REGULAR TOURISM STUFF.
OUR OPERATIVE LOST TRACK OF HER AFTER THAT GAS LEAK EXPLOSION, BUT PICKED HER UP AGAIN AT THE AIRPORT. SHE FLEW STRAIGHT BACK HOME.
SO SHE *DID* GO WHERE SHE TOLD YOU SHE WAS GOING, BUT SHE *WASN'T* DOING WHAT SHE SAID.
SO WHAT *WAS* SHE THERE FOR?

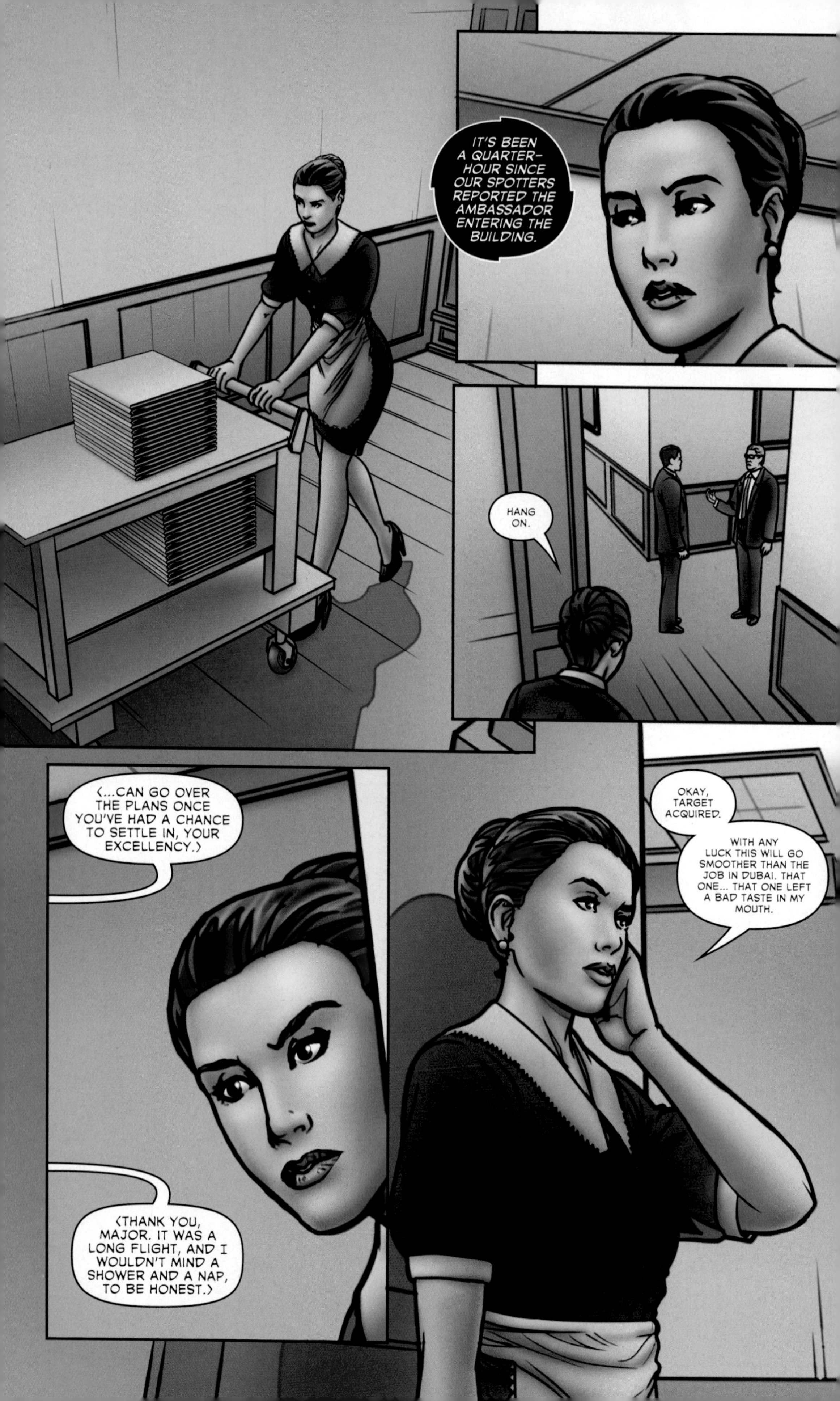
IT'S BEEN A QUARTER-HOUR SINCE OUR SPOTTERS REPORTED THE AMBASSADOR ENTERING THE BUILDING.
HANG ON.
‹...CAN GO OVER THE PLANS ONCE YOU'VE HAD A CHANCE TO SETTLE IN, YOUR EXCELLENCY.›
‹THANK YOU, MAJOR. IT WAS A LONG FLIGHT, AND I WOULDN'T MIND A SHOWER AND A NAP, TO BE HONEST.›
OKAY, TARGET ACQUIRED.
WITH ANY LUCK THIS WILL GO SMOOTHER THAN THE JOB IN DUBAI. THAT ONE... THAT ONE LEFT A BAD TASTE IN MY MOUTH.

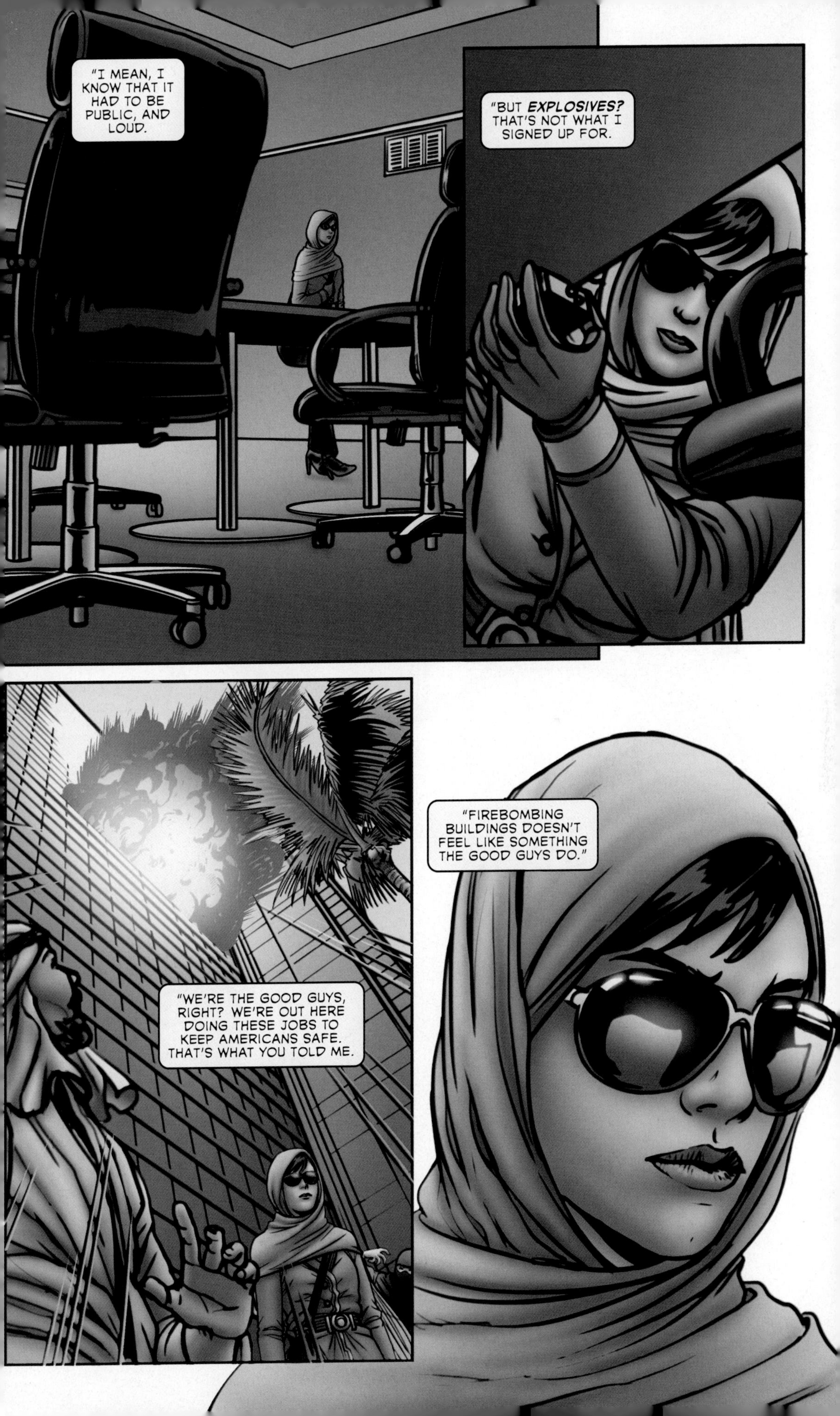
"I MEAN, I KNOW THAT IT HAD TO BE PUBLIC, AND LOUD.
"BUT *EXPLOSIVES?* THAT'S NOT WHAT I SIGNED UP FOR.
"WE'RE THE GOOD GUYS, RIGHT? WE'RE OUT HERE DOING THESE JOBS TO KEEP AMERICANS SAFE. THAT'S WHAT YOU TOLD ME.
"FIREBOMBING BUILDINGS DOESN'T FEEL LIKE SOMETHING THE GOOD GUYS DO."

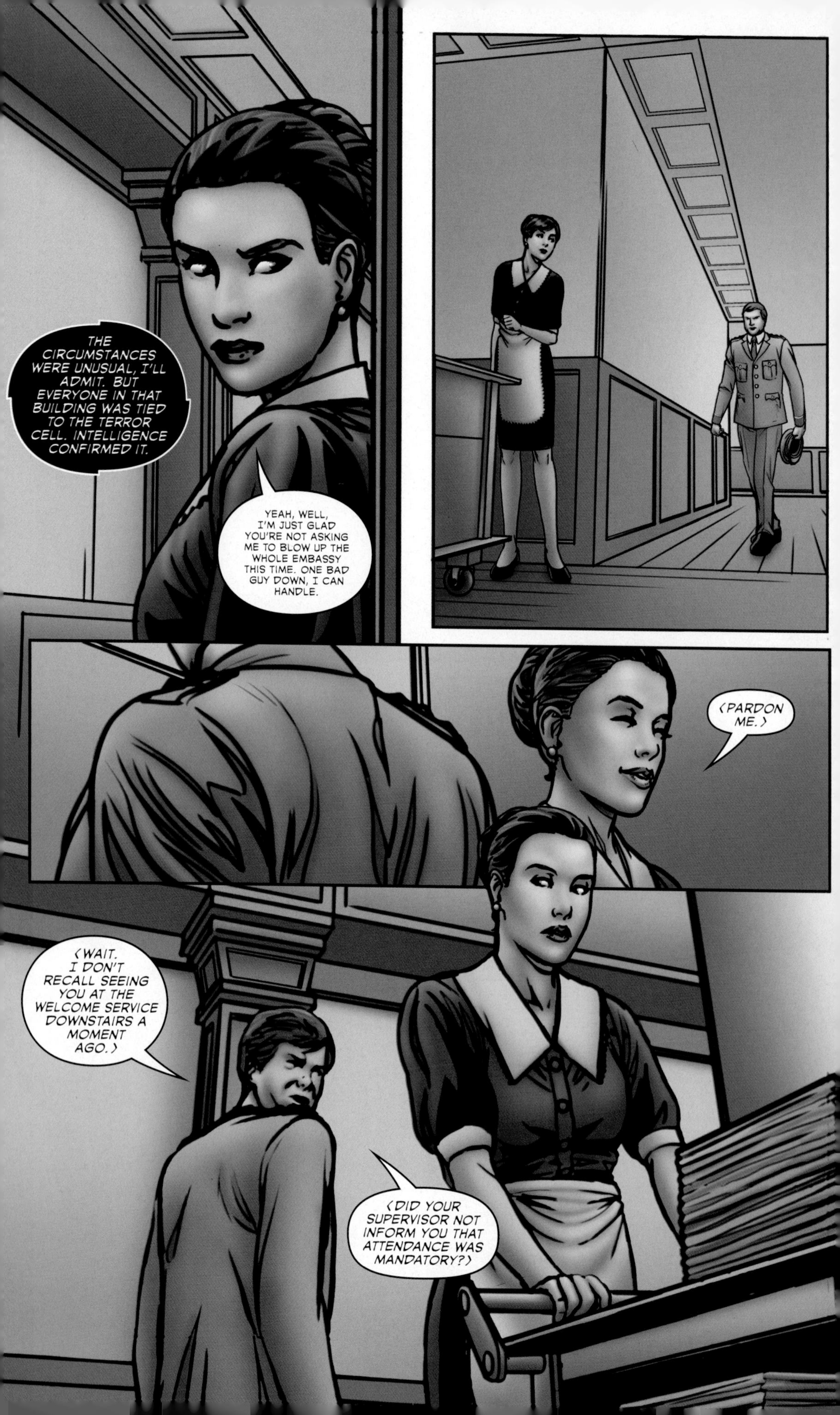
THE CIRCUMSTANCES WERE UNUSUAL, I'LL ADMIT. BUT EVERYONE IN THAT BUILDING WAS TIED TO THE TERROR CELL. INTELLIGENCE CONFIRMED IT.
YEAH, WELL, I'M JUST GLAD YOU'RE NOT ASKING ME TO BLOW UP THE WHOLE EMBASSY THIS TIME. ONE BAD GUY DOWN, I CAN HANDLE.
‹PARDON ME.›
‹WAIT. I DON'T RECALL SEEING YOU AT THE WELCOME SERVICE DOWNSTAIRS A MOMENT AGO.›
‹DID YOUR SUPERVISOR NOT INFORM YOU THAT ATTENDANCE WAS MANDATORY?›

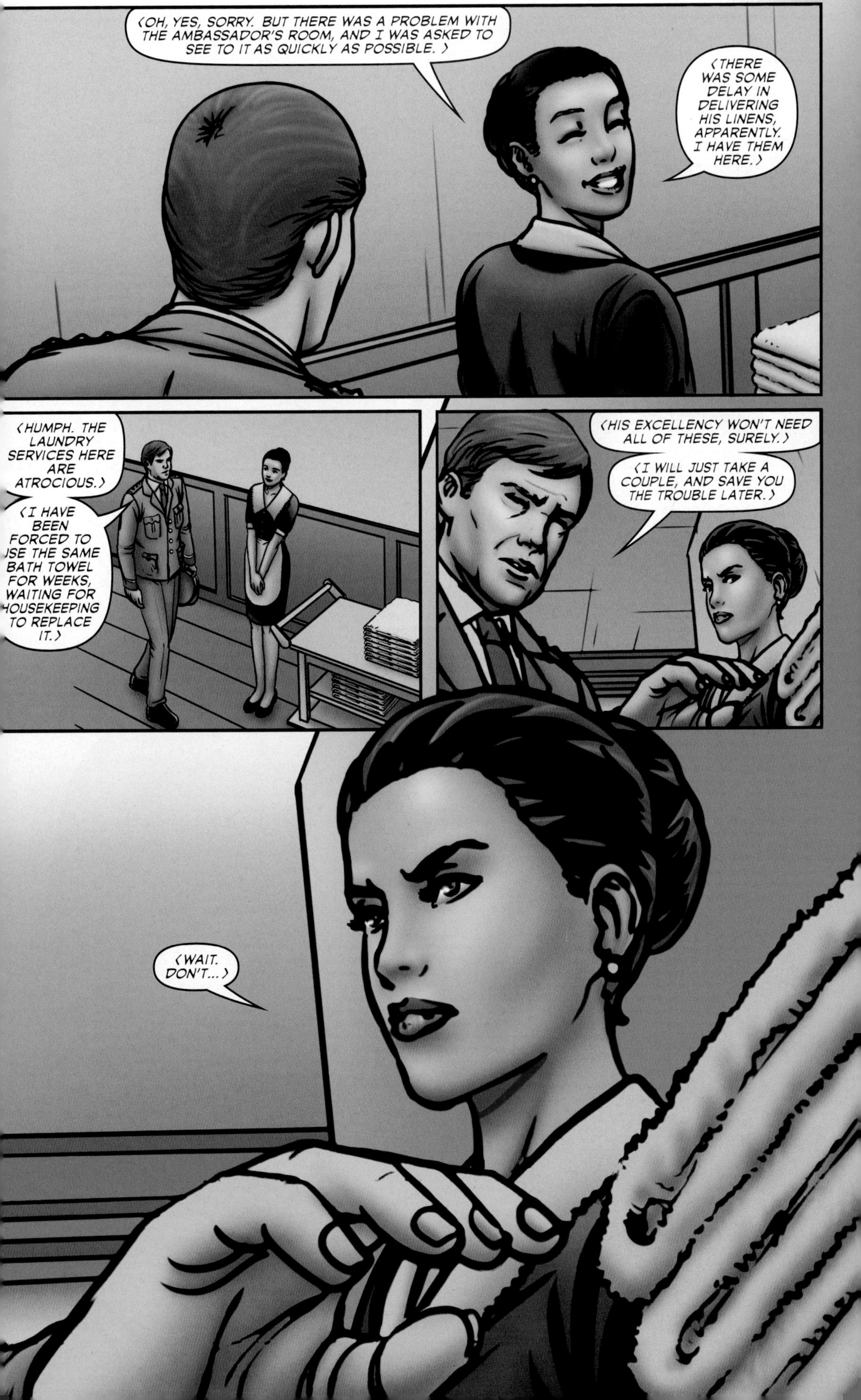
‹OH, YES, SORRY. BUT THERE WAS A PROBLEM WITH THE AMBASSADOR'S ROOM, AND I WAS ASKED TO SEE TO IT AS QUICKLY AS POSSIBLE.›
‹THERE WAS SOME DELAY IN DELIVERING HIS LINENS, APPARENTLY. I HAVE THEM HERE.›
‹HUMPH. THE LAUNDRY SERVICES HERE ARE ATROCIOUS.›
‹I HAVE BEEN FORCED TO USE THE SAME BATH TOWEL FOR WEEKS, WAITING FOR HOUSEKEEPING TO REPLACE IT.›
‹HIS EXCELLENCY WON'T NEED ALL OF THESE, SURELY.›
‹I WILL JUST TAKE A COUPLE, AND SAVE YOU THE TROUBLE LATER.›
‹WAIT. DON'T...›

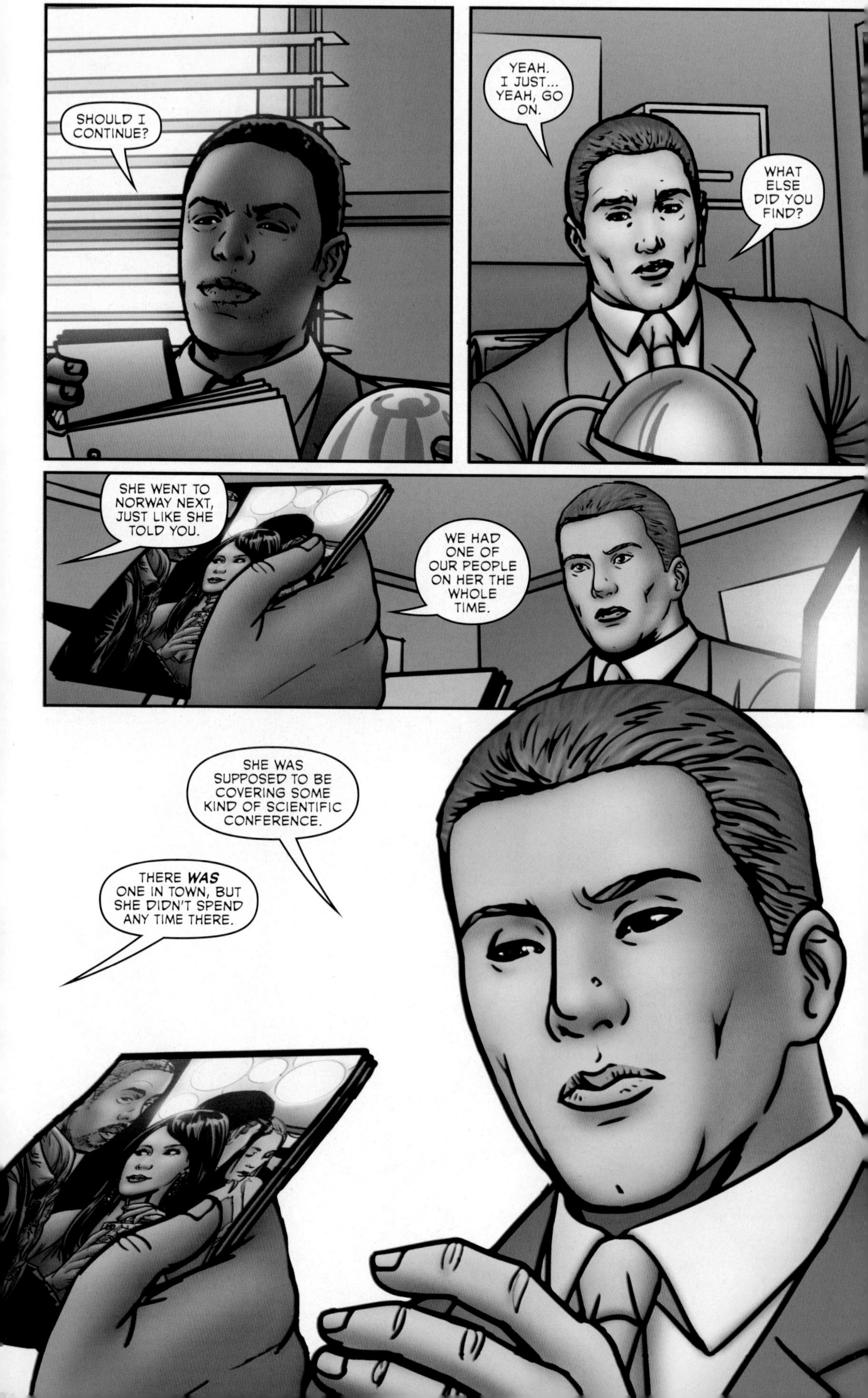
SHOULD I CONTINUE?
YEAH. I JUST... YEAH, GO ON.
WHAT ELSE DID YOU FIND?
SHE WENT TO NORWAY NEXT, JUST LIKE SHE TOLD YOU.
WE HAD ONE OF OUR PEOPLE ON HER THE WHOLE TIME.
SHE WAS SUPPOSED TO BE COVERING SOME KIND OF SCIENTIFIC CONFERENCE.
THERE *WAS* ONE IN TOWN, BUT SHE DIDN'T SPEND ANY TIME THERE.

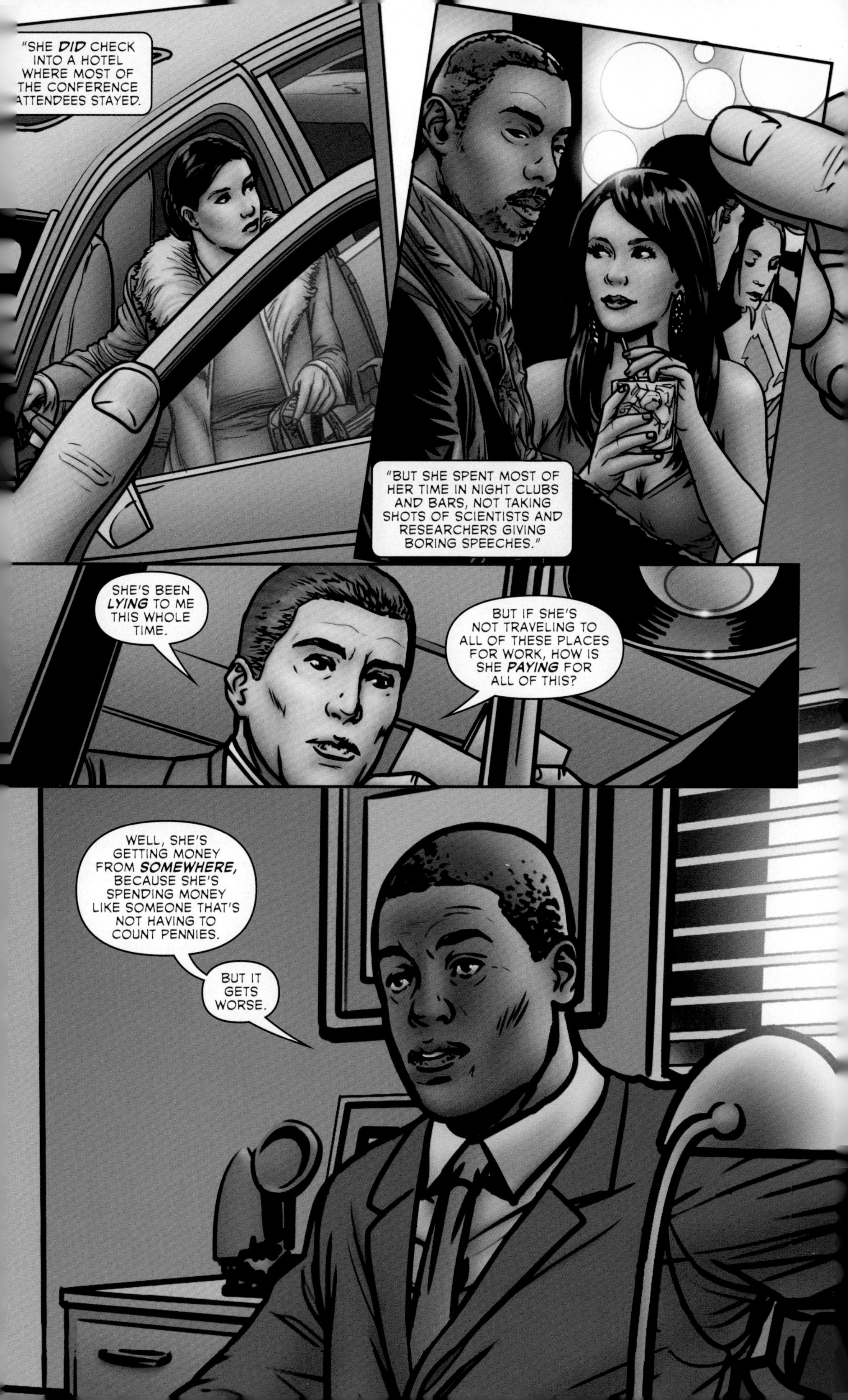
"SHE DID CHECK INTO A HOTEL WHERE MOST OF THE CONFERENCE ATTENDEES STAYED.
"BUT SHE SPENT MOST OF HER TIME IN NIGHT CLUBS AND BARS, NOT TAKING SHOTS OF SCIENTISTS AND RESEARCHERS GIVING BORING SPEECHES."
SHE'S BEEN LYING TO ME THIS WHOLE TIME.
BUT IF SHE'S NOT TRAVELING TO ALL OF THESE PLACES FOR WORK, HOW IS SHE PAYING FOR ALL OF THIS?
WELL, SHE'S GETTING MONEY FROM SOMEWHERE, BECAUSE SHE'S SPENDING MONEY LIKE SOMEONE THAT'S NOT HAVING TO COUNT PENNIES.
BUT IT GETS WORSE.

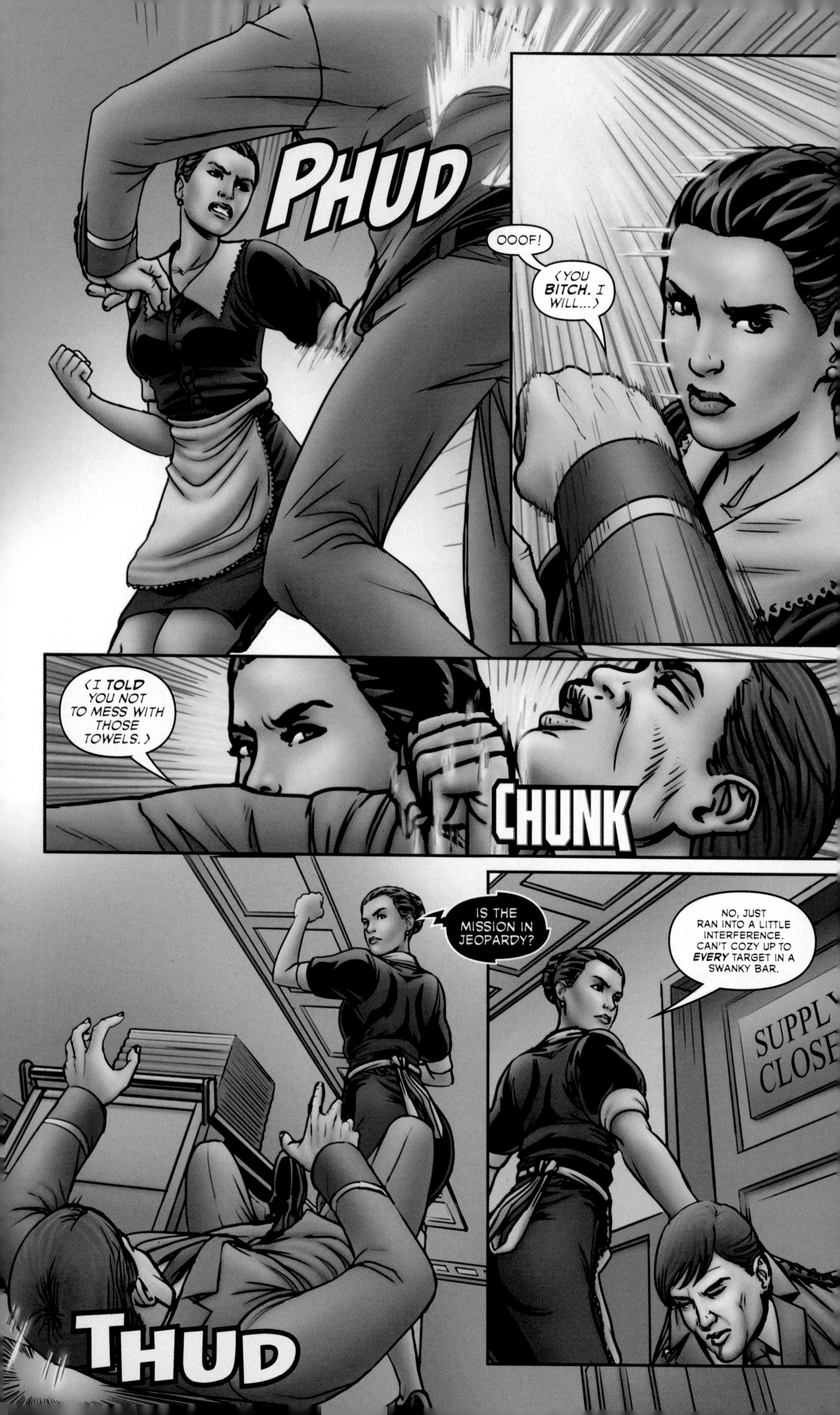
PHUD
OOOF!
‹YOU BITCH. I WILL...›
‹I TOLD YOU NOT TO MESS WITH THOSE TOWELS.›
CHUNK
THUD
IS THE MISSION IN JEOPARDY?
NO, JUST RAN INTO A LITTLE INTERFERENCE. CAN'T COZY UP TO EVERY TARGET IN A SWANKY BAR.

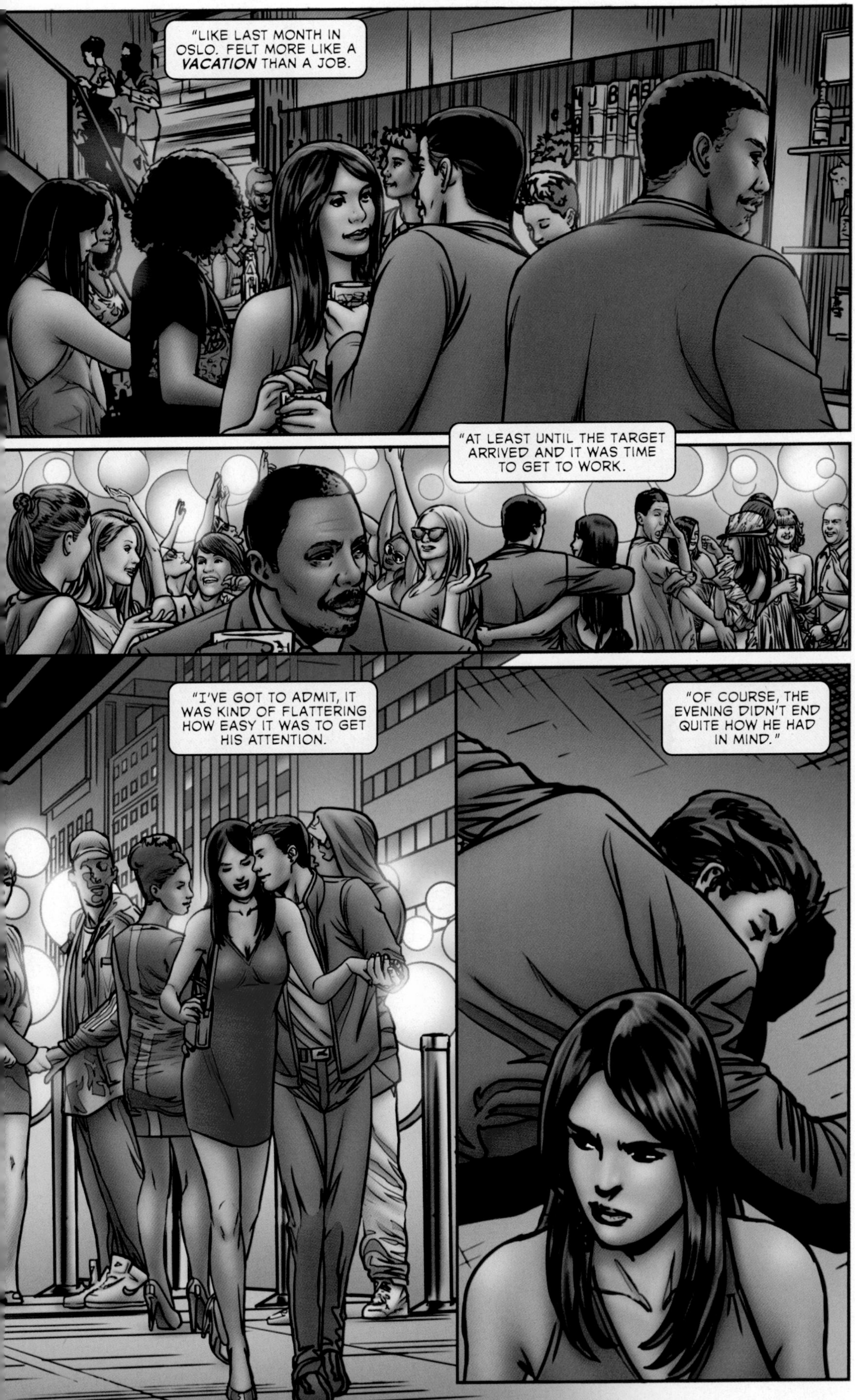
"LIKE LAST MONTH IN OSLO. FELT MORE LIKE A *VACATION* THAN A JOB.
"AT LEAST UNTIL THE TARGET ARRIVED AND IT WAS TIME TO GET TO WORK.
"I'VE GOT TO ADMIT, IT WAS KIND OF FLATTERING HOW EASY IT WAS TO GET HIS ATTENTION.
"OF COURSE, THE EVENING DIDN'T END QUITE HOW HE HAD IN MIND."

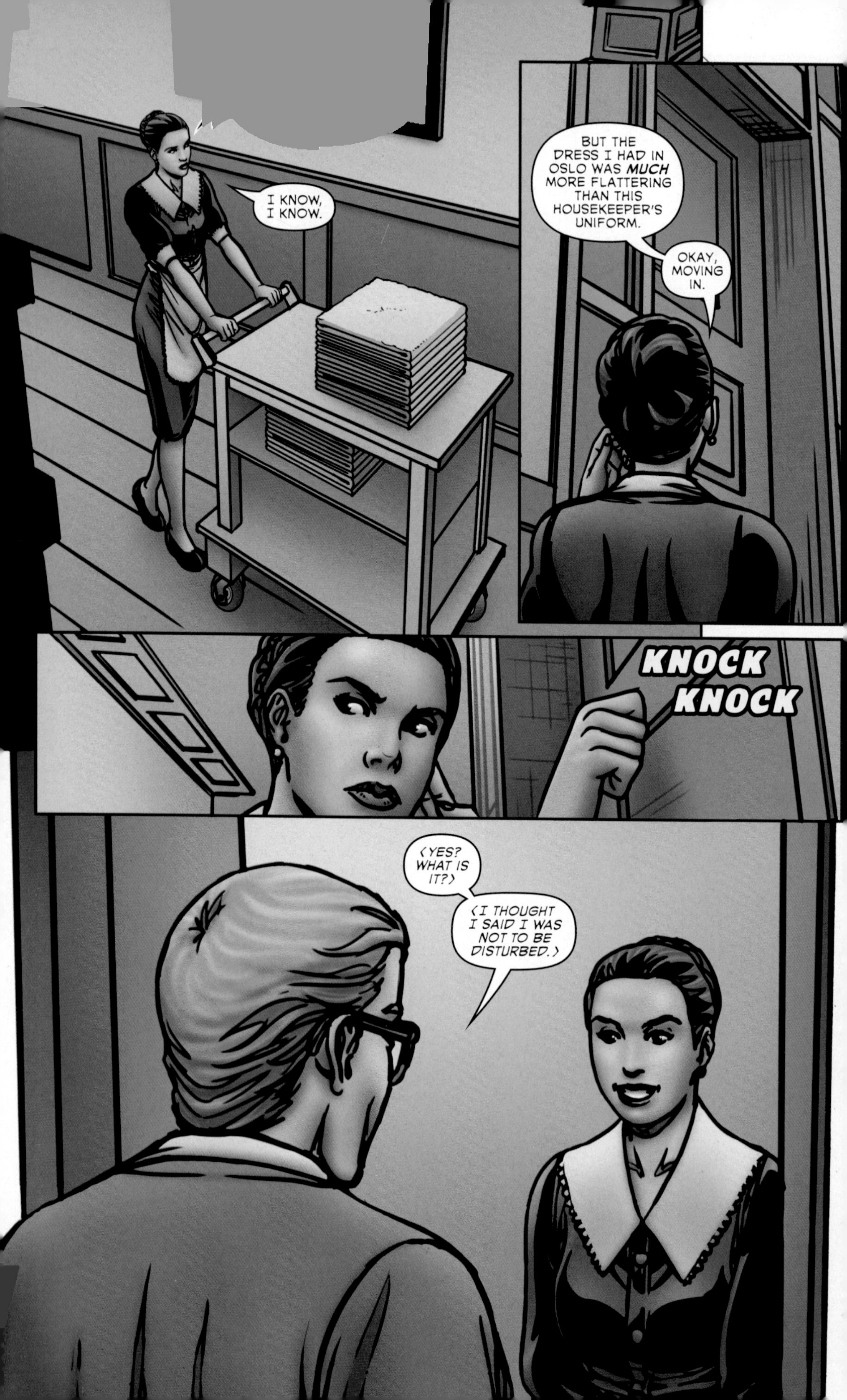
I KNOW, I KNOW.
BUT THE DRESS I HAD IN OSLO WAS *MUCH* MORE FLATTERING THAN THIS HOUSEKEEPER'S UNIFORM.
OKAY, MOVING IN.
KNOCK KNOCK
‹YES? WHAT IS IT?›
‹I THOUGHT I SAID I WAS NOT TO BE DISTURBED.›

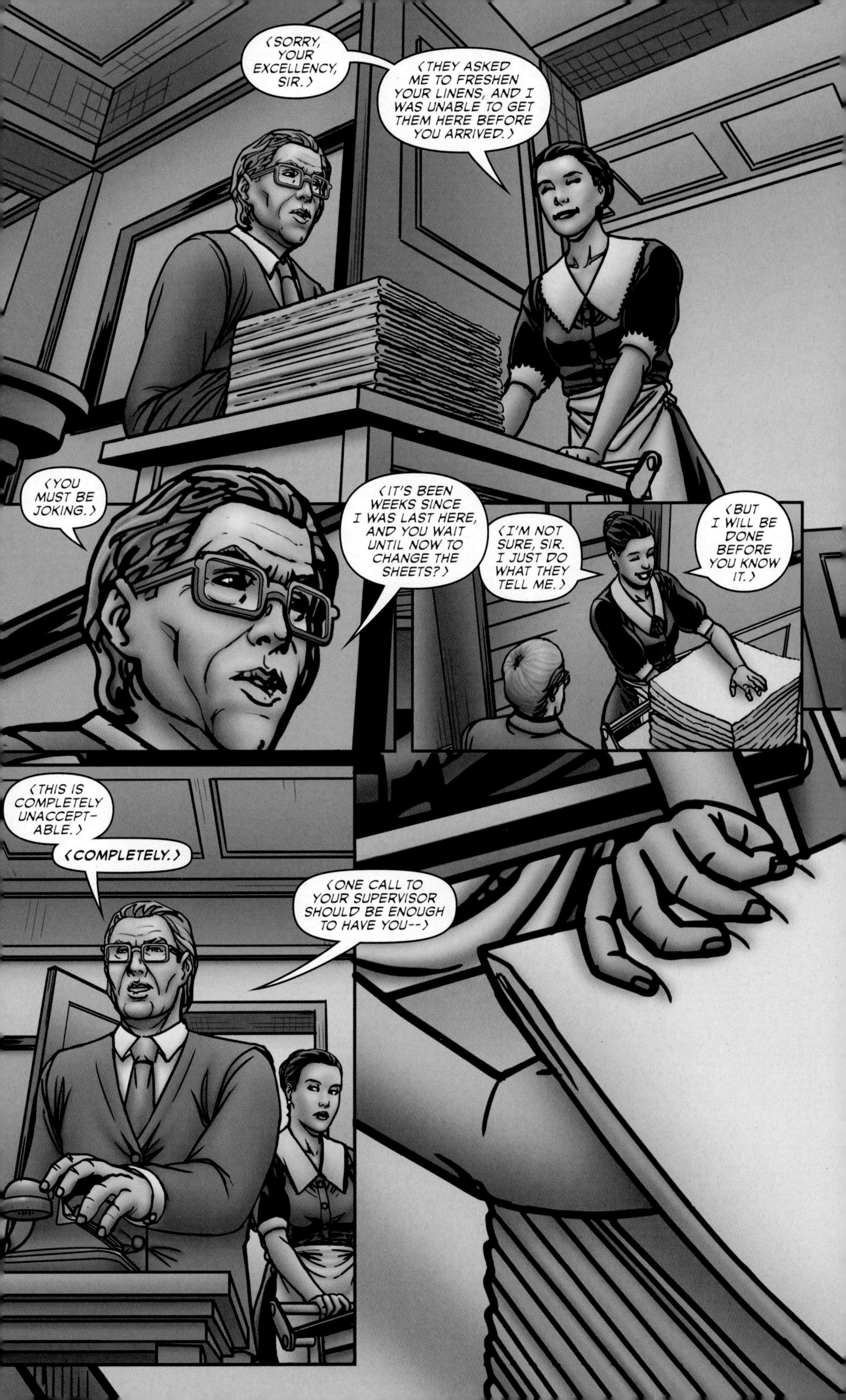
‹SORRY, YOUR EXCELLENCY, SIR.›
‹THEY ASKED ME TO FRESHEN YOUR LINENS, AND I WAS UNABLE TO GET THEM HERE BEFORE YOU ARRIVED.›
‹YOU MUST BE JOKING.›
‹IT'S BEEN WEEKS SINCE I WAS LAST HERE, AND YOU WAIT UNTIL NOW TO CHANGE THE SHEETS?›
‹I'M NOT SURE, SIR. I JUST DO WHAT THEY TELL ME.›
‹BUT I WILL BE DONE BEFORE YOU KNOW IT.›
‹THIS IS COMPLETELY UNACCEPT-ABLE.›
‹COMPLETELY.›
‹ONE CALL TO YOUR SUPERVISOR SHOULD BE ENOUGH TO HAVE YOU--›

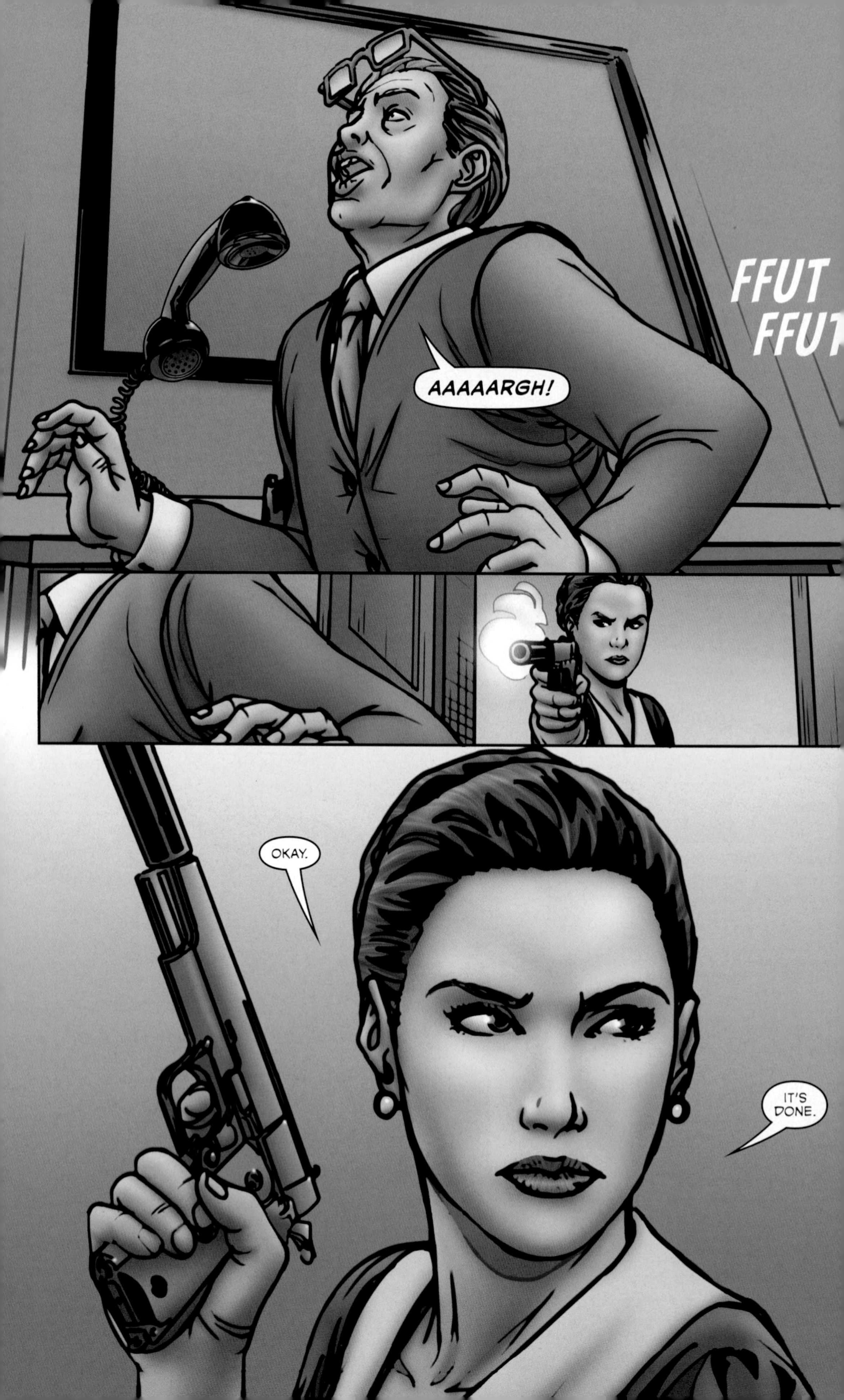
FFUT
FFUT
AAAAARGH!
OKAY.
IT'S DONE.

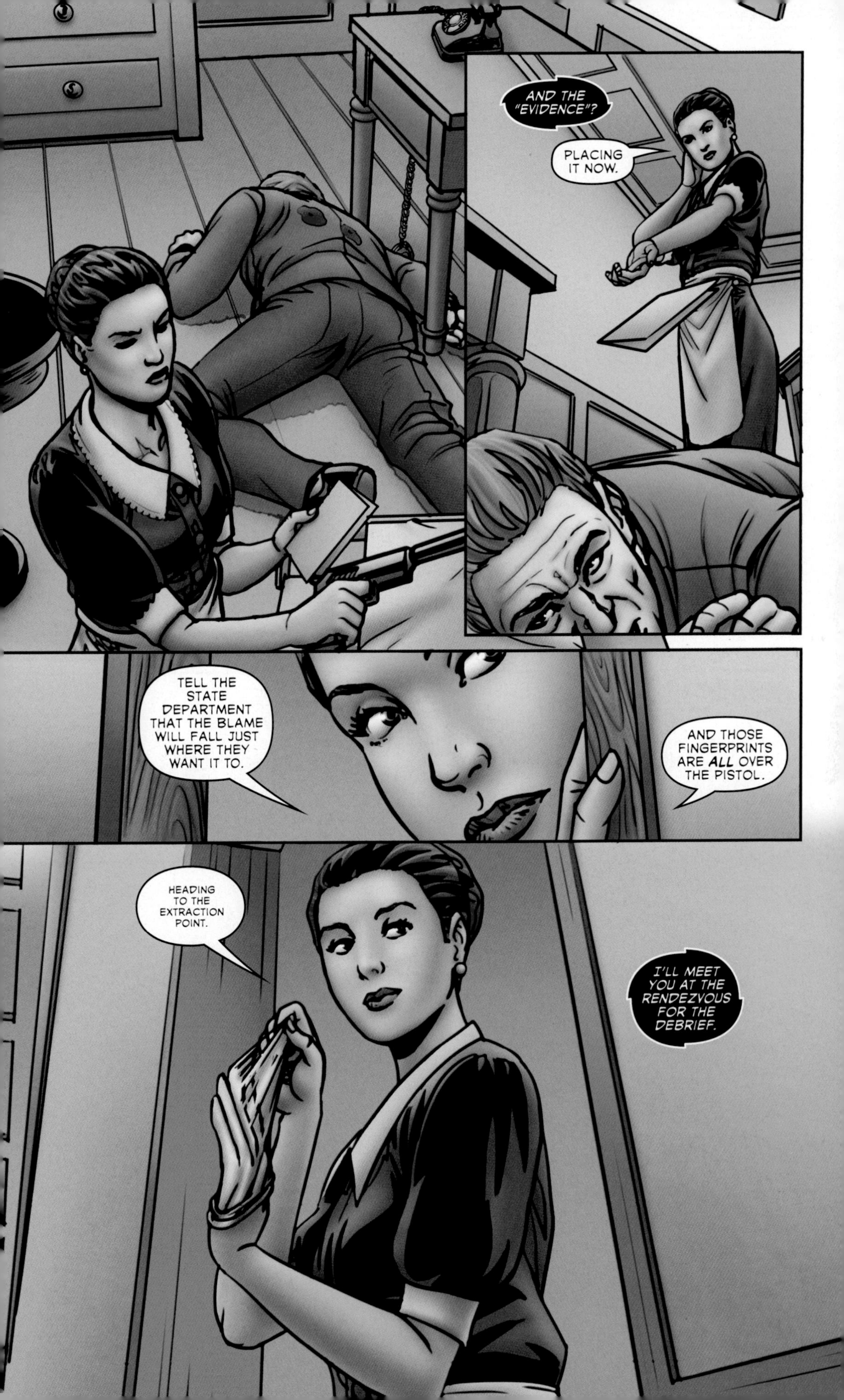
AND THE "EVIDENCE"?
PLACING IT NOW.
TELL THE STATE DEPARTMENT THAT THE BLAME WILL FALL JUST WHERE THEY WANT IT TO.
AND THOSE FINGERPRINTS ARE ALL OVER THE PISTOL.
HEADING TO THE EXTRACTION POINT.
I'LL MEET YOU AT THE RENDEZVOUS FOR THE DEBRIEF.

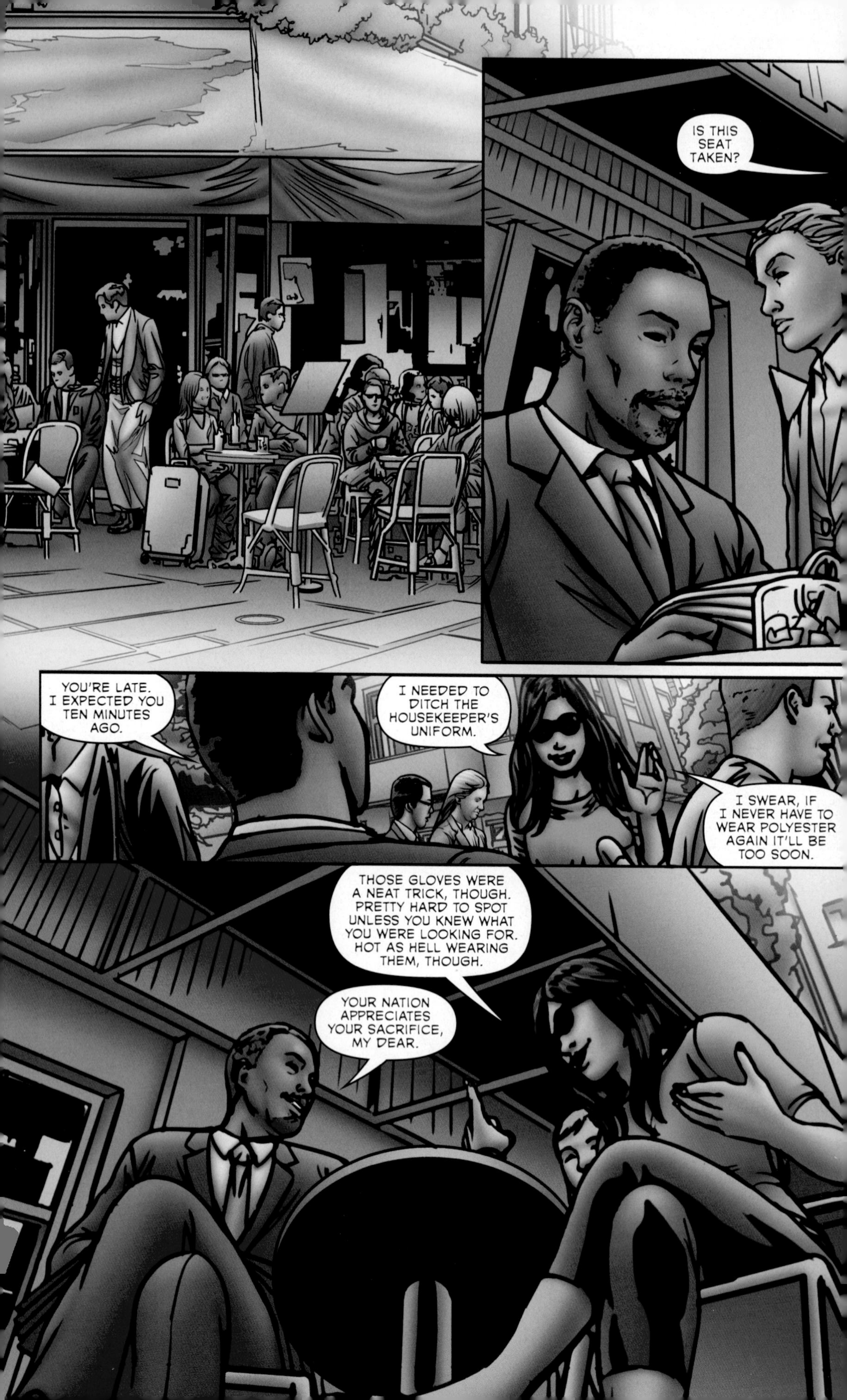
IS THIS SEAT TAKEN?
YOU'RE LATE. I EXPECTED YOU TEN MINUTES AGO.
I NEEDED TO DITCH THE HOUSEKEEPER'S UNIFORM.
I SWEAR, IF I NEVER HAVE TO WEAR POLYESTER AGAIN IT'LL BE TOO SOON.
THOSE GLOVES WERE A NEAT TRICK, THOUGH. PRETTY HARD TO SPOT UNLESS YOU KNEW WHAT YOU WERE LOOKING FOR. HOT AS HELL WEARING THEM, THOUGH.
YOUR NATION APPRECIATES YOUR SACRIFICE, MY DEAR.

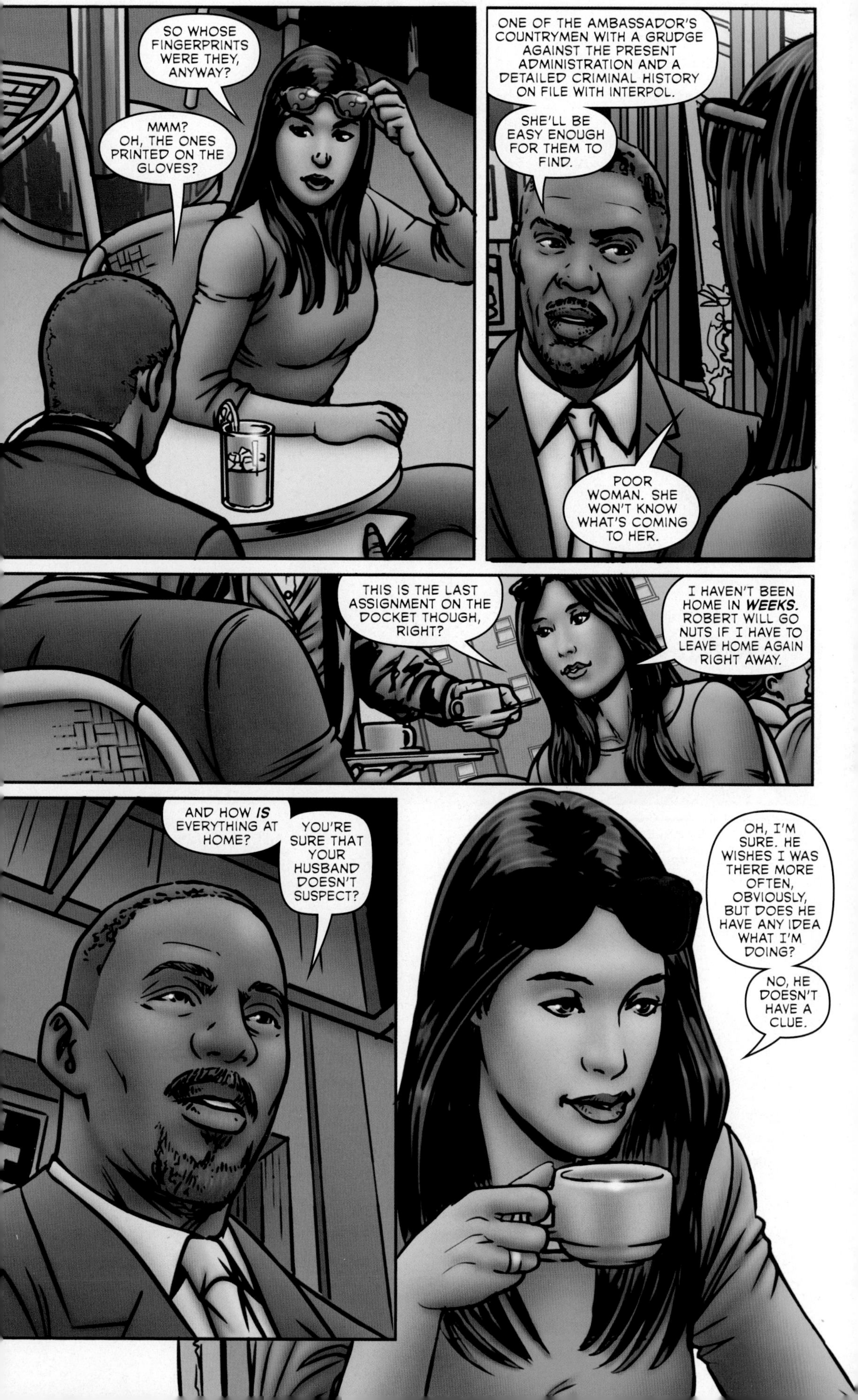
SO WHOSE FINGERPRINTS WERE THEY, ANYWAY?
MMM? OH, THE ONES PRINTED ON THE GLOVES?
ONE OF THE AMBASSADOR'S COUNTRYMEN WITH A GRUDGE AGAINST THE PRESENT ADMINISTRATION AND A DETAILED CRIMINAL HISTORY ON FILE WITH INTERPOL.
SHE'LL BE EASY ENOUGH FOR THEM TO FIND.
POOR WOMAN. SHE WON'T KNOW WHAT'S COMING TO HER.
THIS IS THE LAST ASSIGNMENT ON THE DOCKET THOUGH, RIGHT?
I HAVEN'T BEEN HOME IN *WEEKS.* ROBERT WILL GO NUTS IF I HAVE TO LEAVE HOME AGAIN RIGHT AWAY.
AND HOW *IS* EVERYTHING AT HOME?
YOU'RE SURE THAT YOUR HUSBAND DOESN'T SUSPECT?
OH, I'M SURE. HE WISHES I WAS THERE MORE OFTEN, OBVIOUSLY, BUT DOES HE HAVE ANY IDEA WHAT I'M DOING?
NO, HE DOESN'T HAVE A CLUE.

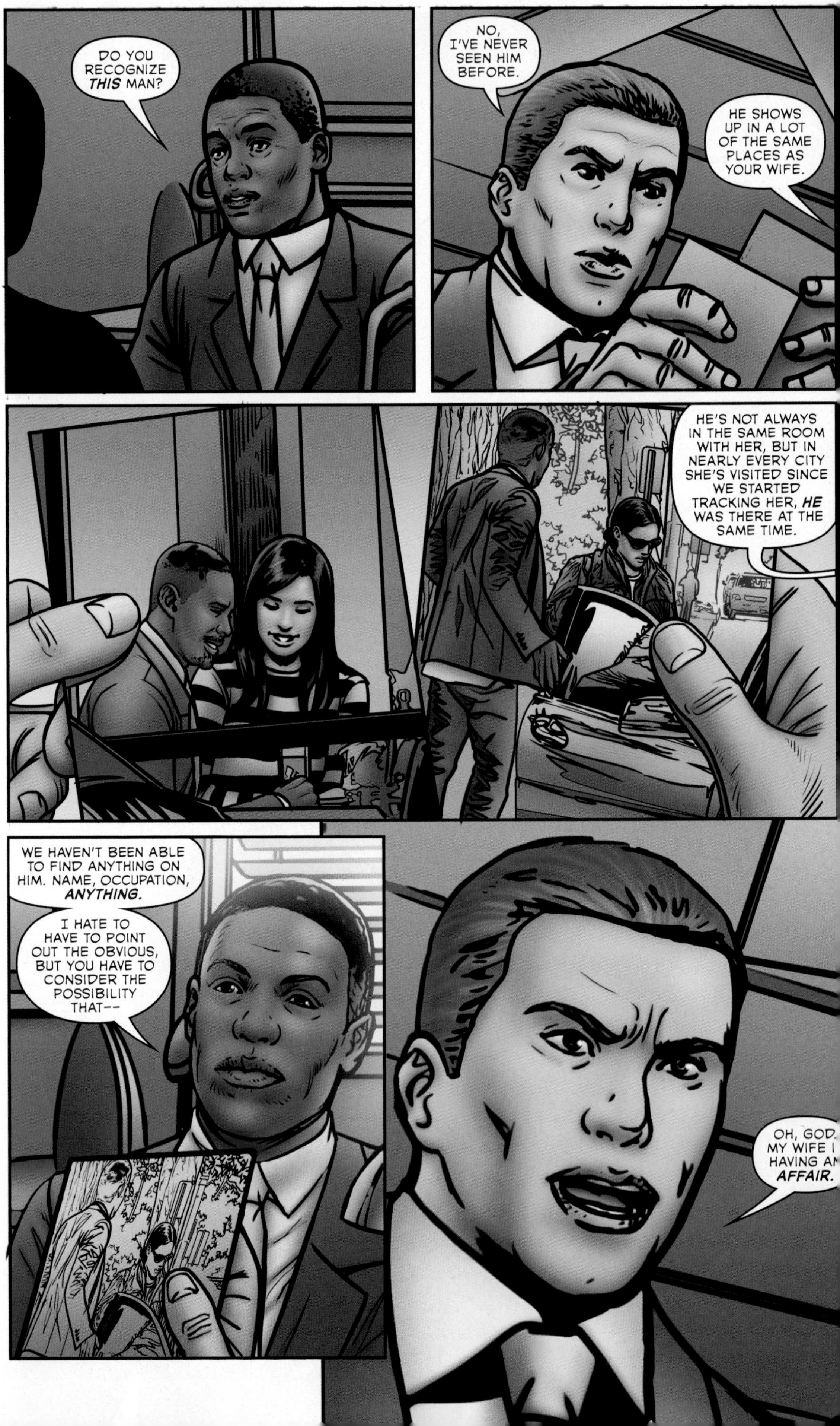
DO YOU RECOGNIZE *THIS* MAN?
NO, I'VE NEVER SEEN HIM BEFORE.
HE SHOWS UP IN A LOT OF THE SAME PLACES AS YOUR WIFE.
HE'S NOT ALWAYS IN THE SAME ROOM WITH HER, BUT IN NEARLY EVERY CITY SHE'S VISITED SINCE WE STARTED TRACKING HER, *HE* WAS THERE AT THE SAME TIME.
WE HAVEN'T BEEN ABLE TO FIND ANYTHING ON HIM. NAME, OCCUPATION, ***ANYTHING.***
I HATE TO HAVE TO POINT OUT THE OBVIOUS, BUT YOU HAVE TO CONSIDER THE POSSIBILITY THAT--
OH, GOD. MY WIFE I HAVING A ***AFFAIR.***

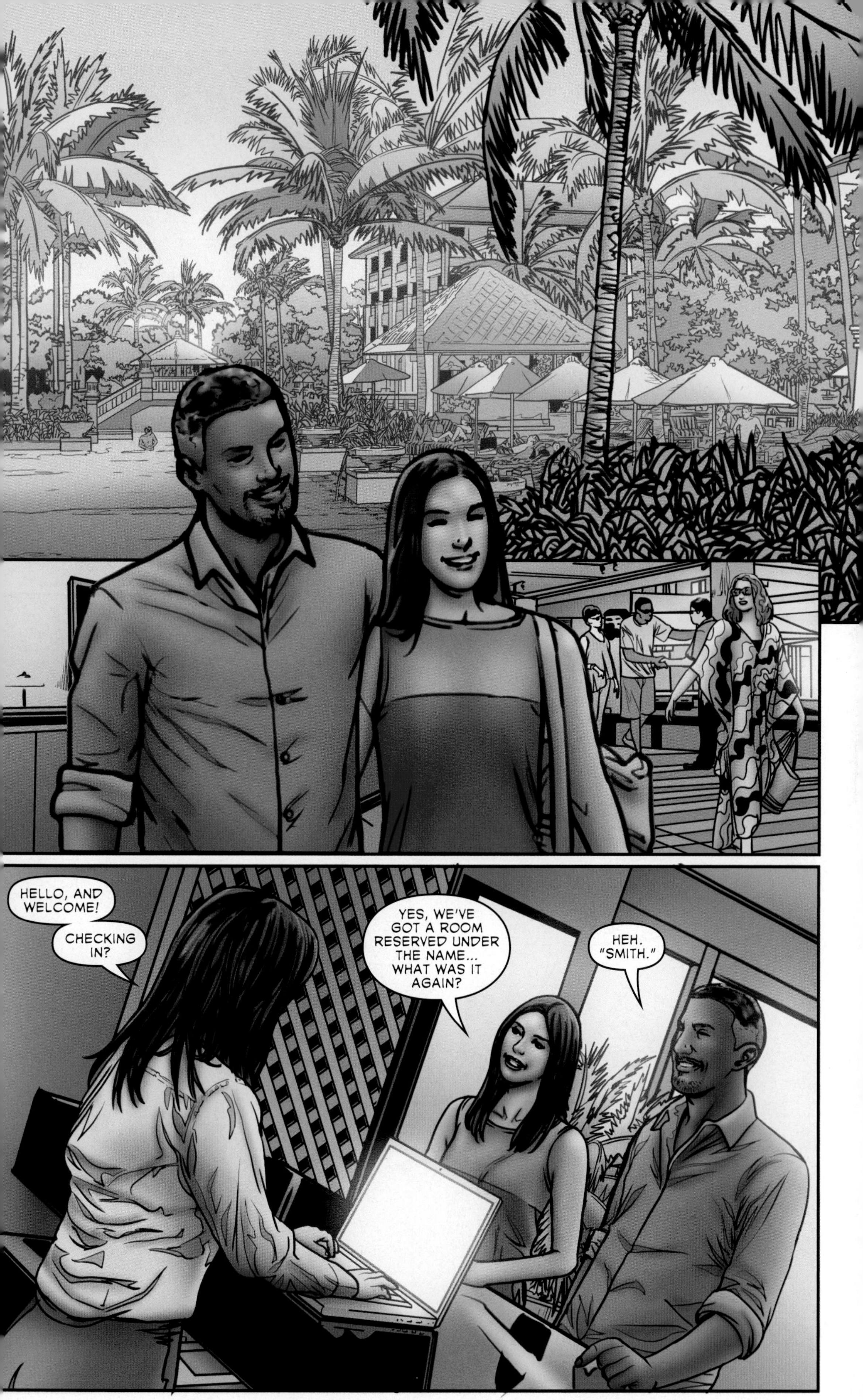
HELLO, AND WELCOME!
CHECKING IN?
YES, WE'VE GOT A ROOM RESERVED UNDER THE NAME... WHAT WAS IT AGAIN?
HEH. "SMITH."

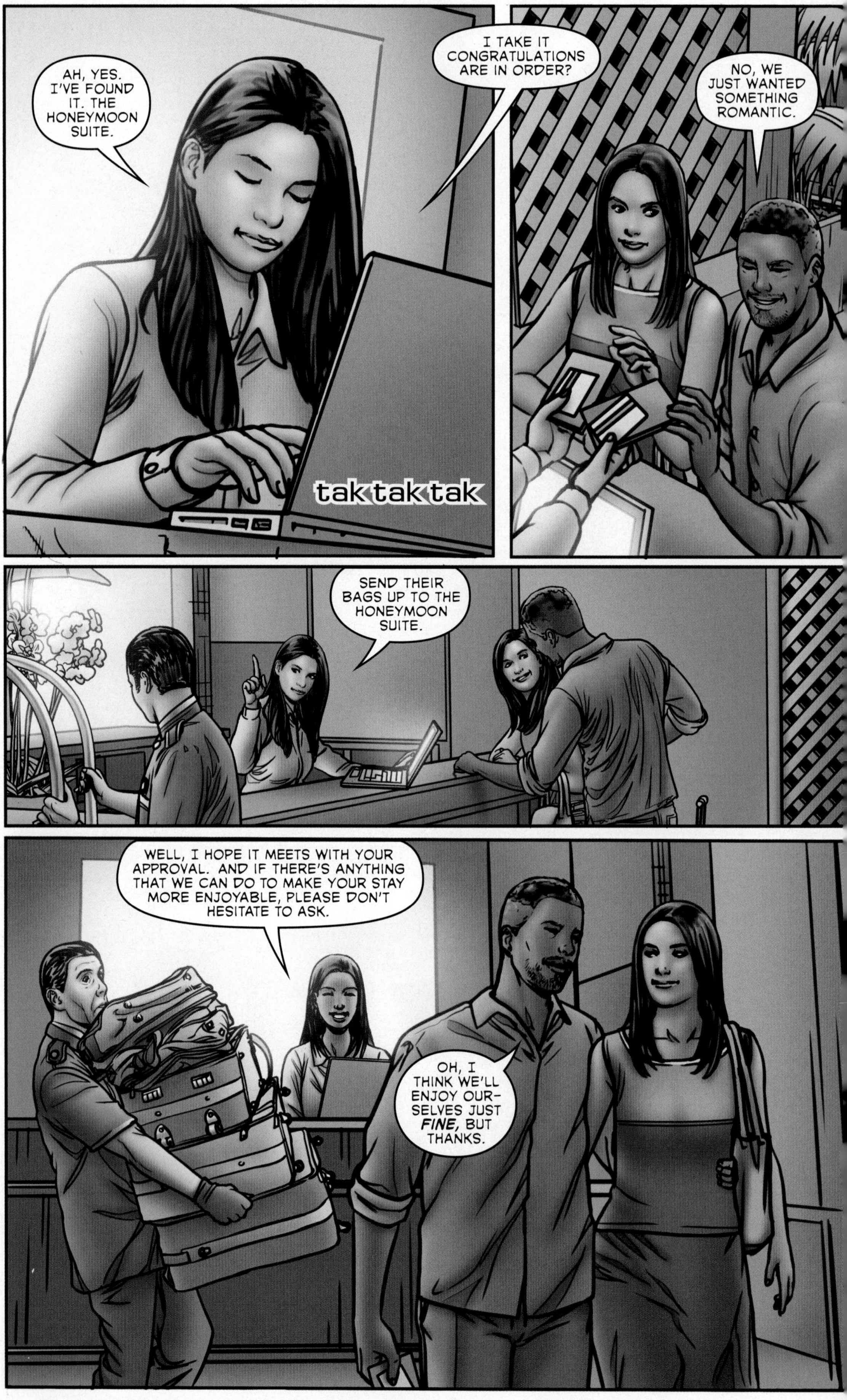
AH, YES. I'VE FOUND IT. THE HONEYMOON SUITE.
tak tak tak
I TAKE IT CONGRATULATIONS ARE IN ORDER?
NO, WE JUST WANTED SOMETHING ROMANTIC.
SEND THEIR BAGS UP TO THE HONEYMOON SUITE.
WELL, I HOPE IT MEETS WITH YOUR APPROVAL. AND IF THERE'S ANYTHING THAT WE CAN DO TO MAKE YOUR STAY MORE ENJOYABLE, PLEASE DON'T HESITATE TO ASK.
OH, I THINK WE'LL ENJOY OUR-SELVES JUST *FINE,* BUT THANKS.

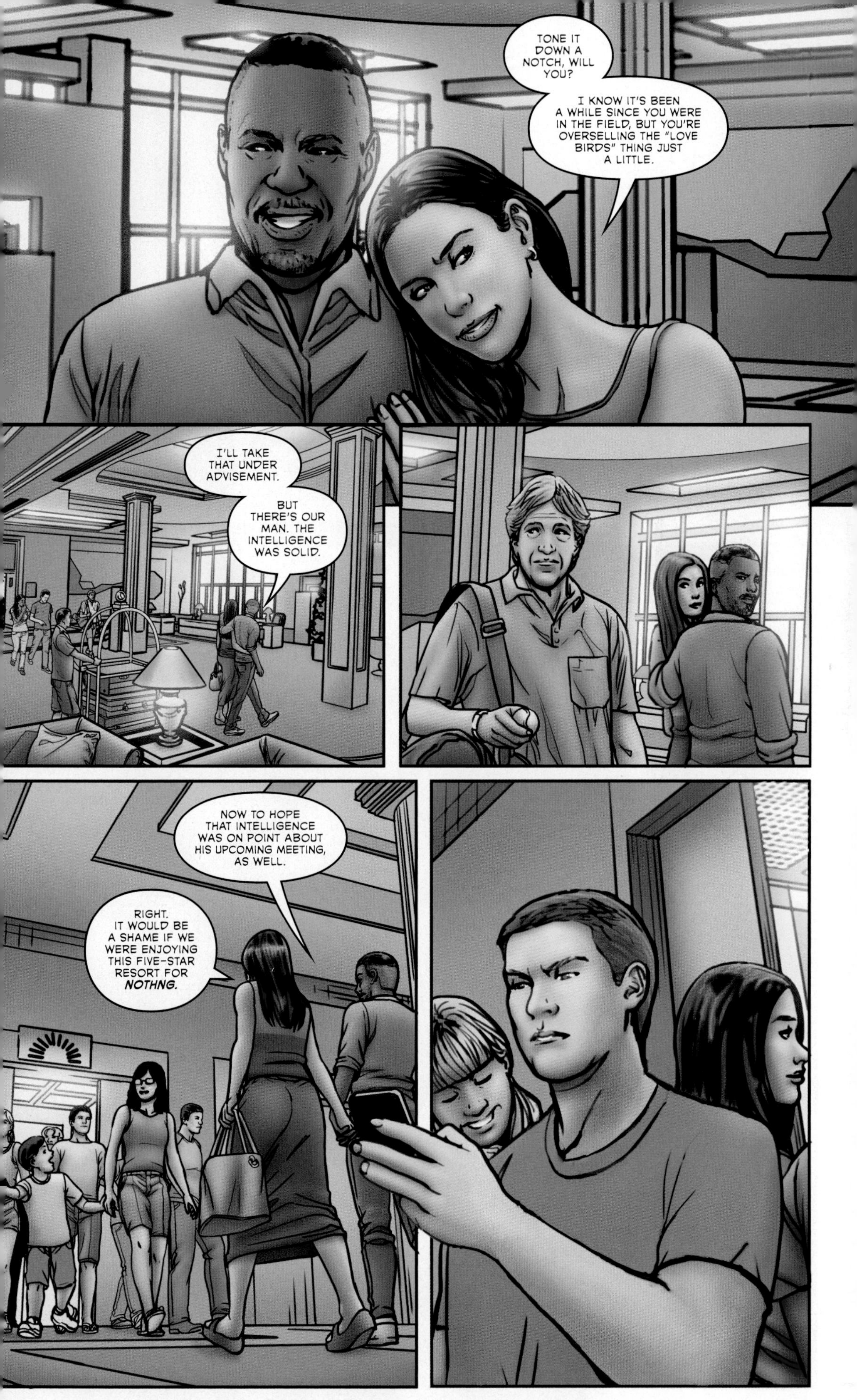
TONE IT DOWN A NOTCH, WILL YOU?
I KNOW IT'S BEEN A WHILE SINCE YOU WERE IN THE FIELD, BUT YOU'RE OVERSELLING THE "LOVE BIRDS" THING JUST A LITTLE.
I'LL TAKE THAT UNDER ADVISEMENT.
BUT THERE'S OUR MAN. THE INTELLIGENCE WAS SOLID.
NOW TO HOPE THAT INTELLIGENCE WAS ON POINT ABOUT HIS UPCOMING MEETING, AS WELL.
RIGHT. IT WOULD BE A SHAME IF WE WERE ENJOYING THIS FIVE-STAR RESORT FOR *NOTHNG.*

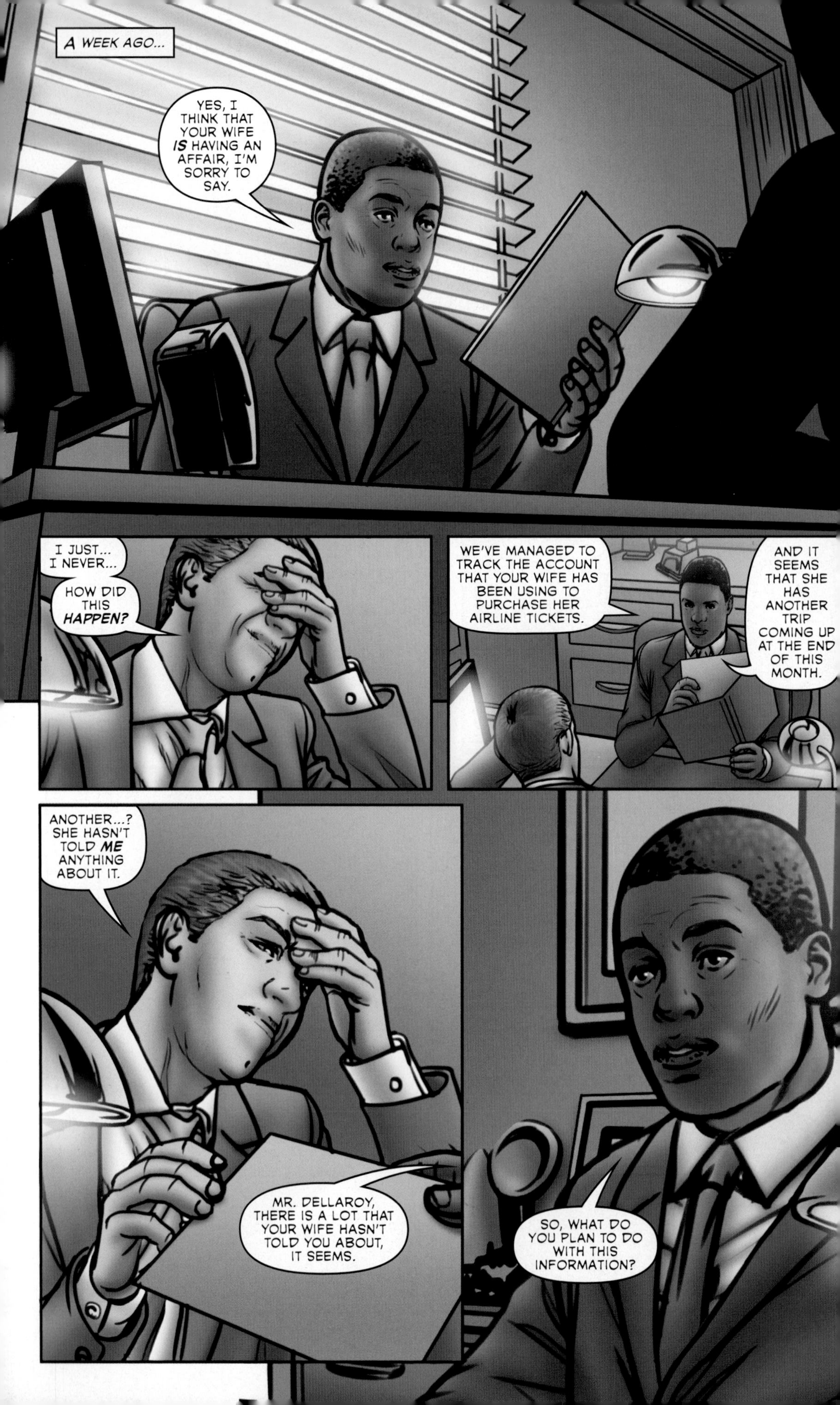
A WEEK AGO...
YES, I THINK THAT YOUR WIFE *IS* HAVING AN AFFAIR, I'M SORRY TO SAY.
I JUST... I NEVER...
HOW DID THIS *HAPPEN?*
WE'VE MANAGED TO TRACK THE ACCOUNT THAT YOUR WIFE HAS BEEN USING TO PURCHASE HER AIRLINE TICKETS.
AND IT SEEMS THAT SHE HAS ANOTHER TRIP COMING UP AT THE END OF THIS MONTH.
ANOTHER...? SHE HASN'T TOLD *ME* ANYTHING ABOUT IT.
MR. DELLAROY, THERE IS A LOT THAT YOUR WIFE HASN'T TOLD YOU ABOUT, IT SEEMS.
SO, WHAT DO YOU PLAN TO DO WITH THIS INFORMATION?

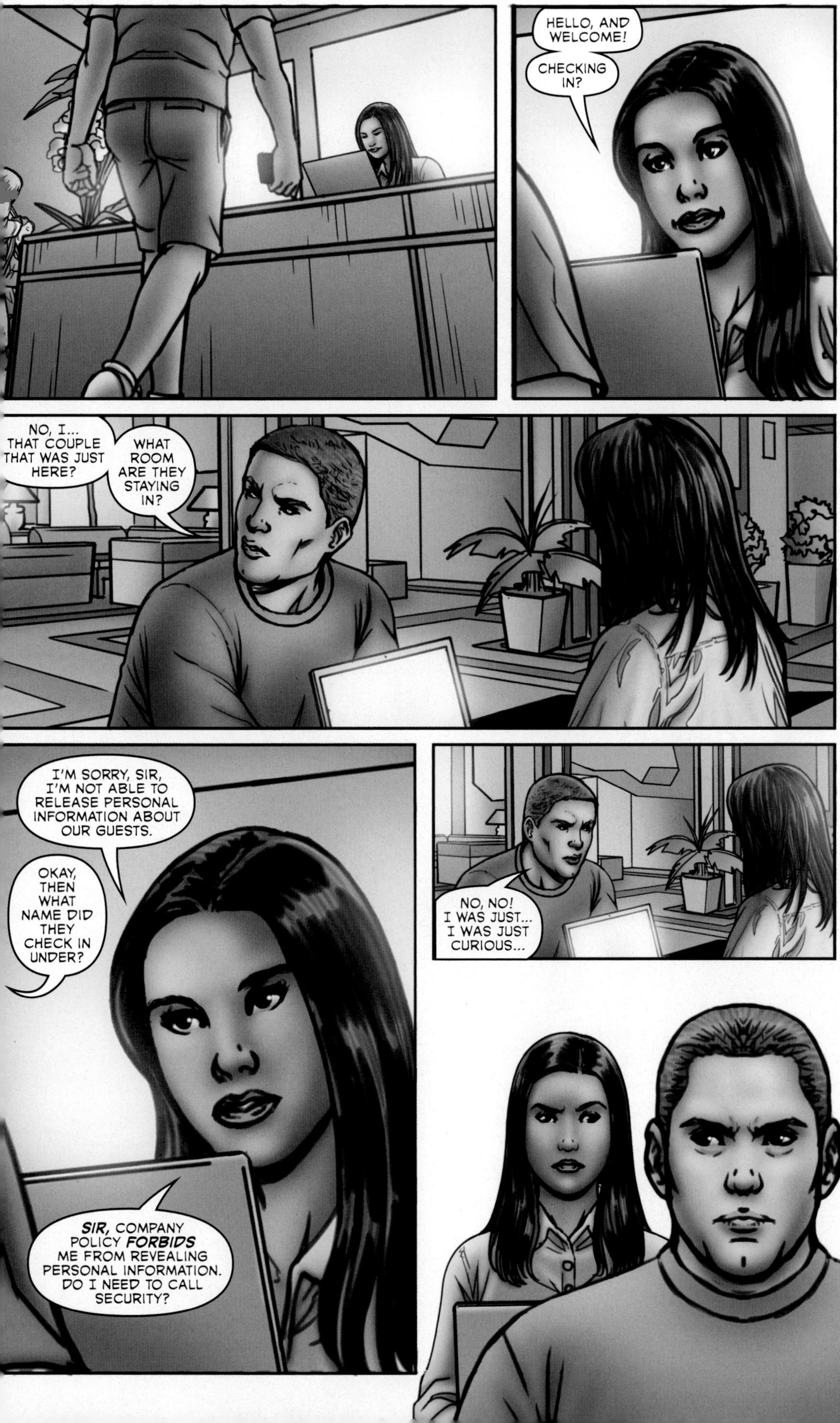
HELLO, AND WELCOME!
CHECKING IN?
NO, I... THAT COUPLE THAT WAS JUST HERE?
WHAT ROOM ARE THEY STAYING IN?
I'M SORRY, SIR, I'M NOT ABLE TO RELEASE PERSONAL INFORMATION ABOUT OUR GUESTS.
OKAY, THEN WHAT NAME DID THEY CHECK IN UNDER?
SIR, COMPANY POLICY FORBIDS ME FROM REVEALING PERSONAL INFORMATION. DO I NEED TO CALL SECURITY?
NO, NO! I WAS JUST... I WAS JUST CURIOUS...

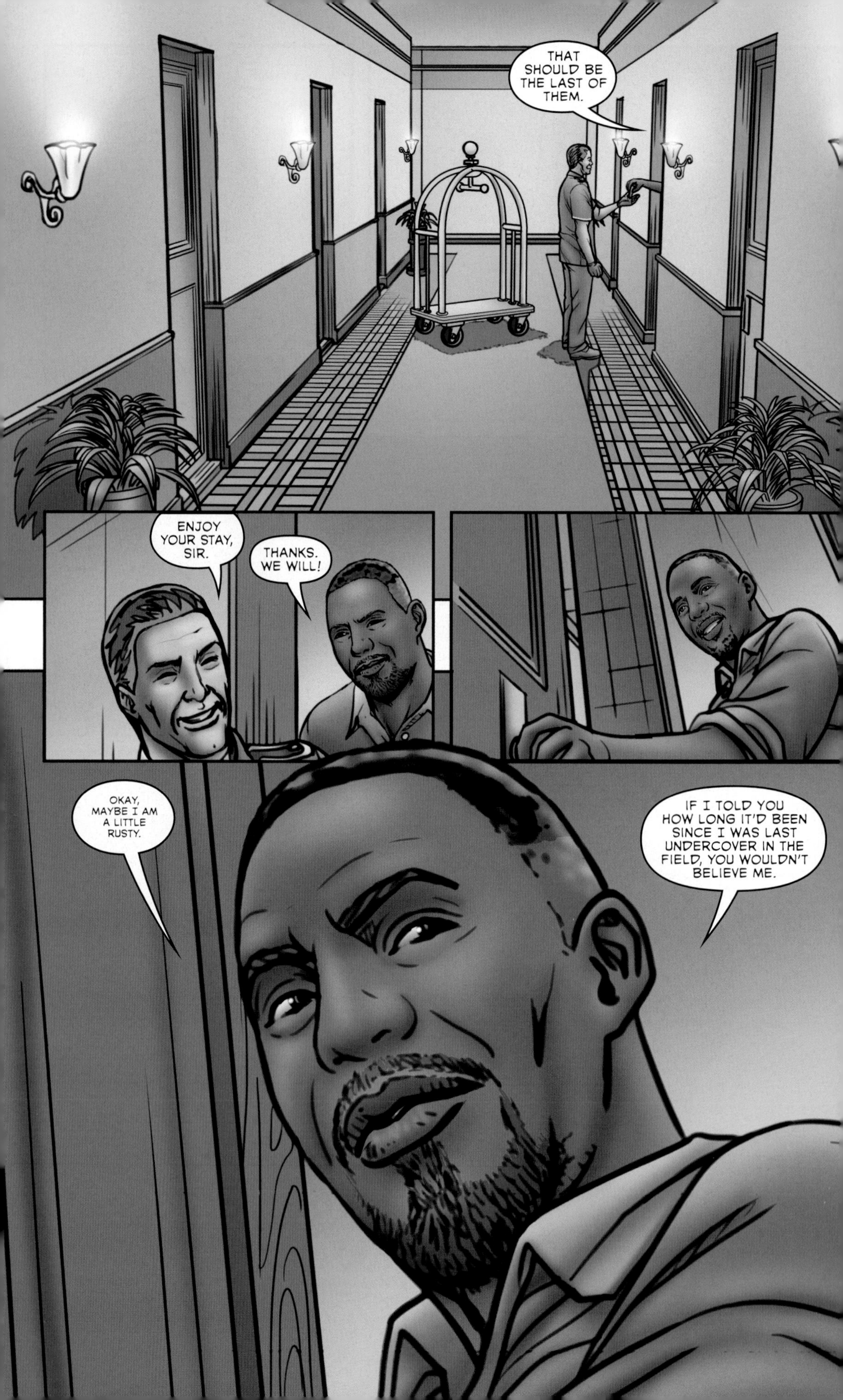
THAT SHOULD BE THE LAST OF THEM.
ENJOY YOUR STAY, SIR.
THANKS. WE WILL!
OKAY, MAYBE I AM A LITTLE RUSTY.
IF I TOLD YOU HOW LONG IT'D BEEN SINCE I WAS LAST UNDERCOVER IN THE FIELD, YOU WOULDN'T BELIEVE ME.

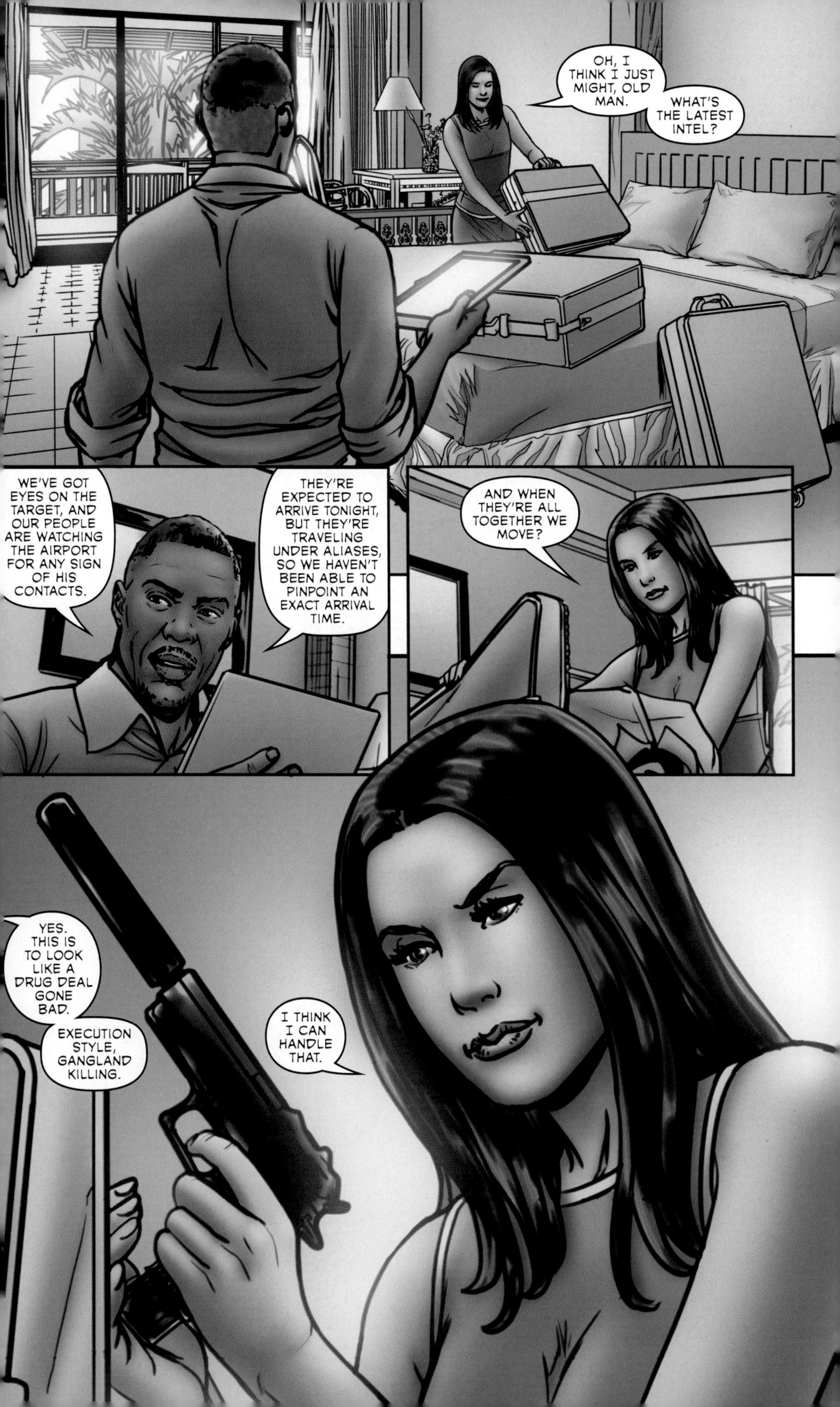

OH, I THINK I JUST MIGHT, OLD MAN.
WHAT'S THE LATEST INTEL?
WE'VE GOT EYES ON THE TARGET, AND OUR PEOPLE ARE WATCHING THE AIRPORT FOR ANY SIGN OF HIS CONTACTS.
THEY'RE EXPECTED TO ARRIVE TONIGHT, BUT THEY'RE TRAVELING UNDER ALIASES, SO WE HAVEN'T BEEN ABLE TO PINPOINT AN EXACT ARRIVAL TIME.
AND WHEN THEY'RE ALL TOGETHER WE MOVE?
YES. THIS IS TO LOOK LIKE A DRUG DEAL GONE BAD.
EXECUTION STYLE, GANGLAND KILLING.
I THINK I CAN HANDLE THAT.

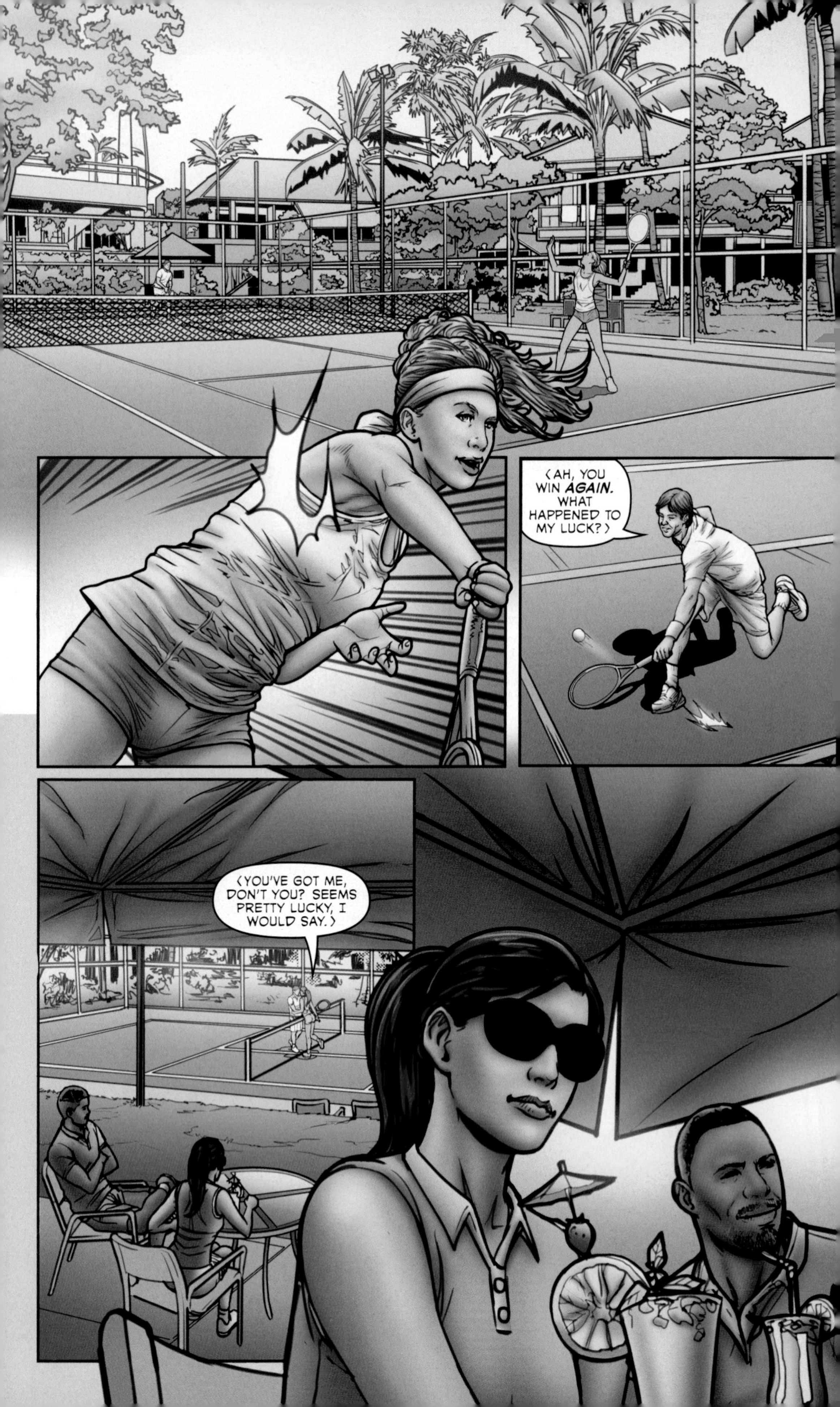

‹AH, YOU WIN AGAIN. WHAT HAPPENED TO MY LUCK?›
‹YOU'VE GOT ME, DON'T YOU? SEEMS PRETTY LUCKY, I WOULD SAY.›

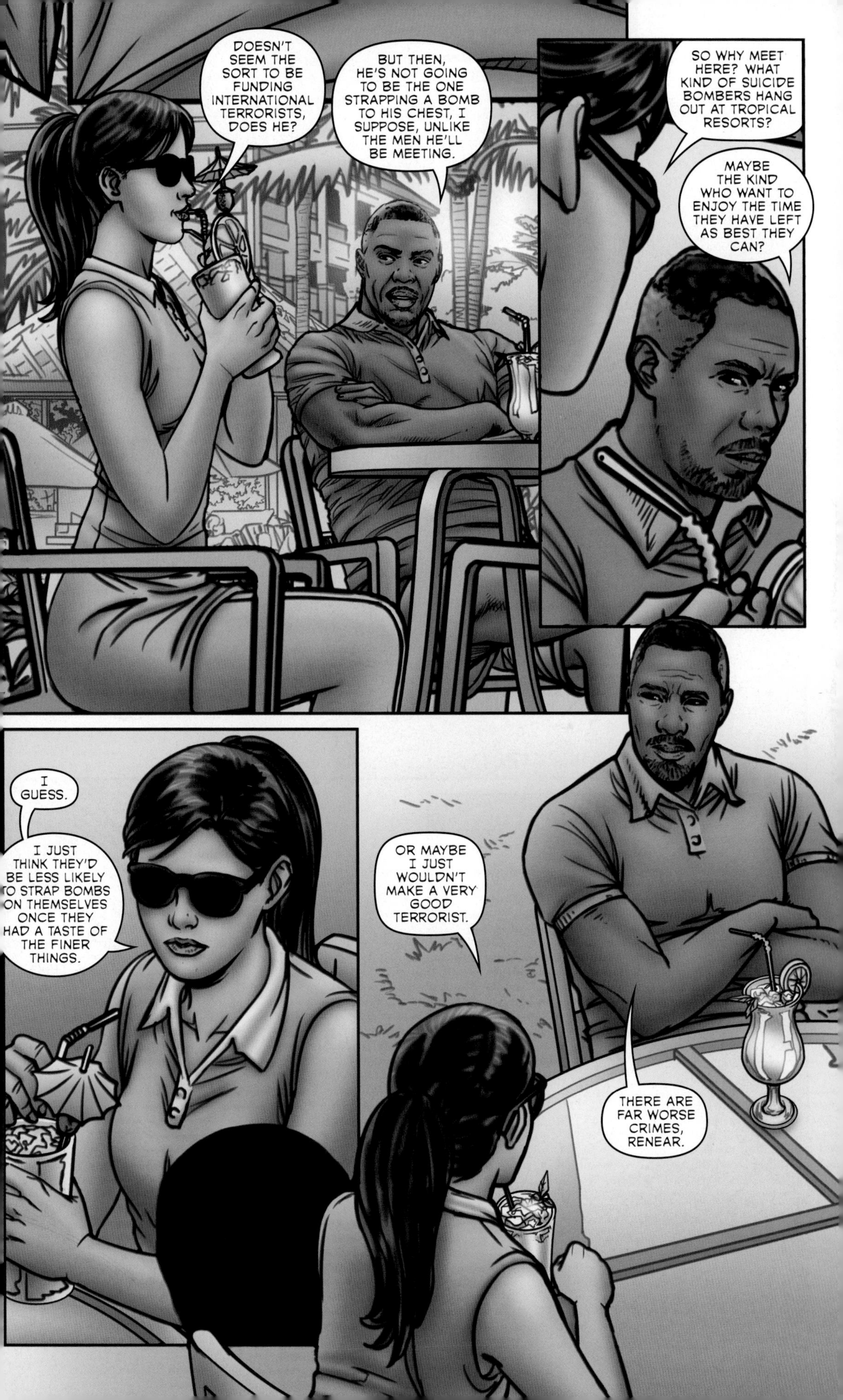
DOESN'T SEEM THE SORT TO BE FUNDING INTERNATIONAL TERRORISTS, DOES HE?
BUT THEN, HE'S NOT GOING TO BE THE ONE STRAPPING A BOMB TO HIS CHEST, I SUPPOSE, UNLIKE THE MEN HE'LL BE MEETING.
SO WHY MEET HERE? WHAT KIND OF SUICIDE BOMBERS HANG OUT AT TROPICAL RESORTS?
MAYBE THE KIND WHO WANT TO ENJOY THE TIME THEY HAVE LEFT AS BEST THEY CAN?
I GUESS.
I JUST THINK THEY'D BE LESS LIKELY TO STRAP BOMBS ON THEMSELVES ONCE THEY HAD A TASTE OF THE FINER THINGS.
OR MAYBE I JUST WOULDN'T MAKE A VERY GOOD TERRORIST.
THERE ARE FAR WORSE CRIMES, RENEAR.

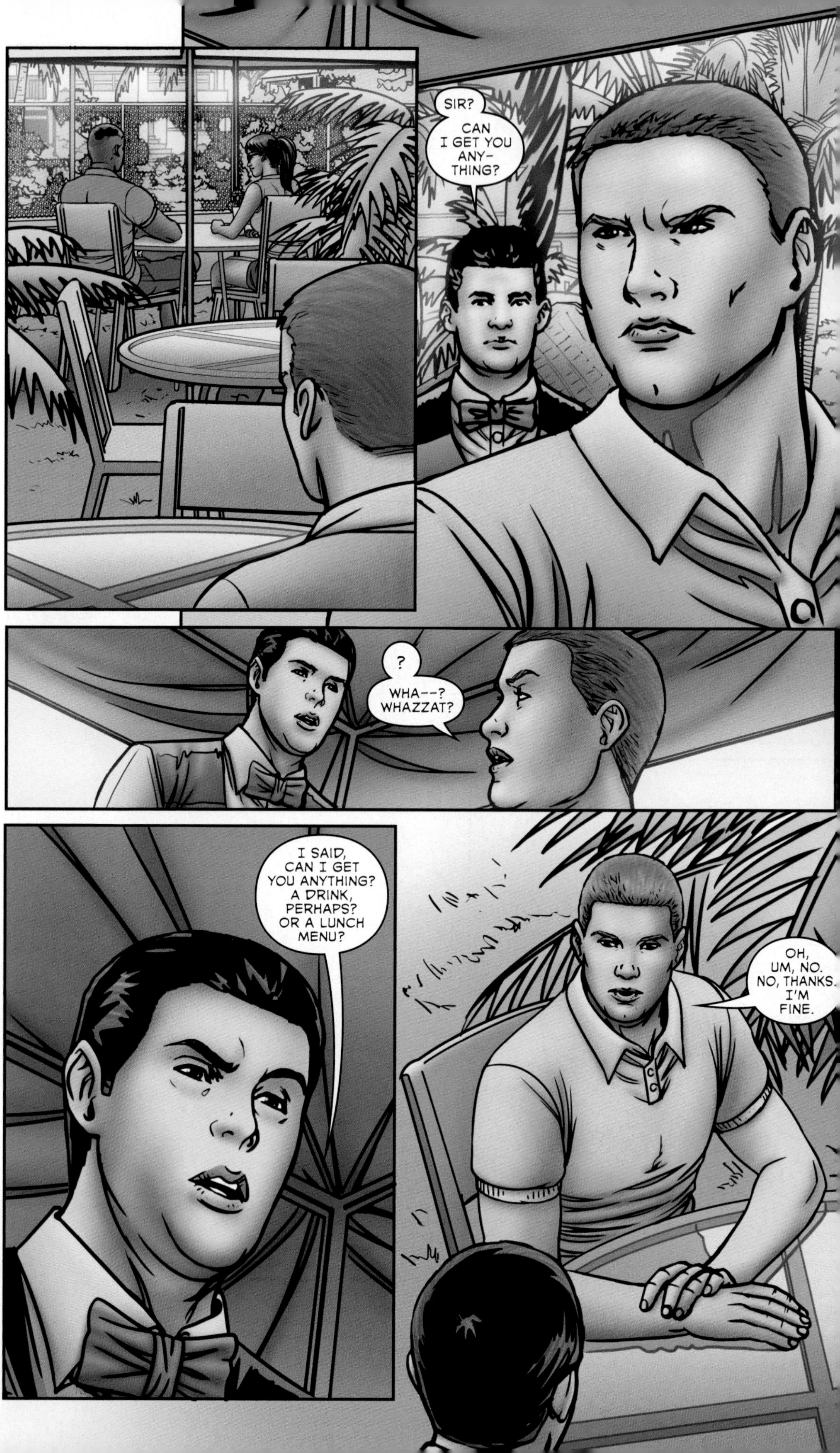
SIR?
CAN I GET YOU ANY-THING?
?
WHA--? WHAZZAT?
I SAID, CAN I GET YOU ANYTHING? A DRINK, PERHAPS? OR A LUNCH MENU?
OH, UM, NO. NO, THANKS. I'M FINE.

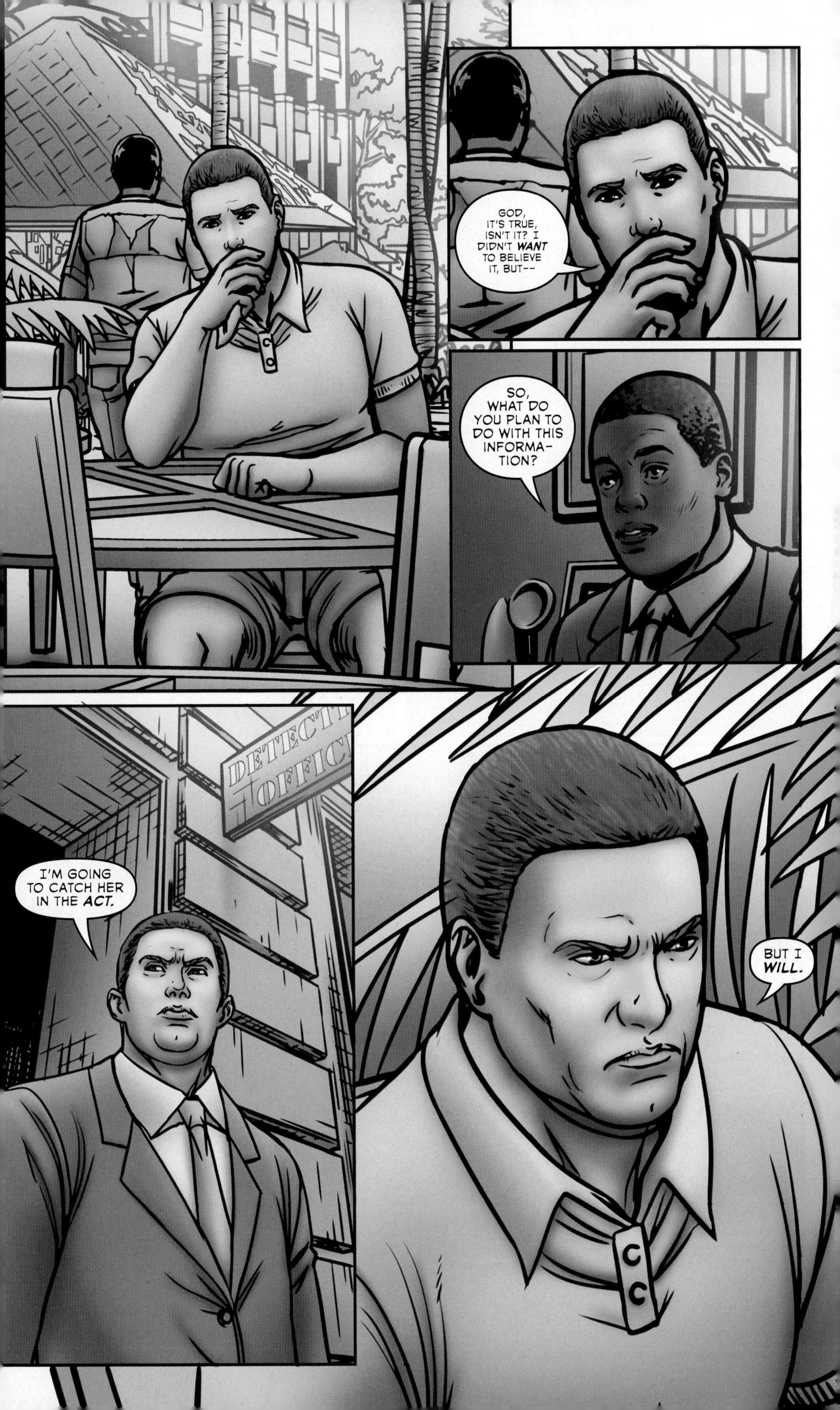
GOD, IT'S TRUE, ISN'T IT? I DIDN'T WANT TO BELIEVE IT, BUT--
SO, WHAT DO YOU PLAN TO DO WITH THIS INFORMATION?
DETECTI OFFIC
I'M GOING TO CATCH HER IN THE ACT.
BUT I WILL.

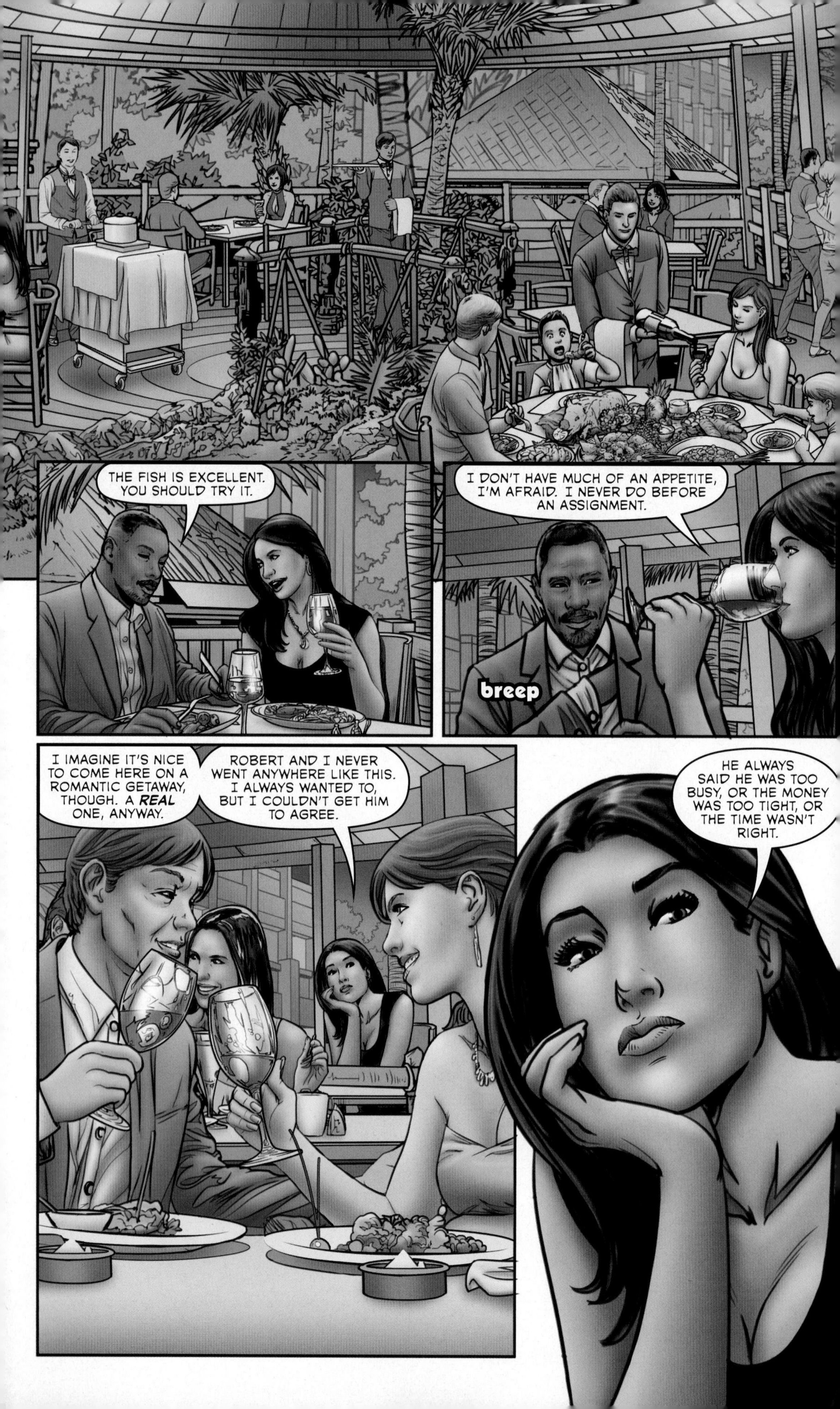
THE FISH IS EXCELLENT. YOU SHOULD TRY IT.
I DON'T HAVE MUCH OF AN APPETITE, I'M AFRAID. I NEVER DO BEFORE AN ASSIGNMENT.
breep
I IMAGINE IT'S NICE TO COME HERE ON A ROMANTIC GETAWAY, THOUGH. A REAL ONE, ANYWAY.
ROBERT AND I NEVER WENT ANYWHERE LIKE THIS. I ALWAYS WANTED TO, BUT I COULDN'T GET HIM TO AGREE.
HE ALWAYS SAID HE WAS TOO BUSY, OR THE MONEY WAS TOO TIGHT, OR THE TIME WASN'T RIGHT.

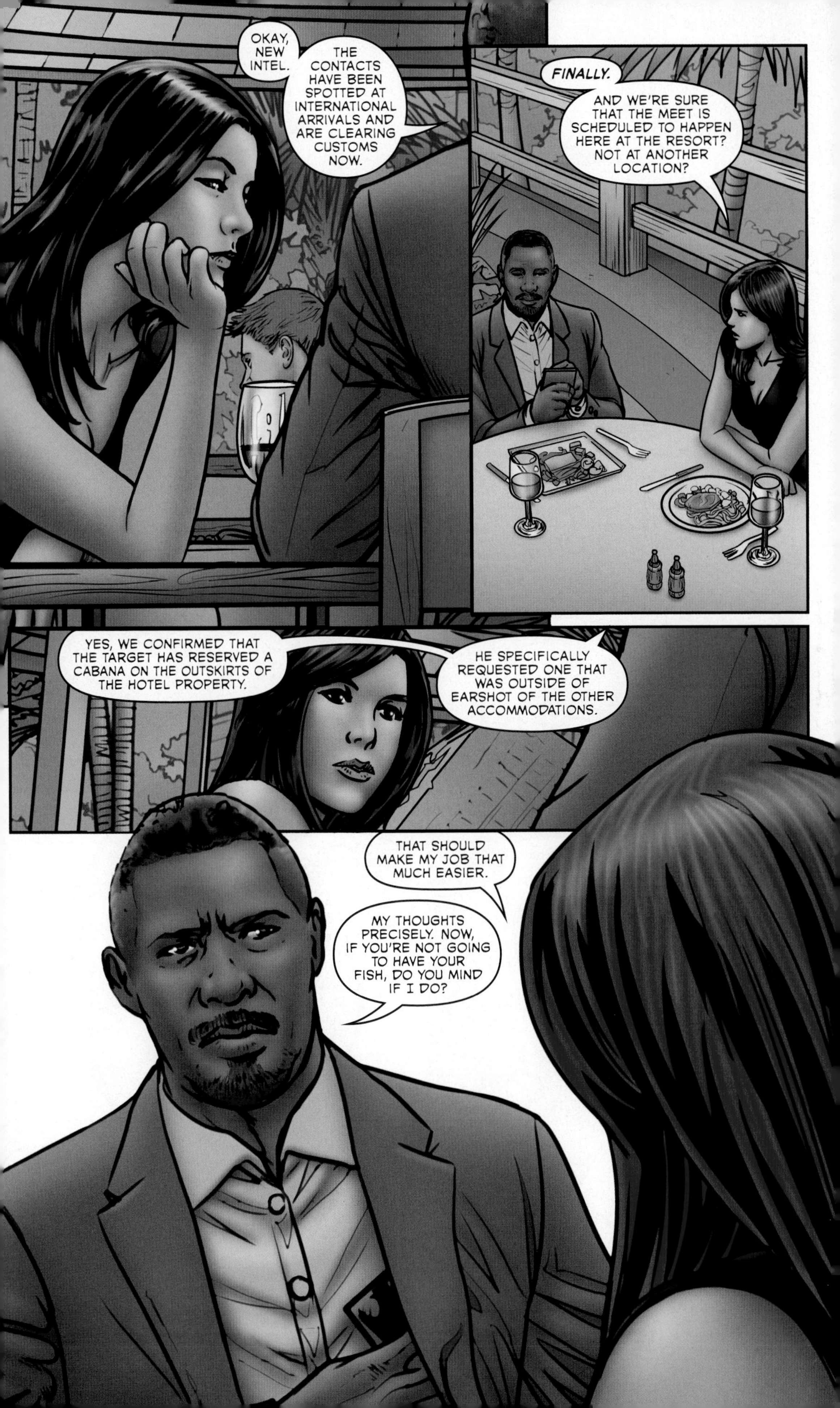
OKAY, NEW INTEL.
THE CONTACTS HAVE BEEN SPOTTED AT INTERNATIONAL ARRIVALS AND ARE CLEARING CUSTOMS NOW.
FINALLY.
AND WE'RE SURE THAT THE MEET IS SCHEDULED TO HAPPEN HERE AT THE RESORT? NOT AT ANOTHER LOCATION?
YES, WE CONFIRMED THAT THE TARGET HAS RESERVED A CABANA ON THE OUTSKIRTS OF THE HOTEL PROPERTY.
HE SPECIFICALLY REQUESTED ONE THAT WAS OUTSIDE OF EARSHOT OF THE OTHER ACCOMMODATIONS.
THAT SHOULD MAKE MY JOB THAT MUCH EASIER.
MY THOUGHTS PRECISELY. NOW, IF YOU'RE NOT GOING TO HAVE YOUR FISH, DO YOU MIND IF I DO?

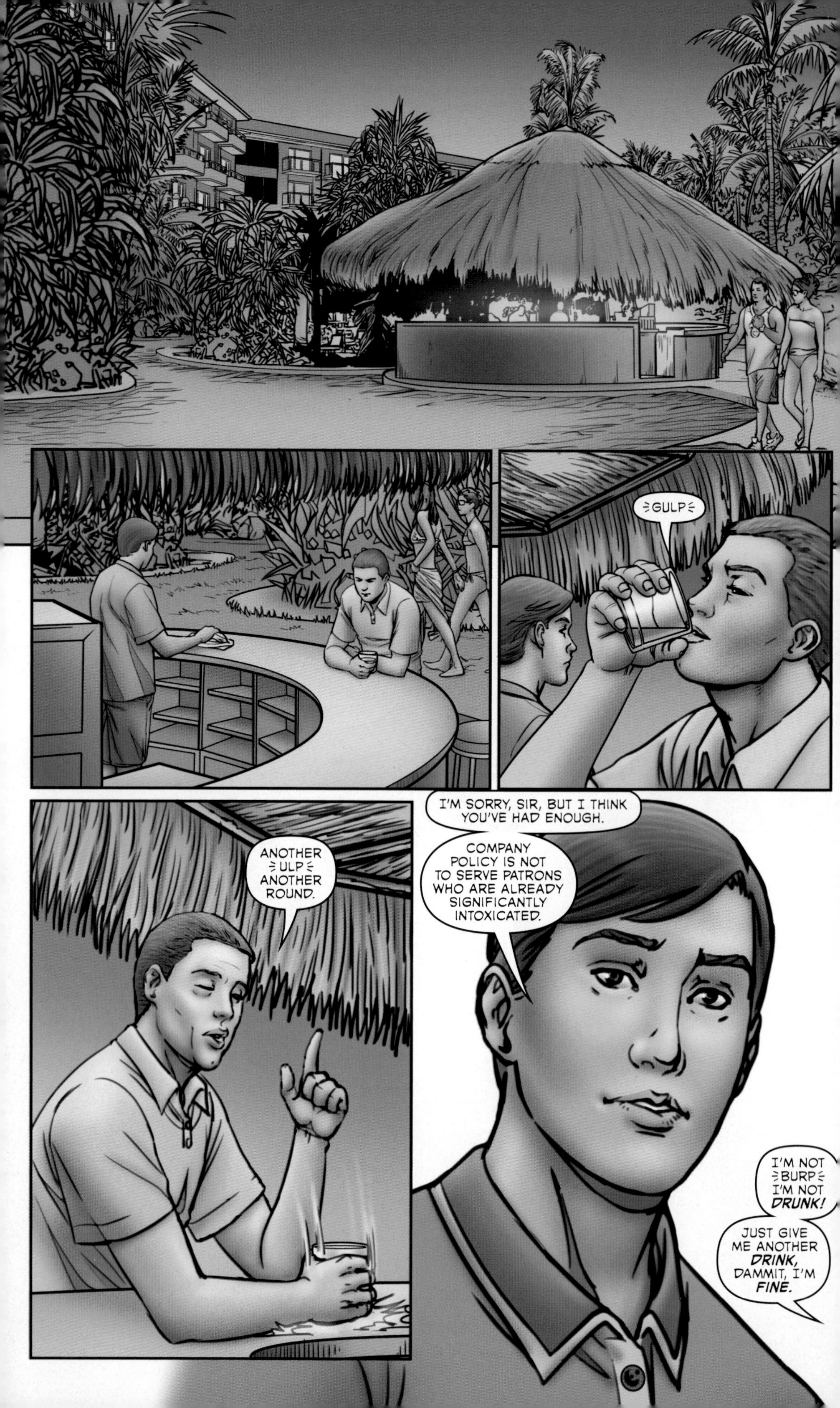
GULP
ANOTHER ULP ANOTHER ROUND.
I'M SORRY, SIR, BUT I THINK YOU'VE HAD ENOUGH.
COMPANY POLICY IS NOT TO SERVE PATRONS WHO ARE ALREADY SIGNIFICANTLY INTOXICATED.
I'M NOT BURP I'M NOT *DRUNK!*
JUST GIVE ME ANOTHER *DRINK,* DAMMIT, I'M *FINE.*

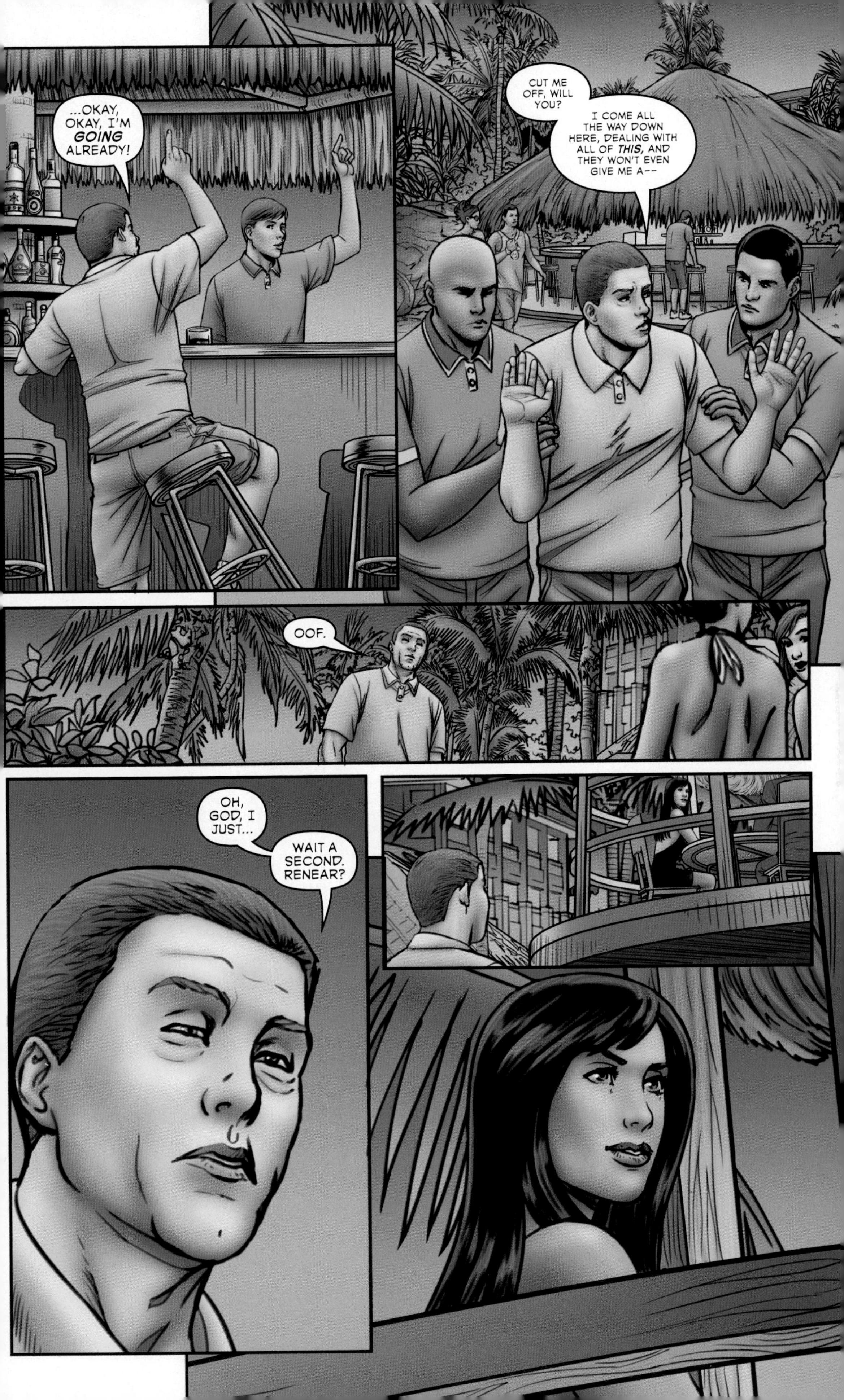
...OKAY, OKAY, I'M GOING ALREADY!
CUT ME OFF, WILL YOU?
I COME ALL THE WAY DOWN HERE, DEALING WITH ALL OF THIS, AND THEY WON'T EVEN GIVE ME A--
OOF.
OH, GOD, I JUST...
WAIT A SECOND. RENEAR?

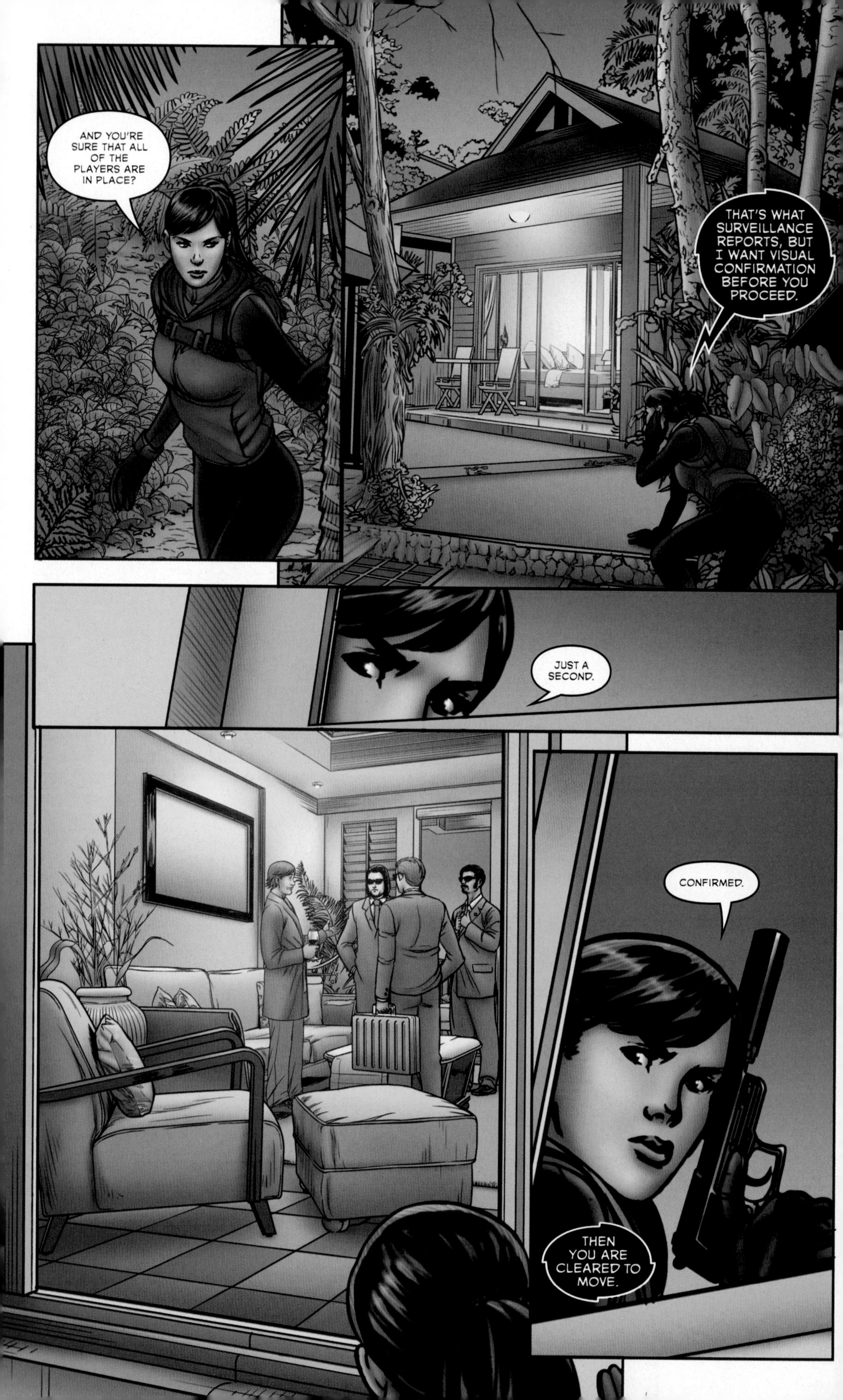
AND YOU'RE SURE THAT ALL OF THE PLAYERS ARE IN PLACE?
THAT'S WHAT SURVEILLANCE REPORTS, BUT I WANT VISUAL CONFIRMATION BEFORE YOU PROCEED.
JUST A SECOND.
CONFIRMED.
THEN YOU ARE CLEARED TO MOVE.

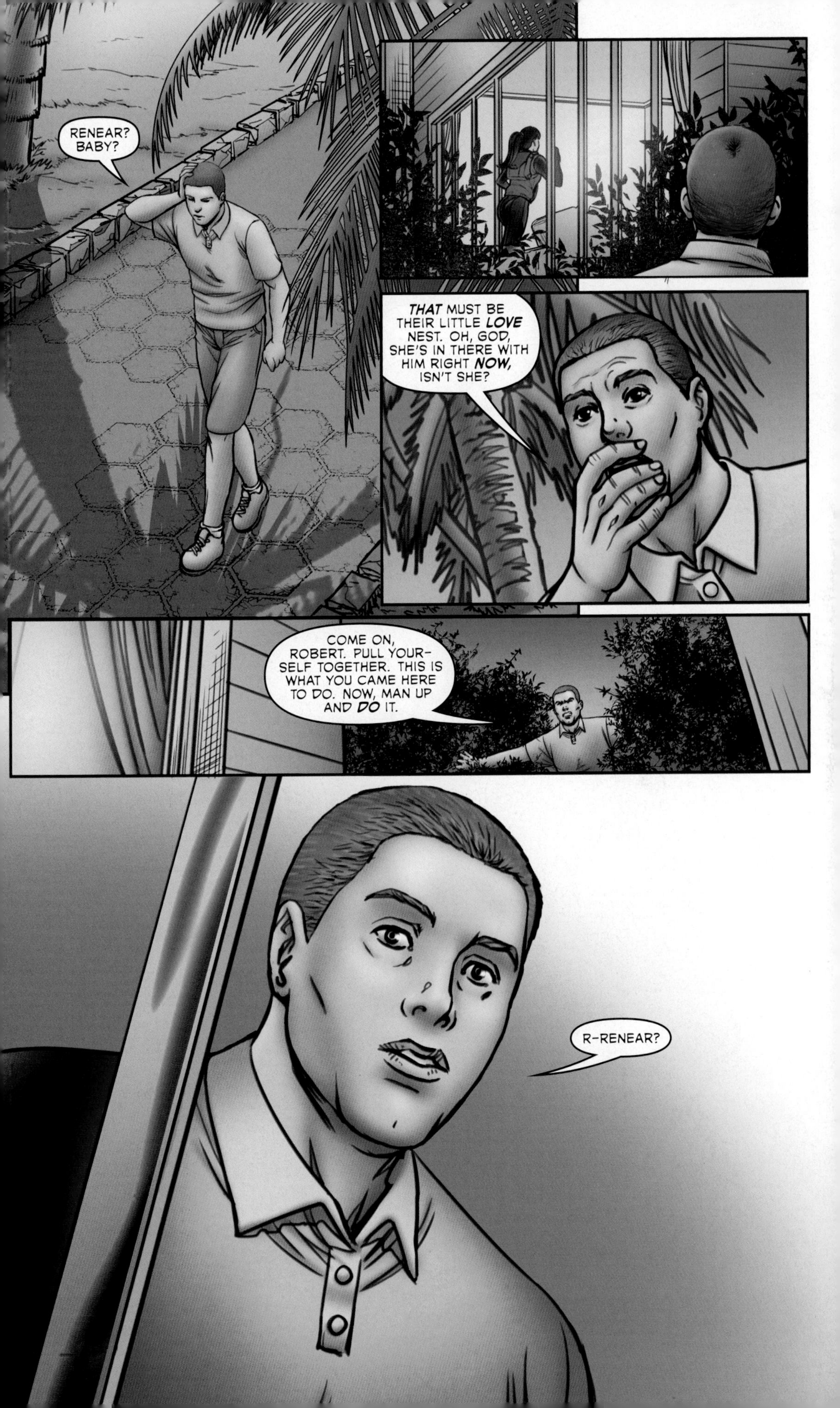
RENEAR? BABY?
THAT MUST BE THEIR LITTLE *LOVE* NEST. OH, GOD, SHE'S IN THERE WITH HIM RIGHT *NOW,* ISN'T SHE?
COME ON, ROBERT. PULL YOURSELF TOGETHER. THIS IS WHAT YOU CAME HERE TO DO. NOW, MAN UP AND *DO* IT.
R-RENEAR?

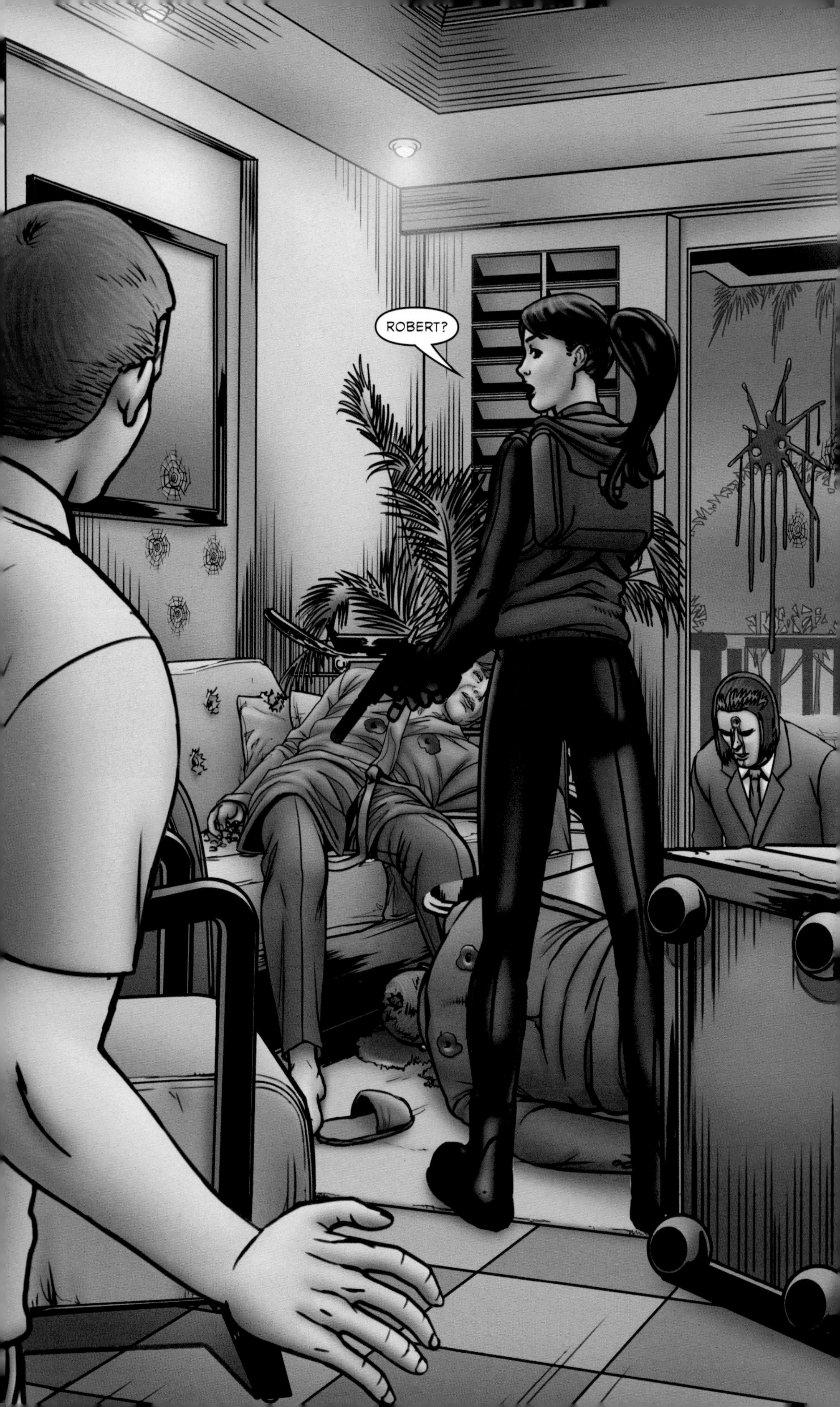
ROBERT?

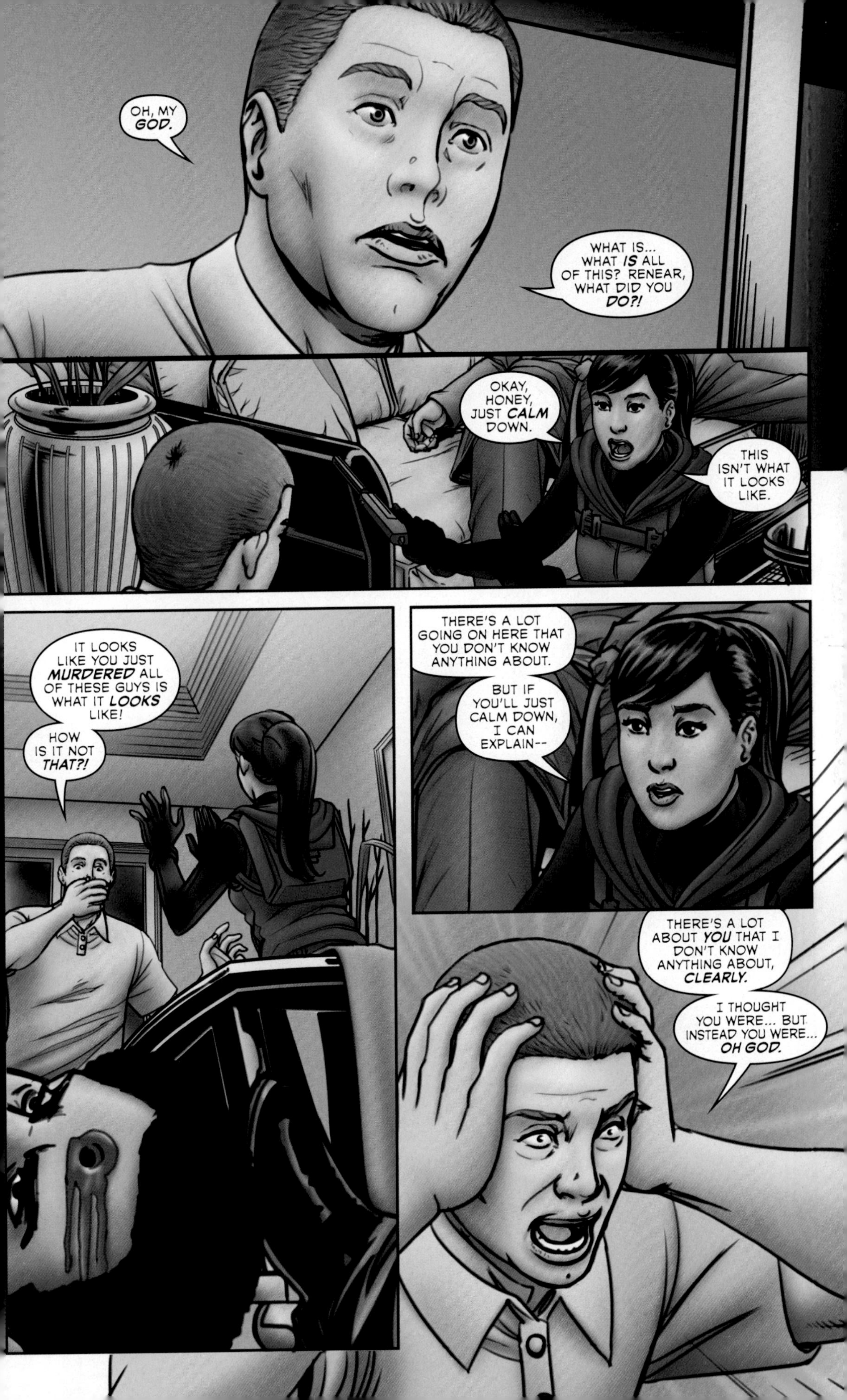
OH, MY GOD.
WHAT IS... WHAT IS ALL OF THIS? RENEAR, WHAT DID YOU DO?!
OKAY, HONEY, JUST CALM DOWN.
THIS ISN'T WHAT IT LOOKS LIKE.
IT LOOKS LIKE YOU JUST MURDERED ALL OF THESE GUYS IS WHAT IT LOOKS LIKE!
HOW IS IT NOT THAT?!
THERE'S A LOT GOING ON HERE THAT YOU DON'T KNOW ANYTHING ABOUT.
BUT IF YOU'LL JUST CALM DOWN, I CAN EXPLAIN--
THERE'S A LOT ABOUT YOU THAT I DON'T KNOW ANYTHING ABOUT, CLEARLY.
I THOUGHT YOU WERE... BUT INSTEAD YOU WERE... OH GOD.

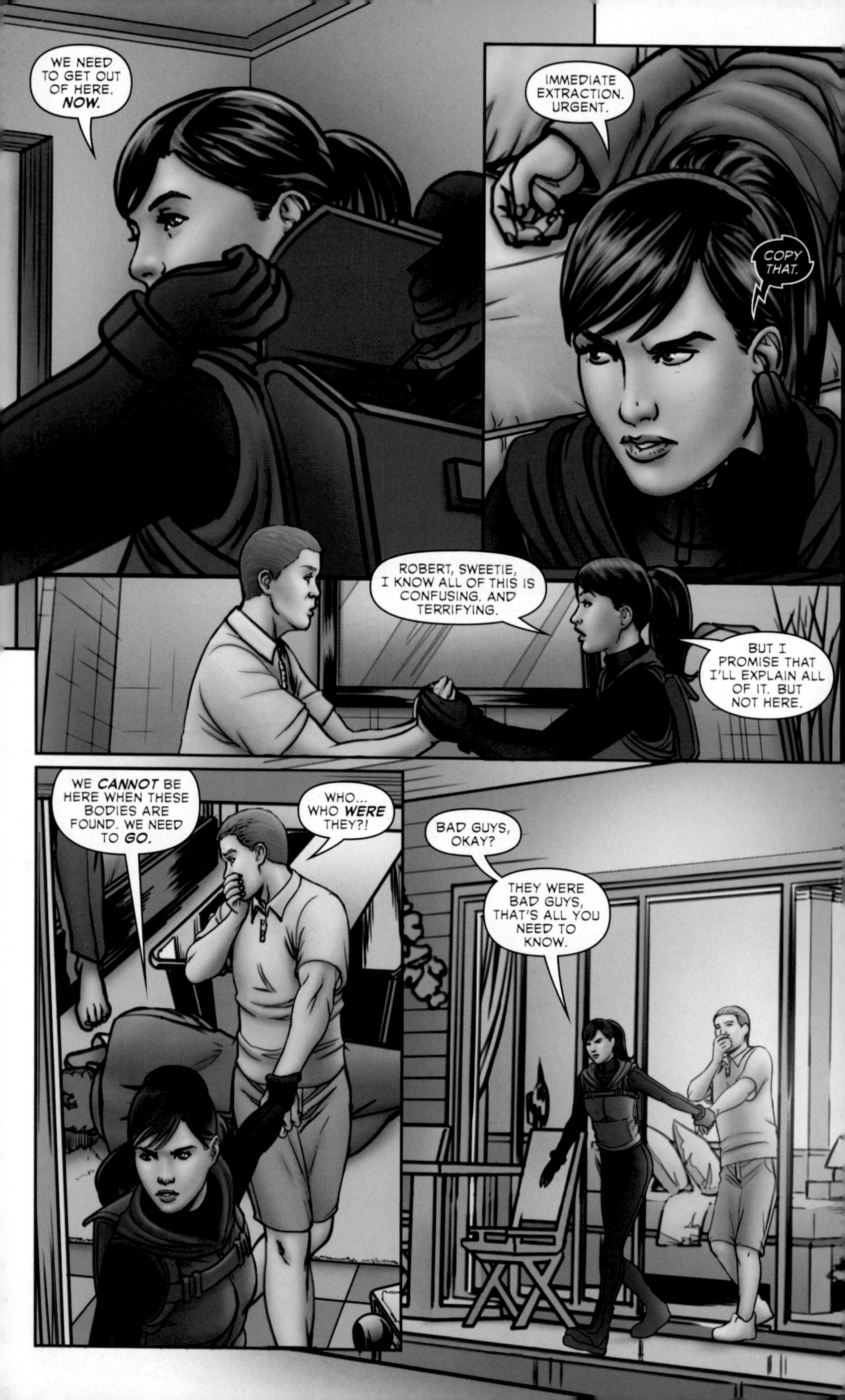
WE NEED TO GET OUT OF HERE. *NOW.*
IMMEDIATE EXTRACTION. URGENT.
COPY THAT.
ROBERT, SWEETIE, I KNOW ALL OF THIS IS CONFUSING. AND TERRIFYING.
BUT I PROMISE THAT I'LL EXPLAIN ALL OF IT. BUT NOT HERE.
WE *CANNOT* BE HERE WHEN THESE BODIES ARE FOUND. WE NEED TO *GO.*
WHO... WHO *WERE* THEY?!
BAD GUYS, OKAY?
THEY WERE BAD GUYS, THAT'S ALL YOU NEED TO KNOW.

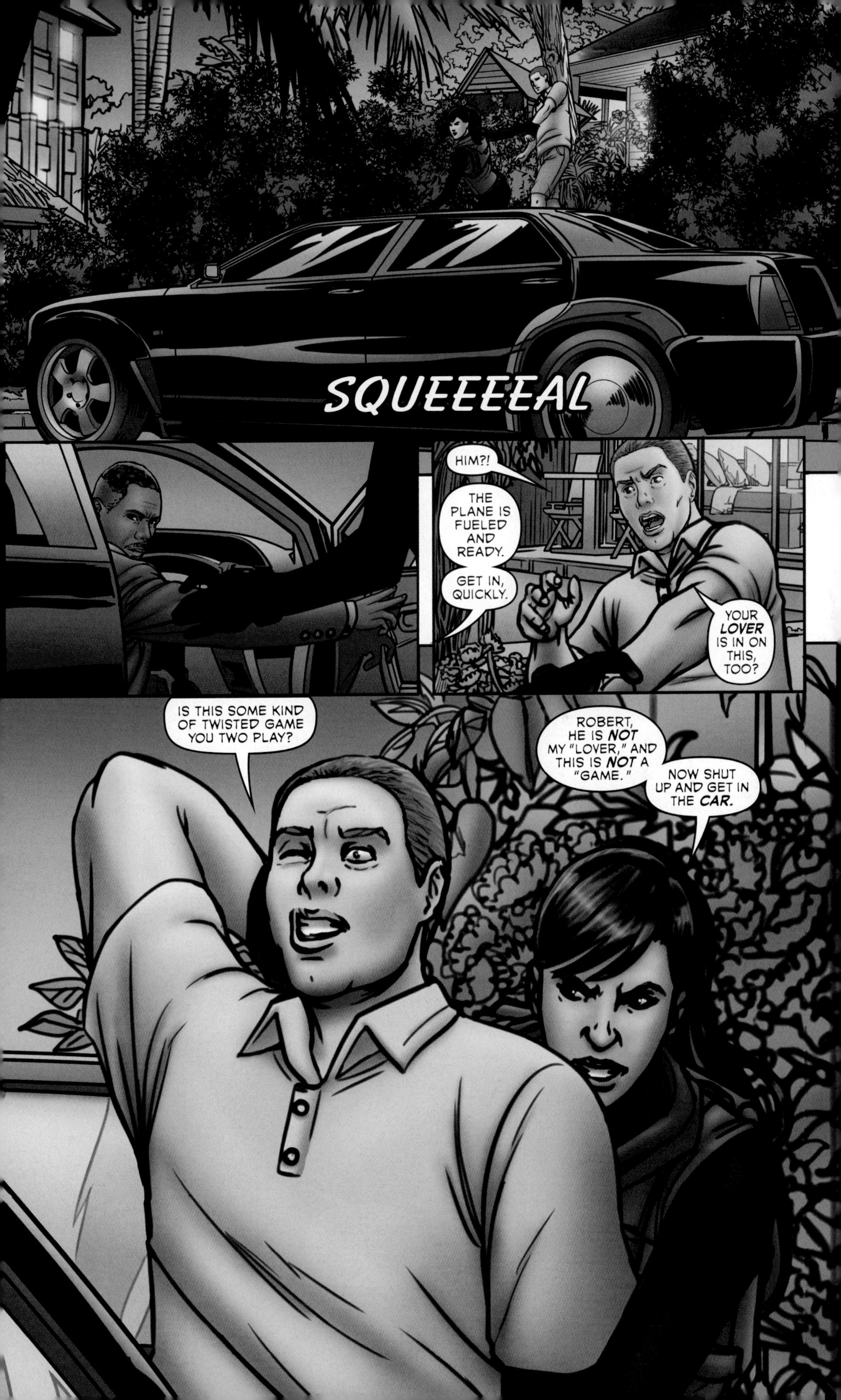
SQUEEEEAL
HIM?!
THE PLANE IS FUELED AND READY.
GET IN, QUICKLY.
YOUR LOVER IS IN ON THIS, TOO?
IS THIS SOME KIND OF TWISTED GAME YOU TWO PLAY?
ROBERT, HE IS NOT MY "LOVER," AND THIS IS NOT A "GAME."
NOW SHUT UP AND GET IN THE CAR.

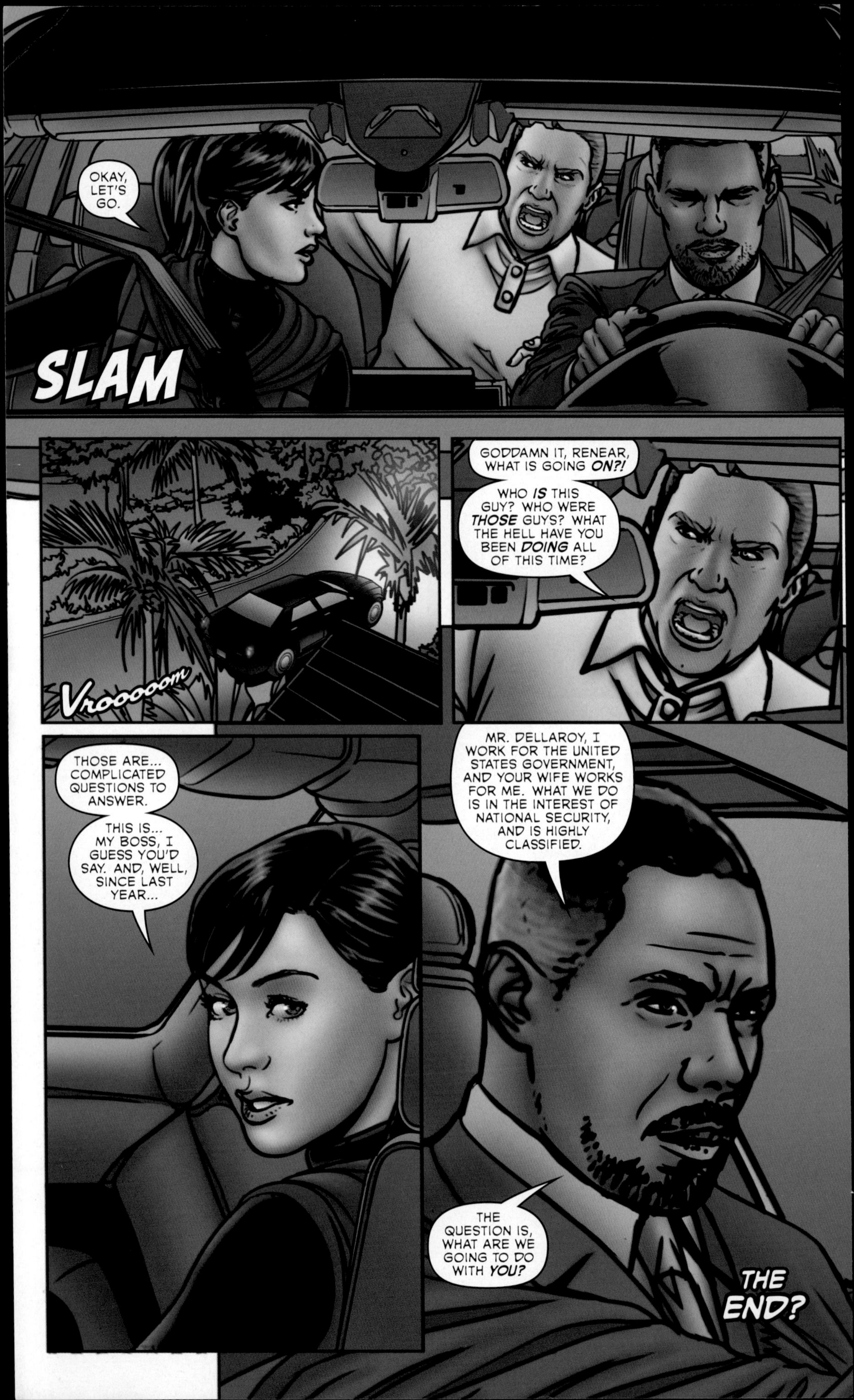
OKAY, LET'S GO.
SLAM
Vrooooom
GODDAMN IT, RENEAR, WHAT IS GOING ON?!
WHO IS THIS GUY? WHO WERE THOSE GUYS? WHAT THE HELL HAVE YOU BEEN DOING ALL OF THIS TIME?
THOSE ARE... COMPLICATED QUESTIONS TO ANSWER.
THIS IS... MY BOSS, I GUESS YOU'D SAY. AND, WELL, SINCE LAST YEAR...
MR. DELLAROY, I WORK FOR THE UNITED STATES GOVERNMENT, AND YOUR WIFE WORKS FOR ME. WHAT WE DO IS IN THE INTEREST OF NATIONAL SECURITY, AND IS HIGHLY CLASSIFIED.
THE QUESTION IS, WHAT ARE WE GOING TO DO WITH YOU?
THE END?

DREW EDWARD JOHNSON
& JAMIE GRANT

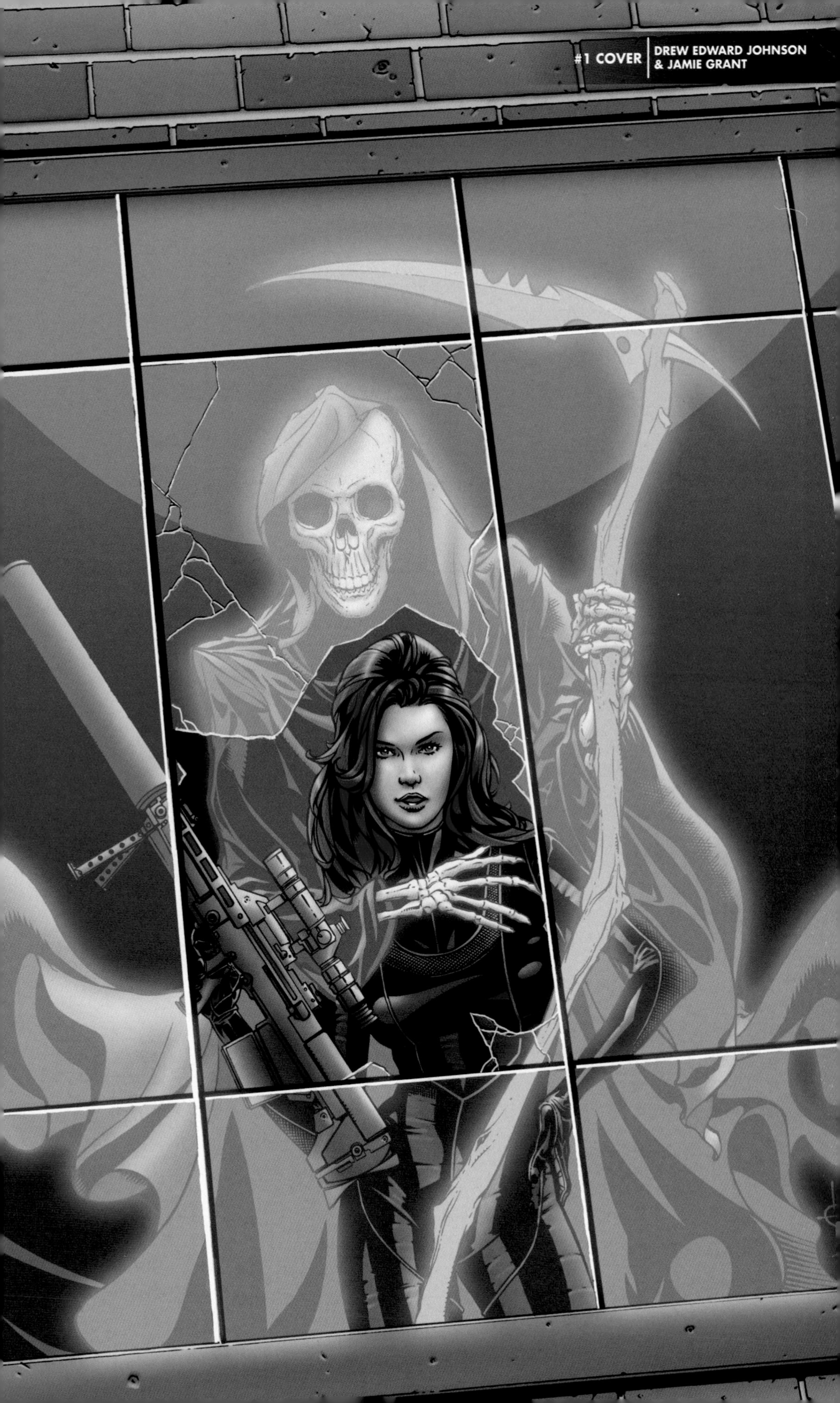

#2 COVER | DREW EDWARD JOHNSON & JAMIE GRANT

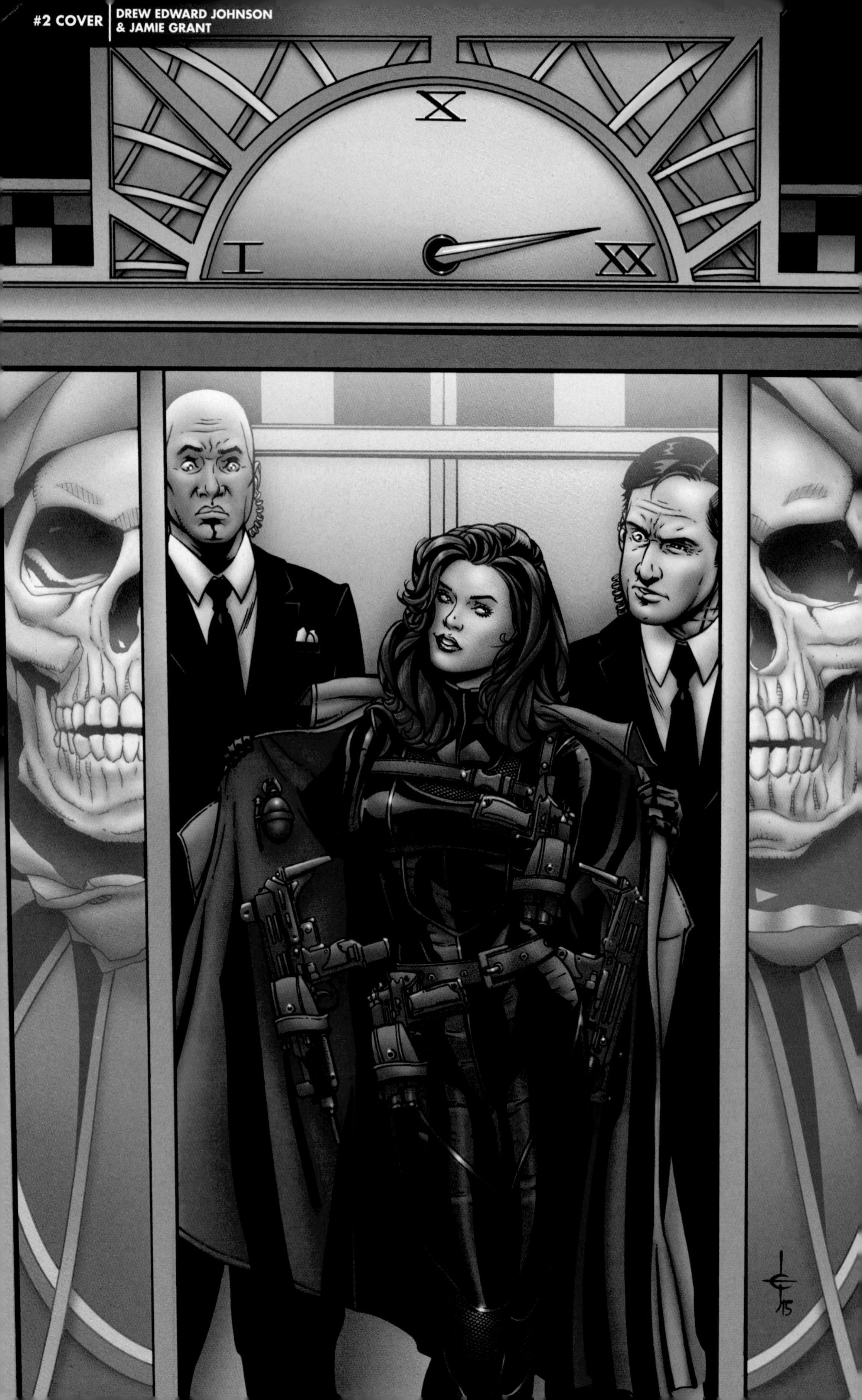

#3 COVER | DREW EDWARD JOHNSON & JAMIE GRANT

#4 COVER | DREW EDWARD JOHNSON & JAMIE GRANT

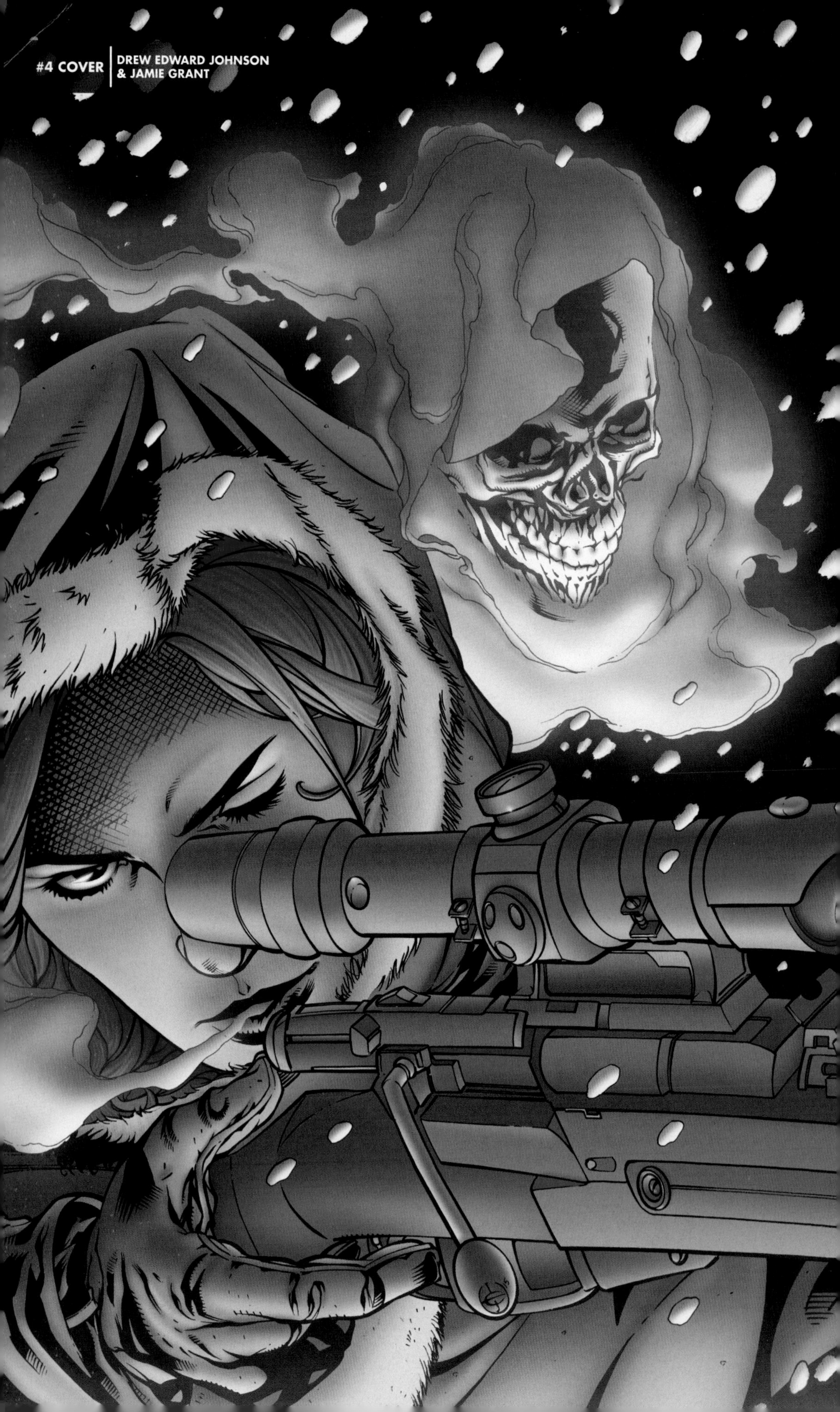

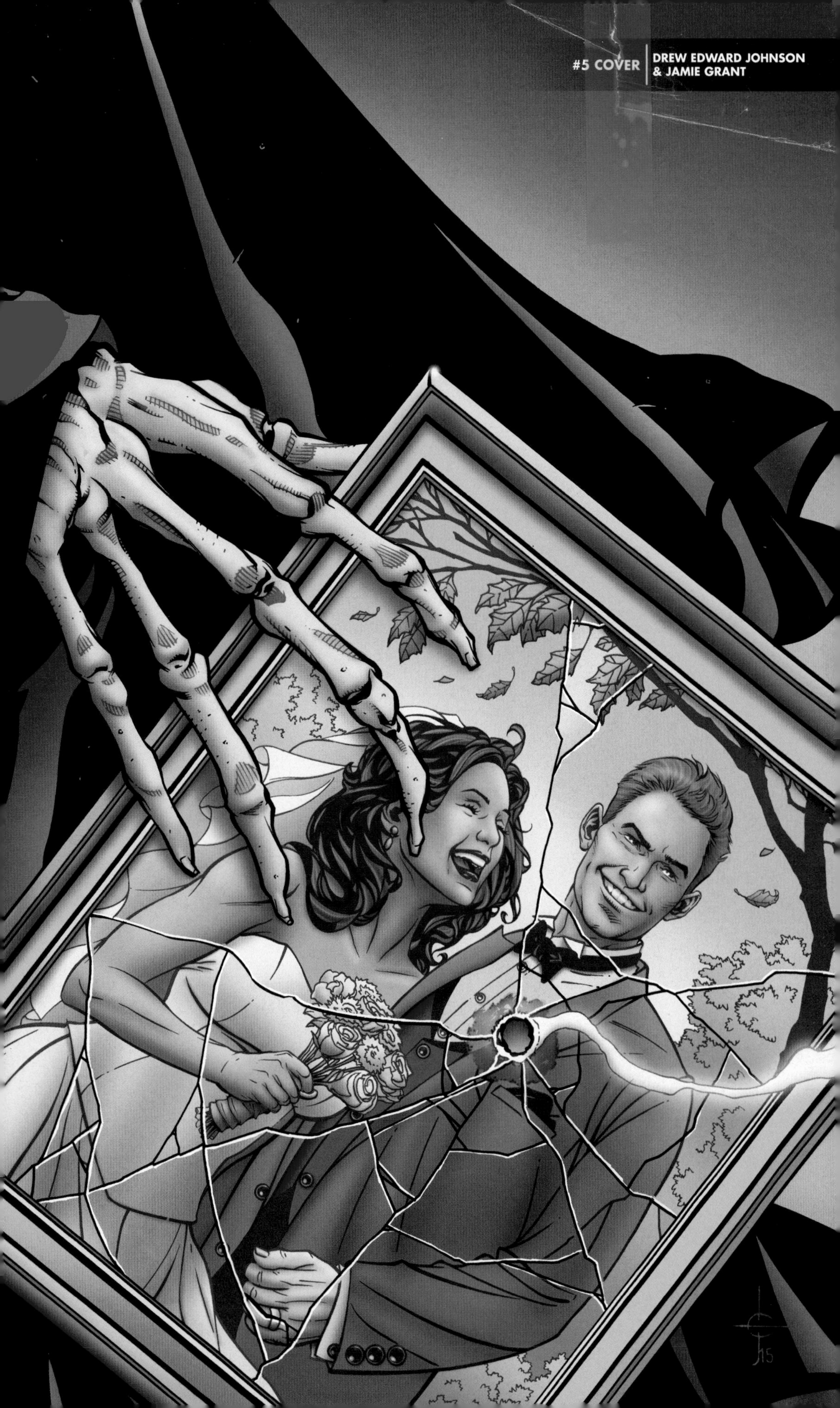
#5 COVER
DREW EDWARD JOHNSON
& JAMIE GRANT

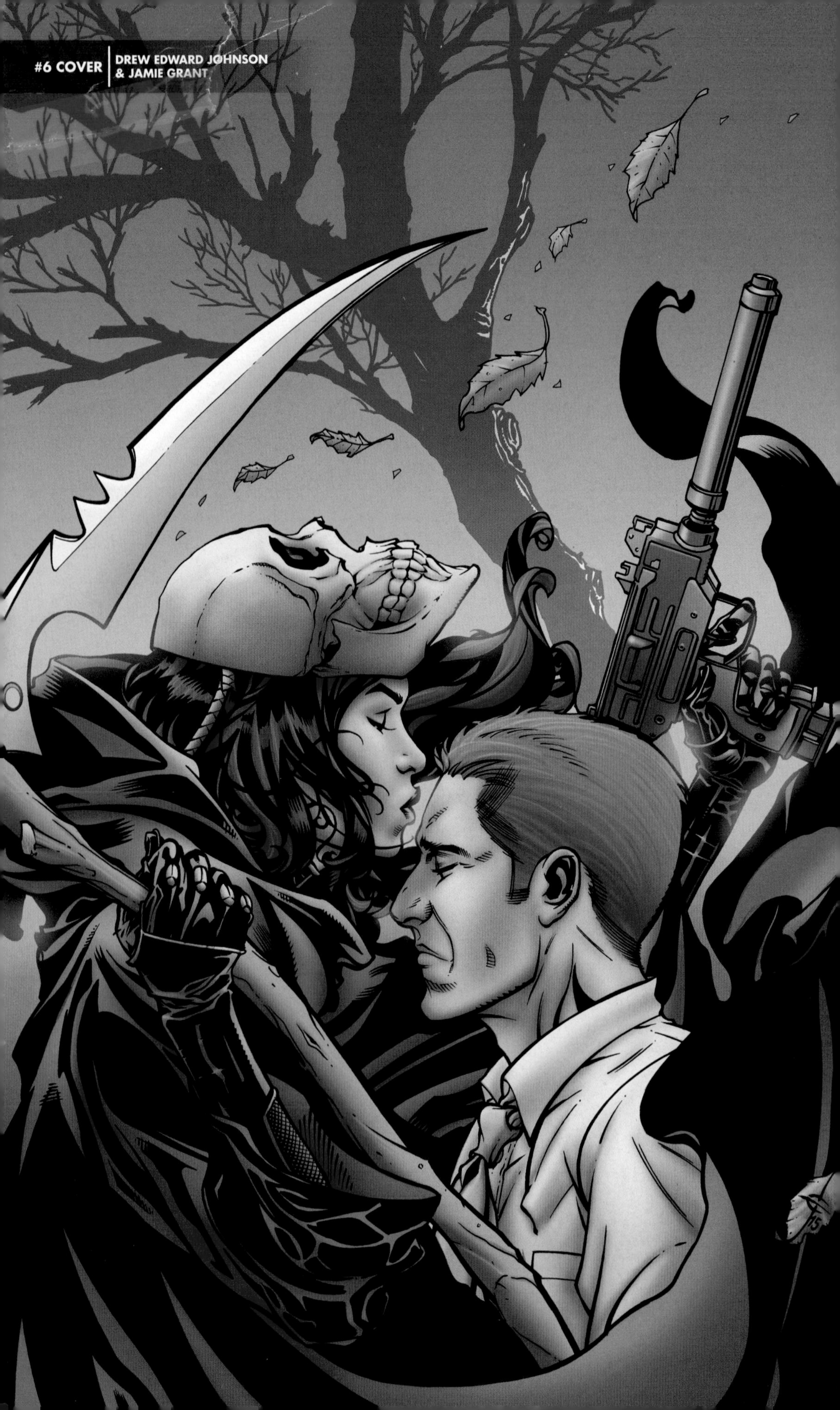

#6 COVER | DREW EDWARD JOHNSON & JAMIE GRANT

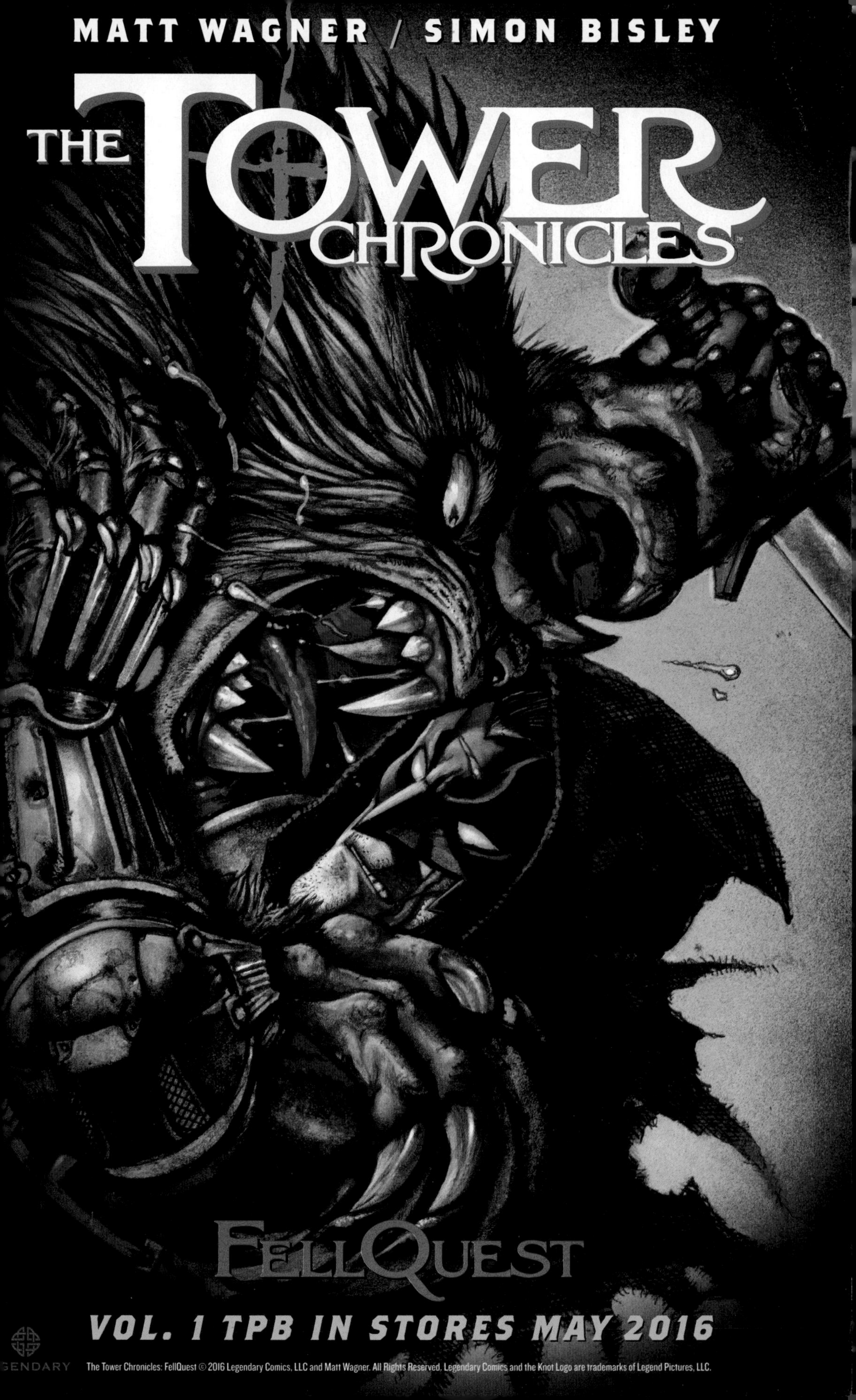
MATT WAGNER / SIMON BISLEY
THE TOWER CHRONICLES
FELLQUEST
VOL. 1 TPB IN STORES MAY 2016
The Tower Chronicles: FellQuest © 2016 Legendary Comics, LLC and Matt Wagner. All Rights Reserved. Legendary Comics and the Knot Logo are trademarks of Legend Pictures, LLC.

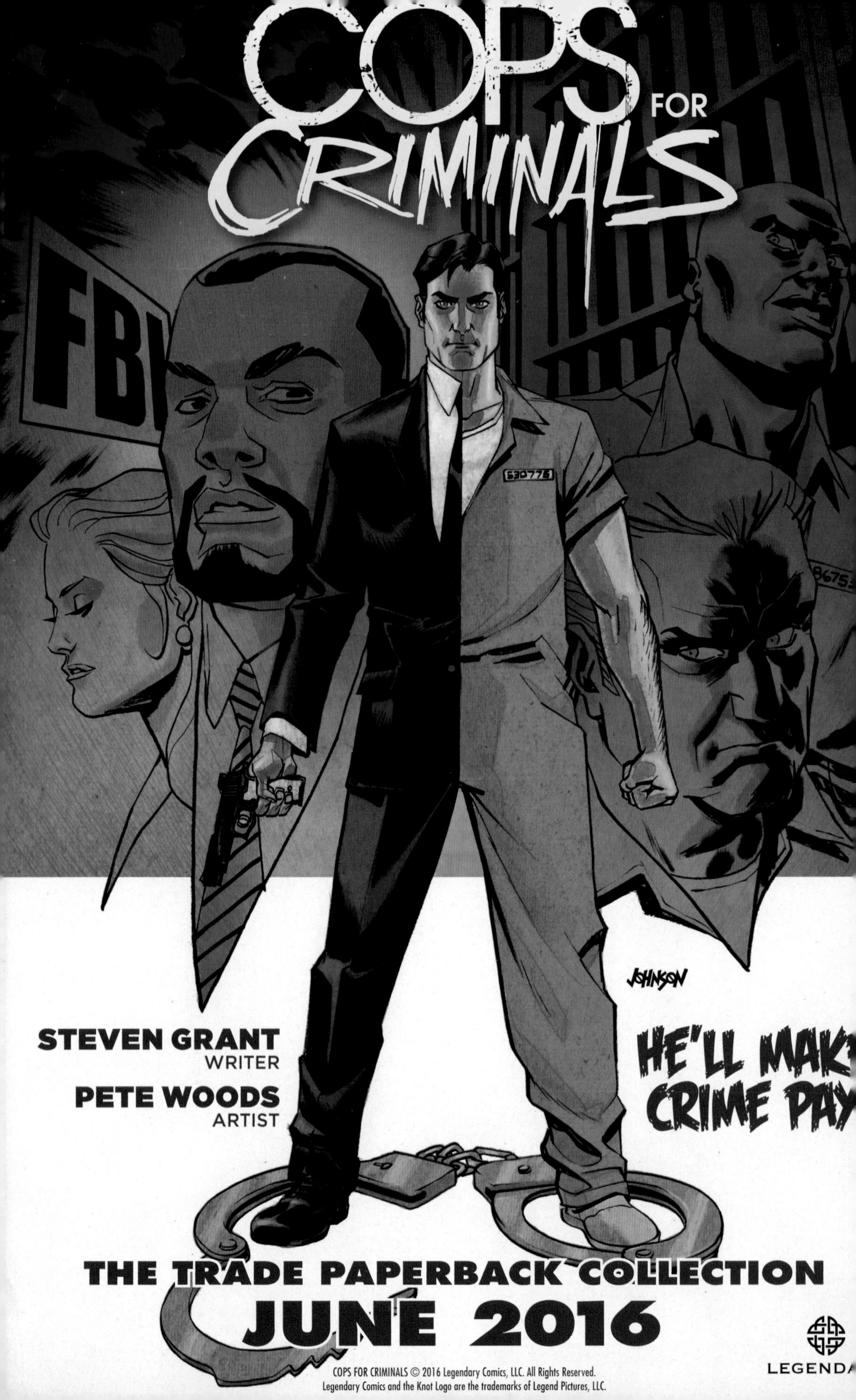
COPS FOR CRIMINALS
FBI
JOHNSON
STEVEN GRANT
WRITER
PETE WOODS
ARTIST
HE'LL MAK
CRIME PAY
THE TRADE PAPERBACK COLLECTION
JUNE 2016
LEGENDA
COPS FOR CRIMINALS © 2016 Legendary Comics, LLC. All Rights Reserved.
Legendary Comics and the Knot Logo are the trademarks of Legend Pictures, LLC.